Cisco Next-Ge
Security Solutions

All-in-one Cisco ASA FirePOWER Services, NGIPS, and AMP

Omar Santos, CISSP No. 463598

Panos Kampanakis, CCIE No. 28561, CISSP No. 367831

Aaron Woland, CCIE No. 20113

Cisco Press

800 East 96th Street

Indianapolis, IN 46240

Cisco Next-Generation Security Solutions: All-in-one Cisco ASA FirePOWER Services, NGIPS, and AMP

Omar Santos, CISSP No. 463598

Panos Kampanakis, CCIE No. 28561, CISSP No. 367831

Aaron Woland, CCIE No. 20113

Copyright © 2016 Cisco Systems, Inc.

Cisco Press logo is a trademark of Cisco Systems, Inc.

Published by:
Cisco Press
800 East 96th Street
Indianapolis, IN 46240 USA

Printed in the United States of America

2   17

Library of Congress Control Number: 2016939800

ISBN-13: 978-1-58714-446-2

ISBN-10: 1-58714-446-8

Warning and Disclaimer

This book is designed to provide information about Cisco Next-Generation Security Solutions. Every effort has been made to make this book as complete and as accurate as possible, but no warranty or fitness is implied.

The information is provided on an "as is" basis. The authors, Cisco Press, and Cisco Systems, Inc. shall have neither liability nor responsibility to any person or entity with respect to any loss or damages arising from the information contained in this book or from the use of the discs or programs that may accompany it.

The opinions expressed in this book belong to the author and are not necessarily those of Cisco Systems, Inc.

Feedback Information

At Cisco Press, our goal is to create in-depth technical books of the highest quality and value. Each book is crafted with care and precision, undergoing rigorous development that involves the unique expertise of members from the professional technical community.

Readers' feedback is a natural continuation of this process. If you have any comments regarding how we could improve the quality of this book, or otherwise alter it to better suit your needs, you can contact us through email at feedback@ciscopress.com. Please make sure to include the book title and ISBN in your message.

We greatly appreciate your assistance.

Trademark Acknowledgments

All terms mentioned in this book that are known to be trademarks or service marks have been appropriately capitalized. Cisco Press or Cisco Systems, Inc. cannot attest to the accuracy of this information. Use of a term in this book should not be regarded as affecting the validity of any trademark or service mark.

Editor-in-Chief: Mark Taub

Product Line Manager: Brett Bartow

Executive Editor: Mary Beth Ray

Development Editor: Christopher Cleveland

Copy Editor: Kitty Wilson

Cover Designer: Chuti Prasertsith

Indexer: James Minkin

Business Operation Manager, Cisco Press: Jan Cornelssen

Managing Editor: Sandra Schroeder

Senior Project Editor: Tracey Croom

Technical Editors: Mason Harris, Foster Lipkey

Composition: Bumpy Design

Proofreader: Kim Wimpsett

Americas Headquarters
Cisco Systems, Inc.
San Jose, CA

Asia Pacific Headquarters
Cisco Systems (USA) Pte. Ltd.
Singapore

Europe Headquarters
Cisco Systems International BV
Amsterdam, The Netherlands

Cisco has more than 200 offices worldwide. Addresses, phone numbers, and fax numbers are listed on the Cisco Website at **www.cisco.com/go/offices.**

CCDE, CCENT, Cisco Eos, Cisco HealthPresence, the Cisco logo, Cisco Lumin, Cisco Nexus, Cisco StadiumVision, Cisco TelePresence, Cisco WebEx, DCE, and Welcome to the Human Network are trademarks; Changing the Way We Work, Live, Play, and Learn and Cisco Store are service marks; and Access Registrar, Aironet, AsyncOS, Bringing the Meeting To You, Catalyst, CCDA, CCDP, CCIE, CCIP, CCNA, CCNP, CCSP, CCVP, Cisco, the Cisco Certified Internetwork Expert logo, Cisco IOS, Cisco Press, Cisco Systems, Cisco Systems Capital, the Cisco Systems logo, Cisco Unity, Collaboration Without Limitation, EtherFast, EtherSwitch, Event Center, Fast Step, Follow Me Browsing, FormShare, GigaDrive, HomeLink, Internet Quotient, IOS, iPhone, iQuick Study, IronPort, the IronPort logo, LightStream, Linksys, MediaTone, MeetingPlace, MeetingPlace Chime Sound, MGX, Networkers, Networking Academy, Network Registrar, PCNow, PIX, PowerPanels, ProConnect, ScriptShare, SenderBase, SMARTnet, Spectrum Expert, StackWise, The Fastest Way to Increase Your Internet Quotient, TransPath, WebEx, and the WebEx logo are registered trademarks of Cisco Systems, Inc. and/or its affiliates in the United States and certain other countries.

All other trademarks mentioned in this document or website are the property of their respective owners. The use of the word partner does not imply a partnership relationship between Cisco and any other company. (0812R)

About the Authors

Omar Santos, CISSP No. 463598, is a principal engineer of Cisco's Product Security Incident Response Team (PSIRT), where he mentors and leads engineers and incident managers during the investigation and resolution of security vulnerabilities in all Cisco products. Omar has held information technology and cybersecurity positions since the mid-1990s. Omar has designed, implemented, and supported numerous secure networks for Fortune 500 companies and the U.S. government. Prior to his current role, he was a technical leader within the World Wide Security Practice and Cisco's Technical Assistance Center (TAC), where he taught, led, and mentored many engineers.

Omar is an active member of the security community, where he leads several industry-wide initiatives and standards bodies. His active role helps businesses, academic institutions, state and local law enforcement agencies, and other participants that are dedicated to increasing the security of critical infrastructure. Omar has delivered numerous technical presentations at conferences worldwide and to Cisco customers and partners, and he has given C-level executive presentations to many organizations. Omar is the author of the following books and video courses:

- *Cisco ASA: All-in-One Firewall, IPS, and VPN Adaptive Security Appliance*

- *Cisco ASA: All-in-One Firewall, IPS, Anti-X, and VPN Adaptive Security Appliance, 2nd edition*

- *Cisco: All-in-One ASA Next-Generation Firewall, IPS, and VPN Services, 3rd edition*

- *Cisco Network Admission Control, Volume: Deployment and Management*

- *End-to-End Network Security: Defense-in-Depth*

- *Network Security with NetFlow and IPFIX: Big Data Analytics for Information Security*

- *CCNA Security 210-260 Complete Video Course*

- *CCNA Security 210-260 Official Cert Guide*

- *Deploying Next-Generation Firewalls LiveLessons*

- *The Current Security Threat Landscape Networking Talks LiveLessons*

- *Cisco Advanced Malware Protection (AMP) LiveLessons*

Panos Kampanakis, CCIE No. 28561, CISSP No. 367831, is a technical marketing engineer in Cisco's Security and Trust Organization (S&TO). He was born in Athens, Greece, and received a five-year degree in electrical and computer engineering from National Technical University of Athens and an MSc from North Carolina State University. His MS thesis was on efficient elliptic curve cryptography and bilinear pairing on sensor networks.

Panos has extensive experience with cryptography, security automation, vulnerability management, and cybersecurity. In his professional career, he has supported and provided security advice to multiple Cisco customers. He has trained and presented on various security topics at Cisco Live for numerous years. He has participated in various security standards bodies, providing common interoperable protocols and languages for security information sharing, cryptography, and PKI. Panos has also worked extensively with Cisco's PSIRT to provide vulnerability mitigations. His current interests include next-generation cryptography, post-quantum cryptography, standards efforts that enable cryptographic implementation interoperability, and IoT security and cryptography. The following are some of his recent publications:

- *Postquantum Preshared Keys for IKEv2 IETF* draft https://tools.ietf.org/html/draft-fluhrer-qr-ikev2

- *BAFi: A Practical Cryptographic Secure Audit Logging Scheme for Digital Forensics.* Security Comm. Networks, doi: 10.1002/sec.1242

- Eric W. Burger, Michael D. Goodman, Panos Kampanakis, and Kevin A. Zhu. 2014. "Taxonomy Model for Cyber Threat Intelligence Information Exchange Technologies," in *Proceedings of the 2014 ACM Workshop on Information Sharing & Collaborative Security* (WISCS '14). ACM, New York, NY, USA, 51-60

- "Security Automation and Threat Information-Sharing Options, Security & Privacy," in *IEEE*, vol.12, no.5, pp.42,51, Sept.-Oct. 2014

- Kampanakis, P.; Perros, H.; Beyene, T., *SDN-Based Solutions for Moving Target Defense Network Protection, A World of Wireless, Mobile and Multimedia Networks (WoWMoM)*, 2014 IEEE 15th International Symposium, vol., no., pp.1,6, 19-19 June 2014

- *IODEF Usage Guidance* IETF draft https://tools.ietf.org/html/draft-ietf-mile-iodef-guidance

- *Next Generation Encryption* on cisco.com

- *Cisco Firewall Best Practices Guide* on cisco.com

In his free time, Panos has a passion for basketball, and he never likes to lose.

Aaron Woland, CCIE No. 20113, is a principal engineer in Cisco's Security Business Group and works with Cisco's largest customers all over the world. His primary job responsibilities include secure access and identity deployments with ISE, solution enhancements, standards development, and futures. Aaron joined Cisco in 2005 and is currently a member of numerous security advisory boards and standards body working groups. Prior to joining Cisco, Aaron spent 12 years as a consultant and technical trainer.

His areas of expertise include network and host security architecture and implementation, regulatory compliance, and route switch and wireless. Aaron is one of six inaugural members of the Hall of Fame for Distinguished Speakers at Cisco Live and is a security columnist for Network World, where he blogs on all things related to identity. His other certifications include GHIC, GSEC, Certified Ethical Hacker, MCSE, VCP, CCSP, CCNP, and CCDP. You can follow Aaron on Twitter @aaronwoland.

Aaron is the author of the following books and courses, as well as many published white papers and design guides:

- *CCNP Security SISAS 300-208 Official Cert Guide*
- *Cisco ISE for BYOD and Secure Unified Access*
- *CCNA Security 210-260 Complete Video Course*

About the Technical Reviewers

Foster Lipkey, SFCE, is a senior member of the Cisco Firepower TAC team supporting Firepower, FireSIGHT, AMP for Endpoints, and Threat Grid, as well as third-party integrations. He has been a leader in developing tools and procedures for supporting the Cisco Firepower and AMP security software platforms. Prior to working for Sourcefire/Cisco, he was an applications solutions specialist as a contractor for the National Cancer Institute (NCI), supporting Java enterprise applications for the NCI's Center for Biomedical Informatics and Information Technology. Foster's primary areas of interest are enterprise security and security automation.

Mason Harris, CCIE No. 5916, is the chief solutions architect at vArmour, a cloud security startup based in Mountain View, California. He is responsible for all enterprise and platform architecture in both private and public cloud deployments. Previously he was a technical solutions architect for Cisco, focusing primarily on security architectures in the data center with Cisco's 27 largest customers. Mason has more than 24 years of experience in systems architecture and is one the few individuals in the world to have attained five CCIE certifications. He also holds the CISSP, GPEN, and GCIH certifications. When not thinking about security topics, Mason can be found backpacking on long trails or at home with his family. A lifelong UNC Tarheels fan, he holds an undergraduate degree from UNC-Chapel Hill and a master's degree from NC State University, with a minor in Arabic.

Dedications

This work is dedicated to those who aim high and constantly try to move science and technology forward.

—*Panos Kampanakis*

I would like to dedicate this book to my lovely wife, Jeannette, and my two beautiful children, Hannah and Derek, who have inspired and supported me throughout the development of this book. I also dedicate this book to my father, Jose, and to the memory of my mother, Generosa. Without their knowledge, wisdom, and guidance, I would not have the goals that I strive to achieve today.

—*Omar Santos*

First and foremost, this book is dedicated to my amazing best friend, fellow adventurer, and wife, Suzanne. To my two awesome and brilliant children, Eden and Nyah, and Mom and Pop. There is nothing in this world more important than family, and my family drives me to be better and do better, every day.

—*Aaron Woland*

Acknowledgments

We would like to thank the technical editors, Foster Lipkey and Mason Harris, for their time and technical expertise. They verified our work and corrected us in all the major and minor mistakes that were hard to find, and they steered us in new directions and to achieve more.

We would like to thank the Cisco Press team, especially Denise Lincoln and Christopher Cleveland, for their patience, guidance, and consideration. Their efforts are greatly appreciated.

Kudos to the Cisco Security Business Group and Cisco Security Services for delivering such great products and services.

Finally, we would like to thank Cisco for enabling us to constantly learn and chase our career aspirations all these years.

Contents at a Glance

Contents

Introduction

This book covers Cisco next-generation network security products and solutions. It provides detailed guidance for designing, configuring, and troubleshooting the Cisco ASA with FirePOWER Services, Cisco next-generation IPS appliances, Cisco Web Security Appliance (WSA), and Cisco Email Security Appliance (ESA) with the new Advanced Malware Protection (AMP) integration, as well as the Cisco AMP Threat Grid malware analysis and threat intelligence and Cisco Firepower Management Center (FMC).

Who Should Read This Book?

This book is a comprehensive guide for any network and/or security professional who has deployed or is planning to deploy Cisco next-generation security products, including the Cisco ASA with FirePOWER Services, Cisco AMP for Networks and Endpoints, and Cisco next-generation IPS appliances (including Firepower). Any security professional who manages or configures Cisco Web Security Appliance (WSA) and Cisco Email Security Appliance (ESA) with the Advanced Malware Protection (AMP) solution will also benefit from this book.

How This Book Is Organized

This book is organized into 12 chapters. It starts with an overview of the Cisco next-generation network security products and then dives into design, configuration, and troubleshooting of the Cisco ASA FirePOWER Services module, Cisco AMP for Networks, Cisco AMP for Endpoints, Cisco AMP for Content Security, and Cisco next-generation IPS. This book also provides an overview of the Cisco AMP Threat Grid malware analysis and threat intelligence. The following are the chapters in this book:

- **Chapter 1, "Fundamentals of Cisco Next-Generation Security":** This chapter starts with an introduction to the new security threat landscape and attack continuum. It then provides an overview of Cisco next-generation network security products, including the Cisco ASA next-generation firewalls and the FirePOWER module; next-generation intrusion prevention systems (NGIPS); an introduction to Advanced Malware Protection (AMP) for Endpoints and AMP for Networks; an overview of AMP Threat Grid; Cisco Email Security; Cisco Web Security; Cisco Identity Services Engine (ISE); Cisco Meraki Cloud Managed MDM and Security Appliances; and the Cisco VPN solutions.

- **Chapter 2, "Introduction to and Design of Cisco ASA with FirePOWER Services":** This chapter covers design topics of the Cisco ASA with FirePOWER Services. It explains the inline versus promiscuous mode deployment and the Cisco ASA Firepower management options. This chapter also provides information about the Cisco ASA FirePOWER Services licensing structure and information about compatibility with other Cisco ASA features. It also covers the Cisco ASA Firepower packet processing order of operations, high-availability design topics, and how to deploy the Cisco ASA FirePOWER Services in the Internet edge, in the data center, and in different VPN scenarios.

- **Chapter 3, "Configuring Cisco ASA with FirePOWER Services":** This chapter starts with instructions on how to perform the initial setup of the Cisco ASA FirePOWER module in Cisco ASA appliances. Then it provides step-by-step configuration guidance on how to redirect traffic to the Cisco ASA FirePOWER module, how to configure the Cisco ASA FirePOWER module using the Adaptive Security Device Manager (ASDM), and how to configure the Cisco ASA FirePOWER module for FireSIGHT Management.

- **Chapter 4, "Troubleshooting Cisco ASA with FirePOWER Services and Firepower Threat Defense (FTD)":** This chapter provides tips on troubleshooting problems in the Cisco ASA and the FirePOWER Services module.

- **Chapter 5, "Introduction to and Architecture of Cisco AMP":** This chapter introduces the Advanced Malware Protection solution, its architectural makeup, and types of clouds. It also provides a step-by-step walk-through for installing an AMP private cloud.

- **Chapter 6, "Cisco AMP for Networks":** This chapter describes how AMP for Networks fits into the AMP architecture, along with the functions of AMP for Networks. It describes and walks through the configuration of malware and file policies for AMP for Networks.

- **Chapter 7, "Cisco AMP for Content Security":** This chapter describes how AMP for Content Security fits within the AMP architecture, describing the components and configuration of File Reputation and File Analysis Services, along with the reporting for those services.

- **Chapter 8, "Cisco AMP for Endpoints":** This chapter dives into Cisco AMP for Endpoints, custom detections, application control, AMP for Endpoints installation, and policy management for applicable operating systems (Windows, Mac, Linux, and Android). The chapter also reviews the usage of the AMP cloud console.

- **Chapter 9, "AMP Threat Grid: Malware Analysis and Threat Intelligence":** AMP Threat Grid is a malware dynamic analysis engine integrated with Cisco AMP. This chapter presents the AMP Threat Grid deployment options, which include a cloud and an on-premises appliance solution. It summarizes the differences between the two and describes when an organization would choose one over the other. It also provides example snapshots of Threat Grid configuration options in the FMC.

- **Chapter 10, "Introduction and Deployment of Cisco Next-Generation IPS":** This chapter presents next-generation IPS (NGIPS) and compares NGIPS to legacy IPS systems. It also describes some basic NGIPS deployment design options and locations based on an organization's security requirements. This chapter then goes over common deployment considerations when designing an IPS deployment. Finally, it closes by going over the NGIPS deployment lifecycle that organizations should follow in order to maximize the benefits of an NGIPS deployment.

- **Chapter 11, "Configuring Cisco Next-Generation IPS":** This chapter introduces the configuration options available in FMC. It presents policy configuration options, IPS rules, Snort, and NGIPS preprocessors and recommendations. It uses various snapshot images to portray the wealth of available configuration options and the intuitive feel of the FMC graphical interface. Finally, it describes performance settings and redundancy configurations. This chapter does not present the ASDM IPS configuration options, which are presented in Chapter 3.

- **Chapter 12, "Reporting and Troubleshooting with Cisco Next-Generation IPS":** The last chapter of this book summarizes the Cisco NGIPS reporting and trouble-shooting capabilities. It describes the analysis capabilities offered in FMC, which include intrusion events, custom reporting, incidents, alerting, and correlation policies. It then provides troubleshooting and health monitoring options that help administrators identify and find the root cause of potential issues in the system.

Command Syntax Conventions

The conventions used to present command syntax in this book are the same conventions used in the IOS Command Reference:

- **Boldface** indicates commands and keywords that are entered literally as shown. In actual configuration examples and output (not general command syntax), boldface indicates commands that are manually input by the user (such as a **show** command).

- *Italics* indicate arguments for which you supply actual values.

- Vertical bars (|) separate alternative, mutually exclusive elements.

- Square brackets [ ] indicate optional elements.

- Braces { } indicate a required choice.

- Braces within brackets [{ }] indicate a required choice within an optional element.

Chapter 1

Fundamentals of Cisco Next-Generation Security

The threat landscape today is very different from that of just a few years ago. Many bad actors are causing major disruptions to enterprises, service providers, and governments with a combination of simple attacks and very sophisticated, well-organized, and well-funded attack campaigns. A large number of these advanced attacks are difficult to detect and remain in networks for long periods of time.

Traditional security products have concentrated on providing high-level visibility into what's happening in the network and denying traffic at the point of entry. However, bad actors do not carry out advanced attacks at a single point in time. Their attack schemes and campaigns use sophisticated methodologies like encrypted traffic, zero-day attacks, command and control (C&C) detection evasion, lateral movement, and evasion techniques to avoid detection.

Cisco creates some of the industry's most comprehensive advanced threat protection security products and services. These products and solutions are designed to provide visibility, policy enforcement, and advanced threat protection across a network and the entire attack continuum. This chapter covers the following topics and Cisco next-generation security products and solutions:

- The new threat landscape and attack continuum

- Cisco ASA 5500-X Series next-generation firewalls and the Cisco ASA with FirePOWER Services

- Cisco Firepower Threat Defense (FTD)

- Next-generation intrusion prevention systems (NGIPS)

- Firepower Management Center (FMC)

- Advanced Malware Protection (AMP) for Endpoints

- AMP for Networks

- AMP Threat Grid

- Cisco Email Security Appliance (ESA)

- Cloud Email Security

- Cisco Web Security Appliance (WSA)

- Cisco Cloud Web Security (CWS)

- Cisco Identity Services Engine (ISE)

- Cisco Meraki cloud-managed MDM

- Cisco Meraki cloud-managed security appliances

- Cisco VPN solutions

Note   This book focuses on the latest next-generation platforms.

The New Threat Landscape and Attack Continuum

Defending against cybersecurity attacks is becoming more challenging every day, and it is not going to get any easier. The threat landscape is evolving to a faster, more effective, and more efficient criminal economy profiting from attacks against users, enterprises, services providers, and governments. The organized cybercrime and exchange of exploits is booming and fueling a very lucrative economy. Bad actors today have a clear understanding of the underlying security technologies and their vulnerabilities. Hacker groups now follow software development lifecycles, just as enterprises do. These bad actors perform quality assurance testing against security products before releasing them into the underground economy. They continue to find ways to evade common security defenses. Attackers follow new techniques such as the following:

- Port and protocol hopping

- Encryption

- Droppers

- Social engineering

- Zero-day attacks

Figure 1-1 illustrates how today's security defenses must be architected.

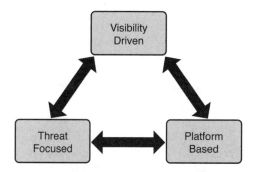

Figure 1-1 *Today's Security Defenses*

Next-generation security defenses must have the following characteristics:

- **Visibility driven**: Defenses must maintain complete visibility and gather data from all potential attack vectors across the network fabric, endpoints (including mobile devices), email and web gateways, virtual machines in the data center, and the cloud.

- **Threat focused**: It is necessary to correlate all collected information with indicators of compromise (IOC) and other contextual information in order for network security administrators to make better decisions and take action. Keeping up with a constantly evolving threat landscape is almost impossible. Access controls reduce the attack surface, but attackers still get through. Security technologies and solutions must focus on understanding, detecting, and blocking attacks. These solutions require continuous analysis and security intelligence delivered from the cloud and shared across all products for better effectiveness.

- **Platform based**: Security now requires an integrated system of agile and open platforms that cover the network, endpoints, users, and the cloud. These platforms must be scalable and centrally managed for device configuration consistency.

The Attack Continuum

You as a security professional need to face the fact that you will get attacked, and eventually some of the devices in your network will be compromised. Security technologies and processes not only should focus on detection but also should provide the capability to mitigate the impact of a successful attack. Figure 1-2 illustrates the attack continuum.

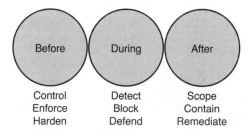

Figure 1-2 *The Attack Continuum*

Security professionals must maintain visibility and control across the extended network during the full attack continuum:

■ Before an attack takes place

■ During an active attack

■ After an attacker starts to damage systems or steal information

Cisco next-generation security products provide protection throughout the attack continuum. Devices such as the Cisco ASA with FirePOWER Services, available on the Cisco ASA 5500-X Series and ASA 5585-X Adaptive Security Appliances; Firepower Threat Defense (FTD); and Cisco Advanced Malware Protection (AMP) provide a security solution that help discover threats and enforce and harden policies before an attack takes place. In addition, you can detect, block, and defend against attacks that have already taken place with next-generation intrusion prevention systems (NGIPS), Email Security, and Web Security Appliance with AMP. These solutions provide the capabilities to contain and remediate an attack to minimize data loss and additional network degradation.

Tip   What is the difference between FirePOWER and Firepower? Cisco uses the term FirePOWER (uppercase *POWER*) when referring to the Cisco ASA FirePOWER Services module and uses Firepower (lowercase *power*) when referring to the FTD unified image and newer software.

Cisco ASA 5500-X Series Next-Generation Firewalls and the Cisco ASA with FirePOWER Services

The members of the Cisco ASA family come in many shapes and sizes, but they all provide a similar set of features. Typically, smaller model numbers represent smaller capacity for throughput. The main standalone appliance model number begins with a 55, but there are also devices in the Cisco ASA family that go into a switch, such as a 6500. Table 1-1 describes the various models of the ASA family.

Table 1-1   *Cisco ASA Models*

Cisco ASA 5500 Series Models	Usage
Cisco ASA 5505	Small offices and branch offices
Cisco ASA 5506-X, Cisco ASA 5506W-X, Cisco ASA 5506H-X	Small offices and branch offices
Cisco ASA 5508-X	Small offices and branch offices
Cisco ASA 5512-X	Small offices and branch offices
Cisco ASA 5515-X	Small offices and branch offices

Cisco ASA 5500 Series Models	Usage
Cisco ASA 5516-X	Medium-sized offices Internet-edge security appliances
Cisco ASA 5525-X	Medium-sized offices Internet-edge security appliances
Cisco ASA 5545-X	Medium-size offices Internet-edge security appliances
Cisco ASA 5555-X	Medium-sized offices Internet-edge security appliances
Cisco ASA 5585-X	Data center and large enterprise networks
Cisco ASA Services Module	Data center and large enterprise networks
Cisco ASAv	Virtual ASA used in many different environments

The Cisco ASA family provides a very comprehensive set of features and next-generation security capabilities. For example, it provides capabilities such as simple packet filtering (normally configured with access control lists [ACLs]) and stateful inspection. The Cisco ASA family also provides support for application inspection/awareness. A Cisco ASA device can listen in on conversations between devices on one side and devices on the other side of the firewall. The benefit of listening in is that the firewall can pay attention to application layer information.

The Cisco ASA family also supports Network Address Translation (NAT), the capability to act as a Dynamic Host Configuration Protocol (DHCP) server or client or both. The Cisco ASA family supports most of the interior gateway routing protocols, including Routing Information Protocol (RIP), Enhanced Interior Gateway Routing Protocol (EIGRP), and Open Shortest Path First (OSPF). It also supports static routing. A Cisco ASA device also can be implemented as a traditional Layer 3 firewall, which has IP addresses assigned to each of its routable interfaces. The other option is to implement a firewall as a transparent (Layer 2) firewall, in which case the actual physical interfaces are not configured with individual IP addresses, but a pair of interfaces operate like a bridge. Traffic that is going across this two-port bridge is still subject to the rules and inspection that can be implemented by the ASA. In addition, a Cisco ASA device is often used as a head-end or remote-end device for VPN tunnels for both remote-access VPN users and site-to-site VPN tunnels. The Cisco ASA family supports IPsec and SSL-based remote-access VPNs. The SSL VPN capabilities include support for clientless SSL VPN and full AnyConnect SSL VPN tunnels.

The Cisco ASA family also provides a basic botnet traffic filtering feature. A *botnet* is a collection of computers that have been compromised and are willing to follow the instructions of someone who is attempting to centrally control them (for example, 200,000 machines all willing [or so commanded] to send a flood of ping requests to the

IP address dictated by the person controlling these devices). Often, users of these computers have no idea that their computers are participating in a coordinated attack. An ASA device works with an external system at Cisco that provides information about the Botnet Traffic Filter Database and so can protect against such attacks.

Cisco introduced the Cisco ASA FirePOWER module as part of the integration of the Sourcefire technology.

Note   Cisco acquired the company Sourcefire to expand its security portfolio. The Cisco ASA FirePOWER module provides NGIPS, Application Visibility and Control (AVC), URL filtering, and AMP. This module runs as a separate application from the classic Cisco ASA software. The Cisco ASA FirePOWER module can be a hardware module on the ASA 5585-X only or a software module that runs in an SSD in all other models.

The Cisco ASA FirePOWER module can be managed by the Firepower Management Center (FMC), formerly known as the FireSIGHT Management Center. The Firepower Management Center and the Cisco ASA FirePOWER module require additional licenses. In all Cisco ASA models except the 5506-X, 5508-X, and 5516-X, the licenses are installed in the FirePOWER module. There are no additional licenses required in a Cisco ASA device. FirePOWER Services running on the Cisco ASA 5506-X, 5508-X, and 5516-X can be managed using Adaptive Security Device Manager (ASDM), and the licenses can be installed using ASDM. In all Cisco ASAs with FirePOWER Services managed by a Firepower Management Center, the license is installed on the Firepower Management Center and used by the module.

Chapter 2, "Introduction to and Design of Cisco ASA with FirePOWER Services," provides a more technical introduction to the Cisco ASA with FirePOWER Services, as well as design guidelines and best practices. Chapter 3, "Configuring Cisco ASA with FirePOWER Services," provides step-by-step instructions on how to configure the Cisco ASA with FirePOWER Services, and Chapter 4, " Troubleshooting Cisco ASA with FirePOWER Services and Firepower Threat Defense (FTD)," provides detailed instructions and tips on how to troubleshoot Cisco ASA with FirePOWER Services deployments.

Note   *Cisco ASA 5500-X Series Next-Generation Firewalls LiveLessons (Workshop): Deploying and Troubleshooting Techniques* (ISBN 978-1-58720-570-5) provides step-by-step instructions on how to deploy, configure, and troubleshoot the firewall features of the Cisco ASA 5500-X Series Next-Generation Firewalls, including an introduction to Cisco ASA with FirePOWER Services.

The Cisco Press book *Cisco ASA: All-in-One Next-Generation Firewall, IPS, and VPN Services*, third edition (ISBN 978-1-58714-307-6), provides an all-in-one guide to the Cisco ASA. Both of these publications provide guidance on how to install, configure, license, maintain, and troubleshoot the newest ASA devices. You learn how to implement authentication, authorization, and accounting (AAA) services, control and provision network access with packet filtering, use context-aware Cisco ASA next-generation firewall services, and take advantage of new NAT/PAT concepts. These publications also provide guidance on how to configure IP routing, application inspection, and QoS and how to implement high availability with failover and elastic scalability with clustering. *Cisco ASA: All-in-One Next-Generation Firewall, IPS, and VPN Services*, third edition, covers the configuration and troubleshooting of site-to-site IPsec VPNs and all forms of remote-access VPNs (IPsec, clientless SSL, and client-based SSL).

Cisco Firepower Threat Defense (FTD)

The Cisco FTD is unified software that includes Cisco ASA features, legacy FirePOWER Services, and new features. FTD can be deployed on Cisco Firepower 4100 and 9300 appliances to provide next-generation firewall (NGFW) services. In addition to being able to run on the Cisco Firepower 4100 Series and the Firepower 9300 appliances, FTD can also run natively on the ASA 5506-X, ASA 5506H-X, ASA 5506W-X, ASA 5508-X, ASA 5512-X, ASA 5515-X, ASA 5516-X, ASA 5525-X, ASA 5545-X, and ASA 5555-X. It is not supported in the ASA 5505 or the 5585-X.

Cisco Firepower 4100 Series

The Cisco Firepower 4100 Series appliances are next-generation firewalls that run the Cisco FTD software and features. There are four models:

- Cisco Firepower 4110, which supports up to 20 Gbps of firewall throughput

- Cisco Firepower 4120, which supports up to 40 Gbps of firewall throughput

- Cisco Firepower 4140, which supports up to 60 Gbps of firewall throughput

- Cisco Firepower 4150, which supports over 60 Gbps of firewall throughput

All of the Cisco Firepower 4100 Series models are one rack-unit (1 RU) appliances and are managed by the Cisco Firepower Chassis Manager.

Cisco Firepower 9300 Series

The Cisco Firepower 9300 appliances are designed for very large enterprises or service providers. They can scale beyond 1 Tbps and are designed in a modular way, supporting Cisco ASA software, Cisco FTD software, and Radware DefensePro DDoS mitigation software.

> **Note**   The Radware DefensePro DDoS mitigation software is available and supported directly from Cisco on Cisco Firepower 4150 and Cisco Firepower 9300 appliances.

Radware's DefensePro DDoS mitigation software provides real-time analysis to protect the enterprise or service provider infrastructure against network and application downtime due to distributed denial of service (DDoS) attacks.

Cisco FTD for Cisco Integrated Services Routers (ISRs)

The Cisco FTD can run on Cisco Unified Computing System (UCS) E-Series blades installed on Cisco ISR routers. Both the FMC and FTD are deployed as virtual machines. There are two internal interfaces that connect a router to an UCS E-Series blade. On ISR G2, Slot0 is a Peripheral Component Interconnet Express (PCIe) internal interface, and UCS E-Series Slot1 is a switched interface connected to the backplane Multi Gigabit Fabric (MGF). In Cisco ISR 4000 Series routers, both internal interfaces are connected to the MGF.

A hypervisor is installed on the UCS E-Series blade, and the Cisco FTD software runs as a virtual machine on it. FTD for ISRs is supported on the following platforms:

- **Cisco ISR G2 Series:** 2911, 2921, 2951, 3925, 3945, 3925E, and 3945E

- **Cisco ISR 4000 Series:** 4331, 4351, 4451, 4321, and 4431

Next-Generation Intrusion Prevention Systems (NGIPS)

As a result of the Sourcefire acquisition, Cisco expanded its NGIPS portfolio with the following products:

- **Cisco FirePOWER 8000 Series appliances:** These high-performance appliances running Cisco FirePOWER Next-Generation IPS Services support throughput speeds from 2 Gbps up through 60 Gbps.

- **Cisco FirePOWER 7000 Series appliances:** These are the base platform for the Cisco FirePOWER **NGIPS** software. Base platforms support throughput speeds from 50 Mbps up through 1.25 Gbps.

- **Virtual next-generation IPS (NGIPSv) appliances for VMware:** These appliances can be deployed in virtualized environments. By deploying these virtual appliances, security administrators can maintain network visibility that is often lost in virtual environments.

Chapter 10, "Introduction to and Deployment of Cisco Next-Generation IPS," provides a more technical introduction of the Cisco NGIPS appliances. Chapter 11,

"Configuring Cisco Next-Generation IPS," provides step-by-step instructions on how to configure Cisco NGIPS appliances, and Chapter 12, "Reporting and Troubleshooting with Cisco Next-Generation IPS," provides detailed instructions and tips on how to troubleshoot Cisco NGIPS deployments.

Firepower Management Center

Cisco Firepower Management Center (FMC) provides a centralized management and analysis platform for the Cisco NGIPS appliances and the Cisco ASA with FirePOWER Services. It provides support for role-based policy management and includes a fully customizable dashboard with advanced reports and analytics. The following are the models of the Cisco FMC appliances:

- **FS750**: Supports a maximum of 10 managed devices (NGIPS or Cisco ASA appliances) and a total of 20 million IPS events.

- **FS2000**: Supports a maximum of 70 managed devices and up to 60 million IPS events.

- **FS4000**: Supports a maximum of 300 managed devices and a total of 300 million IPS events.

- **FMC Virtual Appliance**: Allows you to conveniently provision on your existing virtual infrastructure. It supports a maximum of 25 managed devices and up to 10 million IPS events.

AMP for Endpoints

There are numerous antivirus and antimalware solutions on the market, designed to detect, analyze, and protect against both known and emerging endpoint threats. Before diving into these technologies, you should understand viruses and malicious software (malware). The following are the most common types of malicious software:

- **Computer virus:** Malicious software that infects a host file or system area to perform undesirable outcomes such as erasing data, stealing information, or corrupting the integrity of the system. In numerous cases, these viruses multiply again to form new generations of themselves.

- **Worm:** A virus that replicates itself over the network, infecting numerous vulnerable systems. In most cases, a worm executes malicious instructions on a remote system without user interaction.

- **Mailer or mass-mailer worm:** A type of worm that sends itself in an email message. Examples of mass-mailer worms are Loveletter.A@mm and W32/SKA.A@m (a.k.a. the Happy99 worm), which sends a copy of itself every time the user sends a new message.

- **Logic bomb:** A type of malicious code that is injected into a legitimate application. An attacker can program a logic bomb to delete itself from the disk after it performs the malicious tasks on the system. Examples of these malicious tasks include deleting or corrupting files or databases and executing a specific instruction after certain system conditions are met.

- **Trojan horse:** A type of malware that executes instructions to delete files, steal data, or otherwise compromise the integrity of the underlying operating system. Trojan horses typically use a form of social engineering to fool victims into installing such software in their computers or mobile devices. Trojans can also act as back doors.

- **Back door:** A piece of malware or a configuration change that allows attackers to control the victim's system remotely. For example, a back door can open a network port on the affected system so that the attacker can connect and control the system.

- **Exploit:** A malicious program designed to exploit, or take advantage of, a single vulnerability or set of vulnerabilities.

- **Downloader:** A piece of malware that downloads and installs other malicious content from the Internet to perform additional exploitation on an affected system.

- **Spammer:** Malware that sends spam, or unsolicited messages sent via email, instant messaging, newsgroups, or any other kind of computer or mobile device communications. Spammers send these unsolicited messages with the primary goal of fooling users to click malicious links, reply to emails or other messages with sensitive information, or perform different types of scams. The attacker's main objective is to make money.

- **Key logger:** A piece of malware that captures the user's keystrokes on a compromised computer or mobile device. It collects sensitive information, such as passwords, personal ID numbers (PINs), personal identifiable information (PII), credit card numbers, and more.

- **Rootkit:** A set of tools used by an attacker to elevate his or her privilege to obtain root-level access to be able to completely take control of the affected system.

- **Ransomware:** A type of malware that compromises a system and then demands a ransom from the victim to pay the attacker in order for the malicious activity to cease or for the malware to be removed from the affected system. Two examples of ransomware are Crypto Locker and CryptoWall, and they encrypt the victim's data and demand that the user pay a ransom in order for the data to be decrypted and accessible to the victim.

There are numerous types of commercial and free antivirus software. The following are a few examples of commercial and free options:

- Avast

- AVG Internet Security

- Bitdefender Antivirus Free

- ZoneAlarm PRO ANTIVIRUS+, ZoneAlarm PRO FIREWALL, and ZoneAlarm EXTREME SECURITY

- F-Secure Anti-virus

- Kaspersky Anti-virus

- McAfee AntiVirus

- Panda Antivirus

- Sophos Antivirus

- Norton AntiVirus

- ClamAV

- Immunet AntiVirus

Note ClamAV is an open source antivirus engine sponsored and maintained by Cisco and non-Cisco engineers. You can download ClamAV from www.clamav.net. Immunet is a free community-based antivirus software maintained by Cisco Sourcefire. You can download Immunet from www.immunet.com.

There are numerous other antivirus software companies and products. The following link provides a comprehensive list and comparison of the different antivirus software available on the market: http://en.wikipedia.org/wiki/Comparison_of_antivirus_software.

Personal firewalls and host intrusion prevention systems (HIPS) are software applications that you can install on end-user machines or servers to protect them from external security threats and intrusions. The term *personal firewall* typically applies to basic software that can control Layer 3 and Layer 4 access to client machines. HIPS provides several features that offer more robust security than a traditional personal firewall, such as host intrusion prevention and protection against spyware, viruses, worms, Trojans, and other types of malware.

Today, more sophisticated software makes basic personal firewalls and HIPS obsolete. For example, Cisco Advanced Malware Protection (AMP) for Endpoints provides granular visibility and control to stop advanced threats missed by other security layers. Cisco AMP for Endpoints takes advantage of telemetry from big data, continuous analysis, and advanced analytics provided by Cisco threat intelligence to be able to detect, analyze, and stop advanced malware across endpoints.

Cisco AMP for Endpoints provides advanced malware protection for many operating systems, including Windows, Mac OS X, Android, and Linux.

Attacks are getting very sophisticated and can evade detection of traditional systems and endpoint protection. Today, attackers have the resources, knowledge, and persistence to beat point-in-time detection. Cisco AMP for Endpoints provides mitigation capabilities that go beyond point-in-time detection. It uses threat intelligence from Cisco to perform retrospective analysis and protection. Cisco AMP for Endpoints also provides device and file trajectory capabilities to allow a security administrator to analyze the full spectrum of an attack. Device trajectory and file trajectory support the following file types in Windows and Mac OS X operating systems:

- MSEXE

- PDF

- MSCAB

- MSOLE2

- ZIP

- ELF

- MACHO

- MACHO_UNIBIN

- SWF

- JAVA

Note   The Mac OS X connector does not support SWF files. The Windows connector does not scan ELF, JAVA, MACHO, or MACHO_UNIBIN files at the time of this writing. The Android AMP connector scans APK files.

AMP for Networks

Cisco AMP for Networks provides next-generation security services that go beyond point-in-time detection. It provides continuous analysis and tracking of files and also retrospective security alerts so that a security administrator can take action during and after an attack. The file trajectory feature of Cisco AMP for Networks tracks file transmissions across the network, and the file capture feature enables a security administrator to store and retrieve files for further analysis. Chapter 6, "Cisco AMP for Networks," provides Cisco AMP for Networks configuration and troubleshooting guidance, with step-by-step examples.

AMP Threat Grid

Cisco acquired a security company called ThreatGRID that provides cloud-based and on-premises malware analysis solutions. Cisco integrated Cisco AMP and Threat Grid to provide a solution for advanced malware analysis with deep threat analytics. The Cisco AMP Threat Grid integrated solution analyzes millions of files and correlates them with hundreds of millions of malware samples. This provides a look into attack campaigns and how malware is distributed. This solution provides a security administrator with detailed reports of indicators of compromise and threat scores that help prioritize mitigations and recover from attacks.

Chapter 9, "AMP Threat Grid: Malware Analysis and Threat Intelligence," provides the technical details of the AMP Threat Grid solution.

Email Security Overview

Users are no longer accessing email only from the corporate network or from a single device. Cisco provides cloud-based, hybrid, and on-premises ESA-based solutions that can help protect any dynamic environment. This section introduces these solutions and technologies and explains how users can use threat intelligence to detect, analyze, and protect against both known and emerging threats.

There are several types of email-based threats. The following are the most common:

- **Spam:** Unsolicited email messages that can be advertising a service or (typically) a scam or a message with malicious intent. Email spam continues to be a major threat because it can be used to spread malware.

- **Malware attachments:** Email messages containing malicious software (malware).

- **Phishing:** An attacker's attempt to fool a user that the email communication comes from a legitimate entity or site, such as banks, social media websites, online payment processors, or even corporate IT communications. The goal of a phishing email is to steal a user's sensitive information, such as user credentials, bank account information, and so on.

- **Spear phishing:** Phishing attempts that are more targeted. Spear phishing emails are directed to specific individual or organizations. For instance, an attacker may perform a passive reconnaissance on an individual or organization by gathering information from social media sites (for example, Twitter, LinkedIn, Facebook) and other online resources. Then the attacker may tailor a more directed and relevant message to the victim to increase the probability that the user will be fooled to follow a malicious link, click an attachment containing malware, or simply reply to the email and provide sensitive information. Another phishing-based attack, called *whaling*, specifically targets executives and high-profile users.

Email Security Appliance

The following are the different Email Security Appliance (ESA) models:

- **Cisco X-Series ESA models:**
  - **Cisco X1070:** A high-performance ESA model for service providers and large enterprises

- **Cisco C-Series ESA models:**

  - **Cisco C680:** A high-performance ESA model for service providers and large enterprise

  - **Cisco C670:** An ESA model designed for medium-size enterprises

  - **Cisco C380:** An ESA model designed for medium-size enterprises

  - **Cisco C370:** An ESA model designed for small to medium-size enterprises

  - **Cisco C170:** An ESA model designed for small businesses and branch offices

The Cisco ESA runs the Cisco AsyncOS operating system. Cisco AsyncOS supports numerous features that help mitigate email-based threats.

The following are examples of the features supported by the Cisco ESA:

- **Access control:** Controlling access for inbound senders, according to a sender's IP address, IP address range, or domain name.

- **Anti-spam:** Multilayer filters based on Cisco SenderBase reputation and Cisco antispam integration. The antispam reputation and zero-day threat intelligence are fueled by the Cisco security intelligence and research group named Talos.

- **Network antivirus:** Network antivirus capabilities at the gateway. Cisco partnered with Sophos and McAfee, supporting their antivirus scanning engines.

- **Advanced Malware Protection (AMP):** Allows security administrators to detect and block malware and perform continuous analysis and retrospective alerting.

- **Data loss prevention (DLP):** The ability to detect any sensitive emails and documents leaving the corporation. The Cisco ESA integrates RSA email DLP for outbound traffic.

- **Email encryption:** The ability to encrypt outgoing mail to address regulatory requirements. The administrator can configure an encryption policy on the Cisco ESA and use a local key server or hosted key service to encrypt the message.

- **Email authentication:** A few email authentication mechanisms, including Sender Policy Framework (SPF), Sender ID Framework (SIDF), and DomainKeys Identified Mail (DKIM) verification of incoming mail, as well as DomainKeys and DKIM signing of outgoing mail.

- **Outbreak filters:** Preventive protection against new security outbreaks and email-based scams using Cisco's Security Intelligence Operations (SIO) threat intelligence information.

Note   Cisco SenderBase (see www.senderbase.org) is the world's largest email and web traffic monitoring network. It provides real-time threat intelligence powered by Cisco SIO.

The Cisco ESA acts as the email gateway for an organization, handling all email connections, accepting messages, and relaying messages to the appropriate systems. The Cisco ESA can service email connections from the Internet to users inside a network and from systems inside the network to the Internet. Email connections use Simple Mail Transfer Protocol (SMTP). The ESA services all SMTP connections, by default acting as the SMTP gateway.

Tip   Mail gateways are also known as a mail exchangers (MX).

The Cisco ESA uses listeners to handle incoming SMTP connection requests. A listener defines an email processing service that is configured on an interface in the Cisco ESA. Listeners apply to email entering the appliance from either the Internet or internal systems.

The following listeners can be configured:

- Public listeners for email coming in from the Internet

- Private listeners for email coming from hosts in the corporate (inside) network (These emails are typically from internal groupware, Exchange, POP, or IMAP email servers.)

Cisco ESA listeners are often referred to as *SMTP daemons*, and they run on specific Cisco ESA interfaces. When a listener is configured, the following information must be provided:

- Listener properties such as a specific interface in the Cisco ESA and the TCP port that will be used. The listener properties must also indicate whether it is a public or a private listener.

- The hosts that are allowed to connect to the listener, using a combination of access control rules. An administrator can specify which remote hosts can connect to the listener.

- The local domains for which public listeners accept messages.

Cloud Email Security

Cisco Cloud Email Security provides a cloud-based solution that allows companies to outsource the management of their email security management. The service provides email security instances in multiple Cisco data centers to enable high availability.

Cisco Hybrid Email Security

The Cisco Hybrid Email Security solution combines both cloud-based and on-premises ESAs. This hybrid solution helps Cisco customers reduce their onsite email security footprint and outsource a portion of their email security to Cisco, while still allowing them to maintain control of confidential information within their physical boundaries. Many organizations must comply with regulations that require them to keep sensitive data physically on their premises. The Cisco Hybrid Email Security solution allows network security administrators to remain compliant and to maintain advanced control with encryption, DLP, and onsite identity-based integration.

Web Security Overview

For an organization to be able to protect its environment against web-based security threats, security administrators need to deploy tools and mitigation technologies that go far beyond traditional blocking of known bad websites. Today, you can download malware through compromised legitimate websites, including social media sites, advertisements in news and corporate sites, and gaming sites. Cisco has developed several tools and mechanisms to help customers combat these threats, including and Cisco Web Security Appliance (WSA), Cisco Security Management Appliance (SMA), and Cisco Cloud Web Security (CWS). These solutions enable malware detection and blocking, continuous monitoring, and retrospective alerting.

Web Security Appliance

A Cisco WSA uses cloud-based intelligence from Cisco to help protect an organization before, during, and after an attack. This "lifecycle" is referred to as the *attack continuum*. The cloud-based intelligence includes web (URL) reputation and zero-day threat intelligence from the Talos Cisco security intelligence and research group. This threat intelligence helps security professionals stop threats before they enter the corporate network and also enables file reputation and file sandboxing to identify threats during an attack. Retrospective attack analysis allows security administrators to investigate and provide protection after an attack, when advanced malware might have evaded other layers of defense.

A Cisco WSA can be deployed in explicit proxy mode or as a transparent proxy, using the Web Cache Communication Protocol (WCCP). WCCP was originally developed by Cisco, but several other vendors have integrated this protocol in their products to allow clustering and transparent proxy deployments on networks using Cisco infrastructure devices (routers, switches, firewalls, and so on).

Figure 1-3 illustrates a Cisco WSA deployed as an explicit proxy.

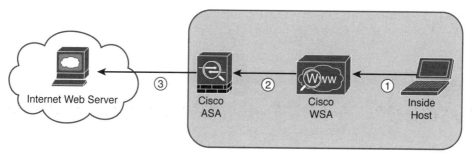

Figure 1-3 *WSA Explicit Proxy Configuration*

The following are the steps illustrated in Figure 1-3:

Step 1.   An internal user makes an HTTP request to an external website. The client browser is configured to send the request to the Cisco WSA.

Step 2.   The Cisco WSA connects to the website on behalf of the internal user.

Step 3.   The firewall (Cisco ASA) is configured to only allow outbound web traffic from the Cisco WSA, and it forwards the traffic to the web server.

Figure 1-4 shows a Cisco WSA deployed as a transparent proxy.

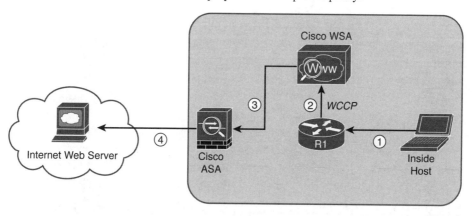

Figure 1-4 *Transparent Proxy Configuration*

The following are the steps illustrated in Figure 1-4:

Step 1.   An internal user makes an HTTP request to an external website.

Step 2.   The internal router (R1) redirects the web request to the Cisco WSA, using WCCP.

Step 3.   The Cisco WSA connects to the website on behalf of the internal user.

Step 4.   The firewall (Cisco ASA) is configured to only allow outbound web traffic from the WSA. The web traffic is sent to the Internet web server.

Figure 1-5 demonstrates how the WCCP registration works. The Cisco WSA is the
WCCP client, and the Cisco router is the WCCP server.

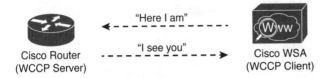

Cisco Router
(WCCP Server)

"Here I am"

"I see you"

Cisco WSA
(WCCP Client)

Figure 1-5   *WCCP Registration*

During the WCCP registration process, the WCCP client sends a registration announce-
ment ("Here I am") every 10 seconds. The WCCP server (the Cisco router, in this
example) accepts the registration request and acknowledges it with an "I see you" WCCP
message. The WCCP server waits 30 seconds before it declares the client as "inactive"
(engine failed). WCCP can be used in large-scale environments. Figure 1-6 shows a cluster of Cisco WSAs, where internal Layer 3 switches redirect web traffic to the cluster.

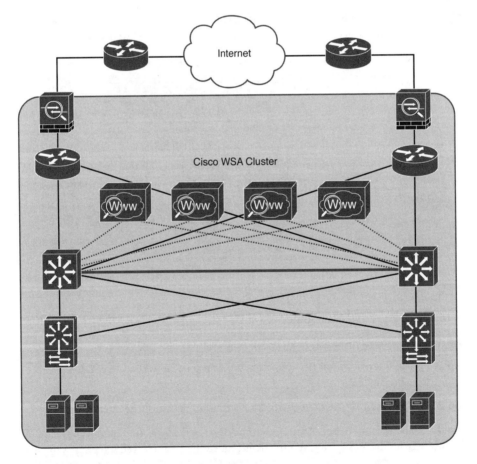

Figure 1-6   *Cisco WSA Cluster Example*

The following are the different Cisco WSA models:

- **Cisco WSA S680:** A high-performance WSA designed for large organizations with 6000 to 12,000 users. A two rack-unit (2 RU) appliance with 16 (2 octa core) CPUs, 32 GB of memory, and 4.8 TB of disk space.

- **Cisco WSA S670:** A high-performance WSA designed for large organizations with 6000 to 12,000 users. A 2 RU appliance with 8 (2 octa core) CPUs, 8 GB of memory, and 2.7 TB of disk space.

- **Cisco WSA S380:** A WSA designed for medium-size organizations with 1500 to 6000 users. A 2 RU appliance with 6 (1 hexa core) CPUs, 16 GB of memory, and 2.4 TB of disk space.

- **Cisco WSA S370:** A WSA designed for medium-size organizations with 1500 to 6000 users. A 2 RU appliance with 4 (1 quad core) CPUs, 4 GB or memory, and 1.8 TB of disk space.

- **Cisco WSA S170:** A WSA designed for small to medium-size organizations with up to 1500 users. A 1 RU appliance with 2 (1 dual core) CPUs, 4 GB of memory, and 500 GB of disk space.

The Cisco WSA runs the Cisco AsyncOS operating system. Cisco AsyncOS supports numerous features that help mitigate web-based threats. The following are examples of these features:

- **Real-time antimalware adaptive scanning:** The Cisco WSA can be configured to dynamically select an antimalware scanning engine based on URL reputation, content type, and scanner effectiveness. Adaptive scanning is a feature designed to increase the "catch rate" of malware that is embedded in images, JavaScript, text, and Adobe Flash files. Adaptive scanning is an additional layer of security on top of Cisco WSA web reputation filters that include support for Sophos, Webroot, and McAfee.

- **Layer 4 traffic monitor:** The Cisco WSA is used to detect and block spyware. It dynamically adds IP addresses of known malware domains to databases of sites to block.

- **Third-party DLP integration:** The Cisco WSA redirects all outbound traffic to a third-party DLP appliance, allowing deep content inspection for regulatory compliance and data exfiltration protection. It enables an administrator to inspect web content by title, metadata, and size and to even prevent users from storing files to cloud services, such as Dropbox and Google Drive.

- **File reputation:** Using threat information from Cisco Talos, this file reputation threat intelligence is updated every 3 to 5 minutes.

■ **File sandboxing:** If malware is detected, the Cisco AMP capabilities can put files in a sandbox to inspect the malware's behavior and combine the inspection with machine-learning analysis to determine the threat level. Cisco Cognitive Threat Analytics (CTA) uses machine-learning algorithms to adapt over time.

■ **File retrospection:** After a malicious attempt or malware is detected, the Cisco WSA continues to cross-examine files over an extended period of time.

■ **Application visibility and control:** The Cisco WSA can inspect and even block applications that are not allowed by the corporate security policy. For example, an administrator can allow users to use social media sites like Facebook but block micro-applications such as Facebook games.

Cisco Security Management Appliance

Cisco Security Management Appliance (SMA) is a Cisco product that centralizes the management and reporting for one or more Cisco ESAs and Cisco WSAs. Cisco SMA enables you to consistently enforce policy and enhances threat protection. Figure 1-7 shows a Cisco SMA that is controlling Cisco ESA and Cisco WSAs in different geographic locations (New York, Raleigh, Paris, and London).

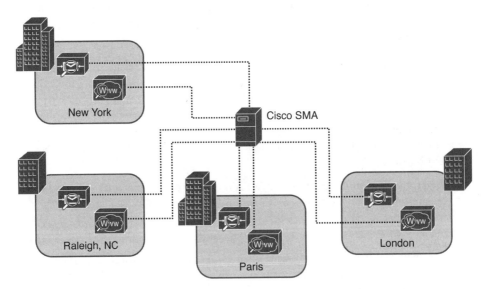

Figure 1-7 *Cisco SMA Centralized Deployment*

The Cisco SMA comes in different models, including physical appliances and the Cisco Content Security Management Virtual Appliance (SMAV):

■ **Cisco SMA M680:** Designed for large organizations with more than 10,000 users

■ **Cisco SMAV M600v:** Designed for organizations with more than 5000 users

- **Cisco SMA M380**: Designed for organizations with 1000 to 10,000 users

- **Cisco SMAV M300v**: Designed for organizations with 1000 to 5000 users

- **Cisco SMA M170**: Designed for small business or branch offices with up to 1000 users

- **Cisco SMAV M100v**: Designed for small business or branch offices with up to 1000 users

Note   Cisco also has a Cisco SMAV M000v that is used for evaluations only.

Cisco Cloud Web Security (CWS)

Cisco CWS is a cloud-based security service that provides worldwide threat intelligence, advanced threat defense capabilities, and roaming user protection. The Cisco CWS service uses web proxies in the Cisco cloud environment that scan traffic for malware and policy enforcement. Cisco customers can connect to the Cisco CWS service directly by using a proxy auto-configuration (PAC) file in the user endpoint or through connectors integrated into the following Cisco products:

- Cisco ISR G2 routers

- Cisco ASA

- Cisco WSA

- Cisco AnyConnect Secure Mobility Client

Organizations using the transparent proxy functionality through a connector can get the most out of their existing infrastructure. In addition, the scanning is offloaded from the hardware appliances to the cloud, reducing the impact to hardware utilization and reducing network latency. Figure 1-8 illustrates how the transparent proxy functionality through a connector works.

In Figure 1-8, the Cisco ASA is enabled with the Cisco CWS connector at a branch office and protects the corporate users at the branch office with these steps:

Step 1.   An internal user makes an HTTP request to an external website (example.org).

Step 2.   The Cisco ASA forwards the request to the Cisco CWS global cloud infrastructure.

Step 3.   Cisco CWS notices that example.org has some web content (ads) that is redirecting the user to a known malicious site.

Step 4.   Cisco CWS blocks the request to the malicious site.

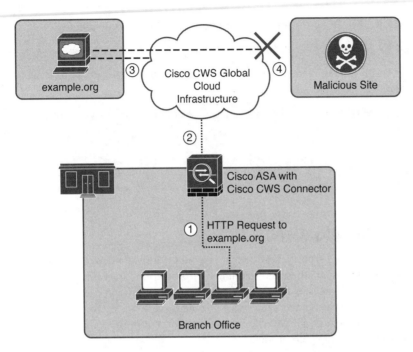

Figure 1-8 *Cisco ASA with Cisco CWS Connector Example*

Cisco Identity Services Engine (ISE)

The Cisco ISE is a comprehensive security identity management solution designed to function as a policy decision point for network access. It allows security administrators to collect real-time contextual information from a network, its users, and devices. Cisco ISE is the central policy management platform in the Cisco TrustSec solution. It supports a comprehensive set of authentication, authorization, and accounting (AAA); posture; and network profiler features in a single device.

Cisco ISE allows security administrators to provide network guest access management and wide-ranging client provisioning policies, including 802.1X environments. The support of TrustSec features such as security group tags (SGTs) and security group access control lists (SGACLs) make the Cisco ISE a complete identity services solution. Cisco ISE supports policy sets, which let a security administrator group sets of authentication and authorization policies.

Cisco ISE provides Network Admission Control (NAC) features, including posture policies, to enforce configuration of end-user devices with the most up-to-date security settings or applications before they enter the network. The Cisco ISE supports the following agent types for posture assessment and compliance:

■ **Cisco NAC Web Agent:** A temporary agent that is installed in end-user machines at the time of login. The Cisco NAC Web Agent is not visible on the end-user machine after the user terminates the session.

- **Cisco NAC Agent:** An agent that is installed permanently on a Windows or Mac OS X client system.

- **AnyConnect ISE Agent:** An agent that is installed permanently on a Windows or Mac OS X client system.

Cisco ISE provides a comprehensive set of features to allow corporate users to connect their personal devices—such as mobile phones, tablets, laptops, and other network devices—to the network. Such a bring-your-own device (BYOD) system introduces many challenges in terms of protecting network services and enterprise data. Cisco ISE provides support for multiple mobile device management (MDM) solutions to enforce policy on endpoints. ISE can be configured to redirect users to MDM onboarding portals and prompt them to update their devices before they can access the network. Cisco ISE can also be configured to provide Internet-only access to users who are not compliant with MDM policies.

Cisco ISE supports the Cisco Platform Exchange Grid (pxGrid), a multivendor, cross-platform network system that combines different parts of an IT infrastructure, such as the following:

- Security monitoring

- Detection systems

- Network policy platforms

- Asset and configuration management

- Identity and access management platforms

Cisco pxGrid has a unified framework with an open **application programming interface** (API) designed in a hub-and-spoke architecture. pxGrid is used to enable the sharing of contextual-based information from a Cisco ISE session directory to other policy network systems, such as Cisco IOS devices and the Cisco ASA.

The Cisco ISE can be configured as a certificate authority (CA) to generate and manage digital certificates for endpoints. Cisco ISE CA supports standalone and subordinate deployments.

Cisco ISE software can be installed on a range of physical appliances or on a VMware server (Cisco ISE VM). The Cisco ISE software image does not support the installation of any other packages or applications on this dedicated platform.

Cisco Meraki Cloud-Managed MDM

Cisco acquired a company called Meraki that provides cloud-managed MDM, cloud-managed wireless devices, and security appliances. Cisco Meraki cloud-based enterprise mobility management allows network administrators to pre-enroll devices or dynamically add users as they try to connect to the corporate network. An administrator can push apps and content or restrict network access based on user groups.

The Cisco Meraki web-based (cloud) dashboard allows administrators to locate, track, monitor, and manage all end-user systems and mobile devices from anywhere in the world.

Note   For more information about Cisco Meraki MDM solutions, visit https://meraki.cisco.com/products/systems-manager.

Cisco Meraki Cloud-Managed Security Appliances

Cisco Meraki also has a series of cloud-managed security appliances that provide the following features:

- Identity-based firewall features that enforce network policy and traffic-shaping rules, VLAN tags, and bandwidth limits for different types of users

- Intrusion prevention to detect and protect network resources

- VPN features to securely connect remote locations using mesh or hub-and-spoke topologies

- Content filtering, anti-malware, and anti-phishing capabilities

- High availability and failover

Note   For more information about Cisco Meraki MDM solutions, go to https://meraki.cisco.com/products.

Cisco VPN Solutions

Numerous enterprises, service providers, and other institutions deploy virtual private networks (VPNs) to provide data integrity, authentication, and data encryption to ensure confidentiality of the packets sent over the Internet or another unprotected network. VPNs are designed to avoid the cost of unnecessary leased lines. Many different protocols are used for VPN implementations, including the following:

- Point-to-Point Tunneling Protocol (PPTP)

- Layer 2 Forwarding (L2F) protocol

- Layer 2 Tunneling Protocol (L2TP)

- Generic routing encapsulation (GRE)

- Multiprotocol Label Switching (MPLS) VPN

- Internet Protocol Security (IPsec)

- Secure Sockets Layer (SSL)

VPN implementations can be categorized into two distinct groups:

- **Site-to-site VPNs:** Enable organizations to establish VPN tunnels between two or more network infrastructure devices in different sites so that they can communicate over a shared medium such as the Internet. Many organizations use IPsec, GRE, or MPLS VPN as site-to-site VPN protocols.

- **Remote-access VPNs:** Enable users to work from remote locations, such as their homes, hotels, and other premises as if they were directly connected to their corporate network. Many organizations use IPsec and SSL VPN for remote-access VPNs.

Cisco provides a comprehensive VPN portfolio, including support for site-to-site VPNs in Cisco IOS devices and the Cisco ASA. Remote-access VPN support includes clientless SSL VPN and full client connections with the Cisco AnyConnect Secure Mobility Client. This book does not cover any VPN topics in detail. *Cisco ASA: All-in-One Next-Generation Firewall, IPS, and VPN Services*, third edition, covers the configuration and troubleshooting of site-to-site IPsec VPNs and all forms of remote-access VPNs (IPsec, clientless SSL, and client-based SSL).

Summary

Cisco makes some of the most complete and advanced security products in the industry. These products and solutions provide visibility, policy enforcement, and advanced threat protection across the network and the entire attack continuum. This chapter introduces the new threat landscape and the attack continuum. It also provides details about the Cisco ASA 5500-X Series next-generation firewalls and the Cisco ASA with FirePOWER Services, Cisco FTD, the Firepower 4100 and 9300 appliances, Cisco's NGIPS, Firepower Management Center, Cisco AMP for Endpoints, Cisco AMP for Networks, and Cisco AMP Threat Grid. It also provides an introduction to email and web security, describing the Cisco ESA, Cloud Email Security, Cisco WSA, and Cisco CWS. This chapter also introduces other Cisco core security products, such as Cisco ISE, Cisco Meraki cloud-managed MDM, and Cisco Meraki cloud-managed security appliances and briefly explains the available Cisco VPN solutions. The chapters that follow focus on the latest next-generation platforms.

Chapter 2

Introduction to and Design of Cisco ASA with FirePOWER Services

This chapter provides an introduction to the Cisco ASA with FirePOWER Services solution. It also provides design guidance and best practices for deploying Cisco ASA with FirePOWER Services. This chapter covers the following topics:

- Introduction to Cisco ASA FirePOWER Services

- Inline versus promiscuous mode

- Cisco ASA FirePOWER management options

- Cisco ASA FirePOWER Services sizing

- Cisco ASA FirePOWER Services licensing

- Compatibility with other Cisco ASA features

- Cisco ASA FirePOWER packet processing order of operations

- Cisco ASA FirePOWER Services and failover

- Cisco ASA FirePOWER Services and clustering

- Deployment of the Cisco ASA FirePOWER Services in the Internet edge

- Deployment of the Cisco ASA FirePOWER Services in VPN scenarios

- Deployment of the Cisco ASA FirePOWER Services in the data center

Introduction to Cisco ASA FirePOWER Services

In Chapter 1, "Fundamentals of Cisco Next-Generation Security," you learned about the different Cisco next-generation security products and technologies. You also learned that those security technologies and processes should not focus solely on detection but should also provide the ability to mitigate the impact of an attack. Organizations must maintain visibility and control across the extended network during the full attack continuum:

- Before an attack takes place

- During an active attack

- After an attacker starts to damage systems or steal information

The Cisco ASA with FirePOWER Services and Cisco's Advanced Malware Protection (AMP) provide a security solution that helps you discover threats and enforce and harden policies before an attack takes place. These technologies and solutions can help you detect, block, and defend against attacks that have already taken place. In Chapter 1 you also learned that the Cisco ASA family has members in many shapes and sizes, and you learned about their uses in small, medium, and large organizations.

Cisco introduced the Cisco ASA FirePOWER Services as part of the integration of the SourceFire technology. Cisco ASA FirePOWER Services provides the following key capabilities:

- **Access control:** This policy-based capability allows a network security administrator to define, inspect, and log the traffic that traverses a firewall. Access control policies determine how traffic is permitted or denied in a network. For instance, you can configure a default action to inspect all traffic or to block or trust all traffic without further inspection. You can also achieve a more complete access control policy with enrichment data based on security threat intelligence. Whether you configure simple or complex rules, you can control traffic based on security zones, network or geographical locations, ports, applications, requested URLs, and per user.

- **Intrusion detection and prevention:** Intrusion detection and prevention help you detect attempts from an attacker to gain unauthorized access to a network or a host, create performance degradation, or steal information. You define intrusion detection and prevention policies based on your access control policies. You can create and tune custom policies at a very granular level to specify how traffic is inspected in a network.

- **AMP and file control:** You can detect, track, capture, analyze, and optionally block the transmission of files, including malware files and nested files inside archive files in network traffic. File control also enables you to detect and block users from sending or receiving files of different specified types over a multitude of application protocols. You can configure file control as part of the overall access control policies and application inspection.

■ **Application programming interfaces (APIs):** Cisco ASA FirePOWER Services supports several ways to interact with the system using APIs.

The Cisco ASA FirePOWER module can be a hardware module on the ASA 5585-X only or a software module that runs in a solid state drive (SSD) in all other Cisco ASA 5500-X models.

Note   The Cisco ASA FirePOWER Services module is not supported in the 5505. For the 5512-X through ASA 5555-X, you must install an SSD. The SSD is standard on the 5506-X, 5508-X, and 5516-X.

Inline versus Promiscuous Mode

The Cisco ASA FirePOWER module can be configured in either of the following modes:

■ Inline mode

■ Promiscuous monitor-only (passive) mode

Inline Mode

When the Cisco ASA FirePOWER module is configured in inline mode, the traffic passes through the firewall policies before it is sent to the Cisco ASA FirePOWER module.

Figure 2-1 illustrates the order of operations when the Cisco ASA FirePOWER module is configured in inline mode.

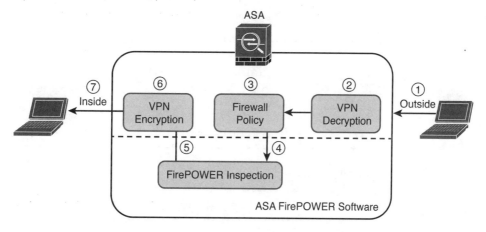

Figure 2-1   *Inline Mode*

1. Network traffic is received on a given interface of the Cisco ASA. In this example, the traffic is received in the outside interface.

2. If IPsec or SSL VPN is configured, the incoming encrypted traffic is decrypted.

3. Firewall policies are applied to the traffic.

4. If the traffic is compliant and allowed by the firewall policies, it is sent to the Cisco ASA FirePOWER module.

5. The Cisco ASA FirePOWER module inspects the traffic and applies its security policies and takes appropriate actions. If traffic is not compliant with security policies or is determined to be malicious, the Cisco ASA FirePOWER module sends back a verdict to the ASA, and the ASA blocks the traffic and alerts the network security administrator. All valid traffic is allowed by the Cisco ASA.

6. If IPsec or SSL VPN is configured, the outgoing traffic is encrypted.

7. The network traffic is sent to the network.

Promiscuous Monitor-Only Mode

When the Cisco ASA FirePOWER module is configured in promiscuous monitor-only mode, a copy of each packet of the traffic that is defined in the service policy is sent to the Cisco ASA FirePOWER module.

Figure 2-2 illustrates the order of operations when the Cisco ASA FirePOWER module is configured in promiscuous monitor-only mode:

1. Network traffic is received on a given interface of the Cisco ASA. In this example, the traffic is received in the outside interface.

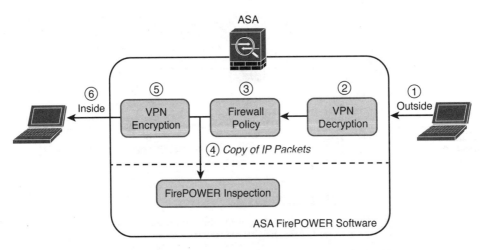

Figure 2-2 *Promiscuous Monitor-Only Mode*

2. If IPsec or SSL VPN is configured, the incoming encrypted traffic is decrypted.

3. Firewall policies are applied to the traffic.

4. If the traffic is compliant and allowed by the firewall policies, a copy of each packet is sent to the Cisco ASA FirePOWER module. If traffic is not compliant with security policies or is determined to be malicious, the Cisco ASA FirePOWER module can be configured to alert the administrator, but it does not block the traffic.

5. If IPsec or SSL VPN is configured, the outgoing traffic is encrypted.

6. The network traffic is sent to the network.

As you can see, the most secure and effective way to configure the Cisco ASA FirePOWER module is in inline mode. You can configure the Cisco ASA FirePOWER module in promiscuous monitor-only mode when you are evaluating and performing capacity planning for a new deployment.

The Cisco ASA FirePOWER module modes are a bit different than those of the Cisco FirePOWER Series of appliances, which support the following deployment modes/options:

- Standalone IPS (active/standby)

- Clustering

- SourceFire Redundancy Protocol (SFRP)

- Bypass and non-bypass modules

Cisco FirePOWER Series next-generation intrusion prevention systems (NGIPS) appliances can be deployed in multiple modes at once:

- Passive

- Inline

- Routed

- Switched

Note   Chapter 10, "Introduction to and Deployment of Cisco Next-Generation IPS," covers the different modes of operations of the Cisco FirePOWER Series NGIPS appliances.

Cisco ASA FirePOWER Management Options

There are several options available for network security administrators to manage the Cisco ASA FirePOWER module. The Cisco ASA FirePOWER module provides a basic command-line interface (CLI) for initial configuration and troubleshooting only. Network security administrators can configure security policies on the Cisco ASA FirePOWER module using either of these methods:

■ Administrators can configure the Cisco Firepower Management Center hosted on a separate appliance or deployed as a virtual machine (VM).

■ Administrators can configure the Cisco ASA FirePOWER module deployed on Cisco ASA 5506-X, 5508-X, and 5516-X using Cisco's Adaptive Security Device Manager (ASDM).

Figure 2-3 shows a Cisco ASA with FirePOWER Services being managed by a Cisco Firepower Management Center (FMC) in a VM.

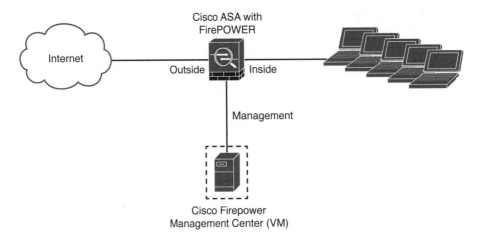

Figure 2-3   *Cisco ASA with FirePOWER Services Managed by a Cisco Firepower Management Center*

In Figure 2-3 the Cisco Firepower Management Center manages the Cisco ASA FirePOWER module via its management interface. The following section provides important information about configuring and accessing the Cisco ASA FirePOWER module management interface.

Accessing the Cisco ASA FirePOWER Module Management Interface in Cisco ASA 5585-X Appliances

In the Cisco ASA 5585-X, the Cisco ASA FirePOWER module includes a separate management interface. All management traffic to and from the Cisco ASA FirePOWER module must enter and exit this management interface, and the management interface cannot be used as a data interface.

The Cisco ASA FirePOWER module needs Internet access to perform several operations, such as automated system software updates and threat intelligence updates. If the module is managed by the Firepower Management Center, the FMC is the one that needs to have Internet access to perform those tasks.

Figure 2-4 shows an example of how you can physically connect the Cisco ASA FirePOWER module management interface to be able to reach the Internet via the Cisco ASA interface.

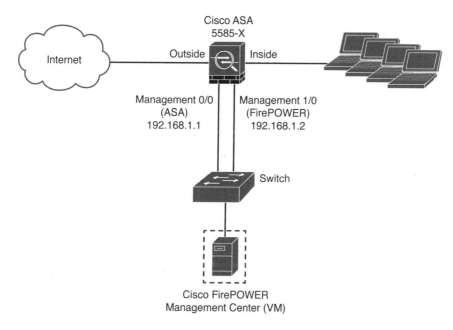

Figure 2-4 *Cisco ASA 5585-X FirePOWER Module Management Interface*

In Figure 2-4, the Cisco ASA 5585-X has two modules:

- A **module** running Cisco ASA software

- A module running FirePOWER Services

The Cisco ASA is managed via the interface named management 0/0 in this example. This interface is configured with the IP address 192.168.1.1. The Cisco ASA FirePOWER module is managed via the interface named management 1/0, configured with the IP address 192.168.1.2. The Cisco ASA FirePOWER module is being managed by a virtual Cisco Firepower Management Center. Both interfaces are connected to a Layer 2 switch in this example.

Note You can use other cabling options with the Cisco ASA FirePOWER module management interface to be able to reach the Internet, depending on how you want to connect your network. However, the example illustrated in Figure 2-4 is one of the most common scenarios.

In order for the Cisco ASA FirePOWER module management interface to have an Internet connection, the default gateway of the Cisco ASA FirePOWER module is set to the Cisco ASA management interface IP address (192.168.1.1 in this example). Figure 2-5 illustrates the logical connection between the Cisco ASA FirePOWER module management interface and the Cisco ASA management interface.

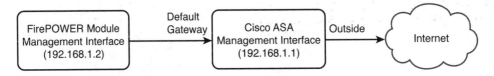

Figure 2-5   *Cisco ASA FirePOWER Module Management Interface*

Accessing the Cisco ASA FirePOWER Module Management Interface in Cisco ASA 5500-X Appliances

In the rest of the Cisco 5500-X appliances, the management interface is shared by the Cisco ASA FirePOWER module and the classic Cisco ASA software. These appliances include the Cisco ASA 5506-X, 5506W-X, 5506H-X, 5508-X, 5512-X, 5515-X, 5516-X, 5525-X, 5545-X, and 5555-X appliances.

Figure 2-6 shows a Cisco ASA 5516-X running Cisco ASA FirePOWER Services.

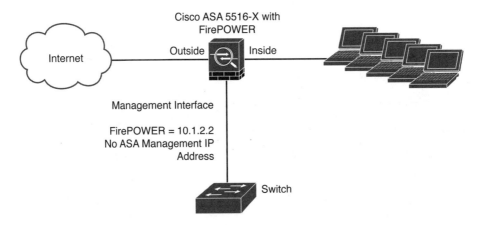

Figure 2-6   *Cisco ASA 5500-X FirePOWER Module Management Interface*

In Figure 2-6, the management interface is used by the Cisco ASA FirePOWER module. The management interface is configured with the IP address 10.1.2.2. You cannot configure an IP address for this interface in the Cisco ASA configuration. For the ASA 5506-X, 5508-X, and 5516-X, the default configuration enables the preceding network deployment; the only change you need to make is to set the module IP address to be on the same network as the ASA inside interface and to configure the module gateway IP address. For other models, you must remove the ASA-configured name and IP address for management 0/0 or 1/1 and then configure the other interfaces as shown in Figure 2-6.

Note   The management interface is considered completely separate from the Cisco ASA, and routing must be configured accordingly.

The Cisco ASA FirePOWER module default gateway is configured to be the inside interface of the Cisco ASA (10.1.2.1), as illustrated in Figure 2-7.

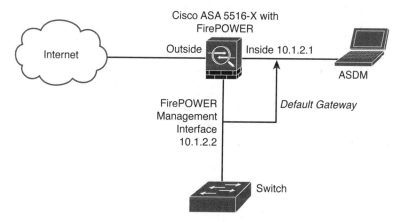

Figure 2-7   *Cisco ASA 5500-X FirePOWER Module Default Gateway*

If you must configure the management interface separately from the inside interface, you can deploy a router or a Layer 3 switch between both interfaces, as shown in Figure 2-8. This option is less common, as you still need to manage the ASA via the inside interface.

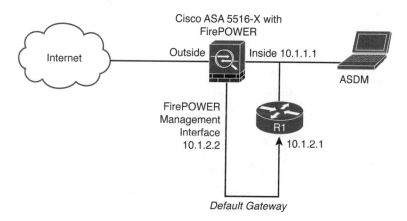

Figure 2-8   *Cisco ASA 5500-X FirePOWER Module Management Interface Connected to a Router*

In Figure 2-8, the Cisco ASA FirePOWER module default gateway is the router labeled R1, with the IP address 10.1.2.1. The Cisco ASA's inside interface is configured with the IP address 10.1.1.1. The Cisco ASA FirePOWER module must have a way to reach the inside interface of the ASA to allow for on-box ASDM management. On the other hand, if you are using FMC, the Cisco ASA FirePOWER module needs to have a way to reach the FMC.

Cisco ASA FirePOWER Services Sizing

It is really important that you understand the capabilities of each Cisco ASA model before you select the one that is appropriate for your specific deployment. Table 2-1 lists the maximum application visibility and control (AVC) and NGIPS throughput on each Cisco ASA–supported model.

Table 2-1   *The Maximum Concurrent Connections and AVC/NGIPS Throughput*

ASA Model	Maximum Concurrent Connections	Maximum AVC and NGIPS Throughput
ASA 5506-X (with Security Plus license)	50,000	125 Mbps
ASA 5506W-X (with Security Plus license)	50,000	125 Mbps
ASA 5506H-X (with Security Plus license)	50,000	125 Mbps
ASA 5508-X	100,000	250 Mbps
ASA 5512-X (with Security Plus license)	100,000	150 Mbps
ASA 5515-X	250,000	250 Mbps
ASA 5516-X	250,000	450 Mbps
ASA 5525-X	500,000	650 Mbps
ASA 5545-X	750,000	1,000 Mbps
ASA 5555-X	1,000,000	1,250 Mbps
ASA 5585-X with SSP10	500,000	2 Gbps
ASA 5585-X with SSP20	1,000,000	3.5 Gbps
ASA 5585-X with SSP40	1,800,000	6 Gbps
ASA 5585-X with SSP60	4,000,000	10 Gbps

For a complete and up-to-date Cisco ASA model comparison, visit Cisco's ASA website, at cisco.com/go/asa.

Cisco ASA FirePOWER Services Licensing

You have already learned that the Cisco ASA FirePOWER module can be managed by the Firepower Management Center or ASDM, in the case of the Cisco ASA 5506-X and 5508-X. The Firepower Management Center and the Cisco ASA FirePOWER module require different licenses. These licenses are installed in the Cisco FirePOWER module and the Cisco Firepower Management Center. There are no additional licenses required in the Cisco ASA.

The following are the different types of Cisco ASA FirePOWER Services licenses:

- Protection

- Control

- Malware

- URL Filtering

Table 2-2 provides a high-level overview of each license.

Table 2-2 *The Different Types of Cisco ASA FirePOWER Services Licenses*

License	Description
Protection	Intrusion detection and prevention File control Security intelligence filtering
Control	User and application control
Malware	Advanced malware protection (network-based malware detection and blocking)
URL Filtering	Category and reputation-based URL filtering

The Protection License

The Protection license enables a network security administrator to perform intrusion detection and prevention, file control, and security intelligence filtering. The intrusion detection and prevention capabilities are used to analyze network traffic for intrusions and exploits, to alert the network security administrator and optionally block offending packets. File control allows network security administrators to detect and (optionally) block users from sending or receiving files of specific types over specific application protocols.

Note The Malware license also allows you to inspect and block a set of file types, based on malware intelligence and dispositions. The Malware license is covered later in this chapter.

Security intelligence filtering allows network security administrators to blacklist different hosts/IP addresses before the traffic is analyzed by access control rules. Cisco provides dynamic feeds, allowing a network security administrator to immediately blacklist connections based on the Cisco threat intelligence capabilities, fueled by Cisco's research organization, Talos. You can also configure this to be monitor only.

> **Tip**   You can configure access control policies without a license; however, if you do this, you will not be able to apply the policy until the Protection license is added to the Cisco ASA FirePOWER module. If the Protection license is for some reason deleted, the Cisco ASA FirePOWER module ceases to detect intrusions and file events, and it is not able to reach the Internet for either Cisco-provided or third-party security intelligence information.
>
> A Protection license is required with all the other licenses (Control, Malware, and URL Filtering licenses). If the Protection license is disabled or deleted, this has a direct effect on any other licenses installed.

The Control License

The Control license allows a network security administrator to implement user and application control. The administrator does this by adding user and application settings to access control rules. As with the Protection license, you can add user and application conditions to access control rules without a Control license. You cannot apply the policy until the Control license is installed and enabled in the Cisco ASA FirePOWER module, however.

The URL Filtering License

The URL Filtering license allows a network security administrator to implement access control rules that determine what traffic can pass through the firewall, based on URLs requested by monitored hosts. The Cisco ASA FirePOWER module obtains information about those URLs from the Cisco cloud, as illustrated in Figure 2-9.

You can configure individual URLs or groups of URLs to be allowed or blocked by the Cisco ASA FirePOWER module without a URL Filtering license; however, you cannot use URL category and reputation data to filter network traffic without a URL Filtering license. The example in Figure 2-9 applies to Cisco ASA FirePOWER modules managed by ASDM. If the Cisco ASA FirePOWER module is managed by the FMC, the URL categorization and reputation information is received from Cisco by the FMC and then sent to the managed devices (that is, Cisco ASA FirePOWER modules, NGIPS, FTD, etc.).

> **Note**   The URL Filtering license is a subscription-based license.

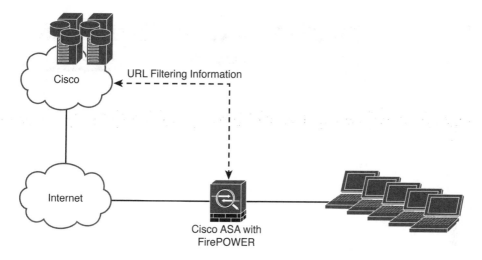

Figure 2-9 *URL Filtering Information Obtained from Cisco's Cloud*

The Malware License

The Malware license enables Advanced Malware Protection (AMP) in the Cisco ASA FirePOWER module. With AMP you can detect and block malware potentially being transmitted over the network.

Malware detection is configured as part of a file policy, which you then associate with one or more access control rules.

Note   Step-by-step examples of how to configure the Cisco ASA FirePOWER module are provided in Chapter 3, "Configuring Cisco ASA with FirePOWER Services."

Viewing the Installed Cisco ASA FirePOWER Module Licenses

You can view the installed licenses in the Cisco ASA FirePOWER module by navigating to **System > Licenses** in the Cisco Firepower Management Center. The Licenses page lists all the licenses in the devices managed by the Cisco Firepower Management Center, as shown in Figure 2-10.

In Figure 2-10, a Cisco ASA 5515-X is being managed by the Cisco Firepower Management Center. The Protection, Control, Malware, and URL Filtering licenses are enabled.

Another way to view the installed licenses in the Cisco ASA FirePOWER module is by navigating to **Devices > Device Management** in the Cisco Firepower Management Center. Then click the device for which you want to see the details, as shown in Figure 2-11.

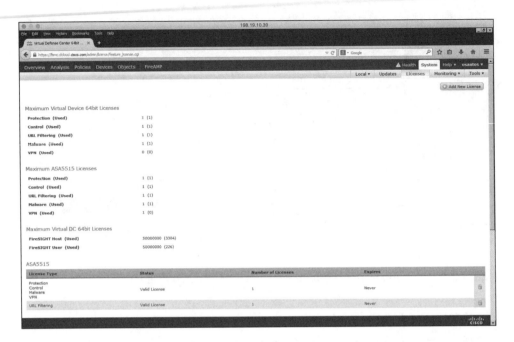

Figure 2-10   *Cisco Firepower Management Center Licenses Page*

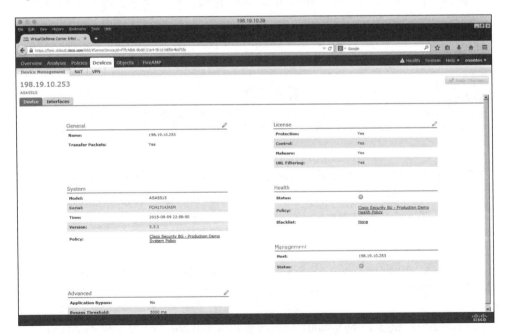

Figure 2-11   *Cisco Firepower Management Center Device Management*

Adding a License to the Cisco ASA FirePOWER Module

This section covers how to add a license to the Cisco ASA FirePOWER module after you receive the activation key provided by Cisco when you purchase the license. The following are the steps to add a license:

Step 1.   Navigate to **System > Licenses** in the Cisco Firepower Management Center, as shown in Figure 2-12.

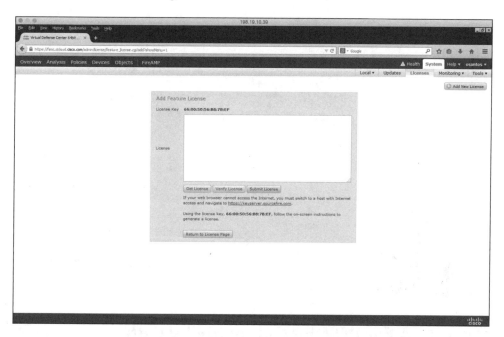

Figure 2-12   *Adding a New License in the FMC*

Step 2.   Click **Add New License** on the Licenses page.

Step 3.   Copy and paste the license into the **License** field and click **Submit License**. If you do not have the license, follow the instructions onscreen to obtain your license.

If you are configuring the Cisco ASA FirePOWER module using ASDM, you can manage and install FirePOWER licenses by navigating to **Configuration > ASA FirePOWER Configuration > Licenses**, as shown in Figure 2-13.

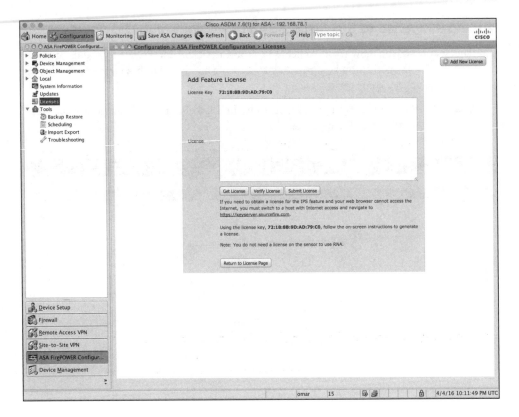

Figure 2-13   *Adding a New License in ASDM*

Cisco ASA FirePOWER Compatibility with Other Cisco ASA Features

The Cisco ASA FirePOWER module provides advanced HTTP inspection and other advanced application inspection features. To take advantage of these features, you do not configure traditional HTTP inspection in the Cisco ASA.

In addition, the Mobile User Security (MUS) feature is not compatible with the Cisco ASA FirePOWER module. You must disable MUS if it is enabled in the Cisco ASA.

All other Cisco ASA application inspections are compatible with the Cisco ASA FirePOWER module.

Cisco ASA FirePOWER Packet Processing Order of Operations

When the Cisco ASA FirePOWER module is deployed, the Cisco ASA processes all ingress packets against access control lists (ACLs), connection tables, Network Address

Translation (NAT), and application inspections before traffic is forwarded to the FirePOWER Services module. In order for the Cisco ASA to redirect packets to the Cisco ASA FirePOWER module, you need to configure redirection policies using the Cisco ASA Modular Policy Framework (MPF), as illustrated in Figure 2-14.

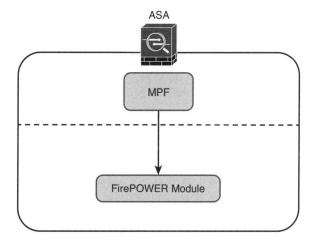

Figure 2-14 *Cisco ASA MPF, Redirecting Traffic to the Cisco ASA FirePOWER Module*

Note Chapter 3 covers how to configure the Cisco ASA MPF to redirect traffic to the Cisco ASA FirePOWER module.

Figure 2-15 shows the Cisco ASA packet processing order of operations.

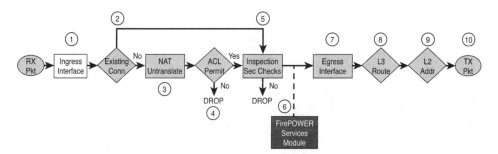

Figure 2-15 *The Cisco ASA Packet Processing Order of Operations*

The following steps are illustrated in Figure 2-15:

Step 1. A packet is received on a given interface of the Cisco ASA. If a VPN is configured, the packet is decrypted at this point. If ACL bypass is configured for VPN traffic, the Cisco ASA proceeds to step 5.

Step 2.   The Cisco ASA checks to see if there is an existing connection for the source and destination hosts for that specific traffic. If there is an existing connection, the Cisco ASA bypasses the ACL checks and performs application inspection checks and proceeds to step 5.

Step 3.   If there is no existing connection for that traffic, the Cisco ASA performs the NAT checks (or untranslate process).

Step 4.   The Cisco ASA allows or denies traffic based on the rules in the configured ACLs.

Step 5.   If traffic is allowed, the Cisco ASA performs application inspection.

Step 6.   The Cisco ASA forwards the packet to the Cisco ASA FirePOWER module. If promiscuous monitor-only mode is configured, only a copy of the packet is sent to the Cisco ASA FirePOWER module. If the Cisco ASA FirePOWER module is configured in inline mode, the packet is inspected and dropped if it does not conform to security policies. If the packet is compliant with security policies and Cisco ASA FirePOWER module protection capabilities, it is sent back to the ASA for processing.

Step 7.   The Cisco ASA determines the egress interface based on NAT or Layer 3 routing.

Step 8.   Layer 3 routing is performed.

Step 9.   Layer 2 address lookup occurs.

Step 10.   The packet is sent to the network.

Figure 2-16 shows the packet flow in the Cisco ASA 5585-X.

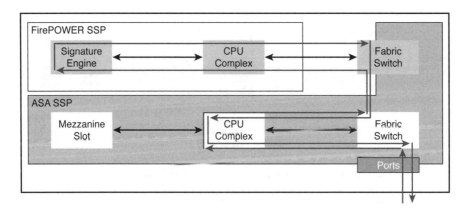

Figure 2-16   *The Packet Flow in the Cisco ASA 5585-X*

In Cisco ASA 5585-X appliances, the SSP running Cisco ASA software processes all ingress and egress packets. No packets are directly processed by the Cisco ASA FirePOWER module (SSP) except for the Cisco ASA FirePOWER module management port.

Cisco ASA FirePOWER Services and Failover

The Cisco ASA supports high availability using failover and clustering. This section covers the deployment of the Cisco ASA FirePOWER module in failover scenarios. Clustering is covered later in this chapter.

The Cisco ASA supports two types of failover:

- Active/standby

- Active/active

In active/standby failover, one unit in a failover pair is always active, and the other one is in standby. Figure 2-17 illustrates active/standby failover.

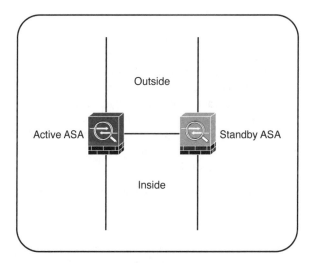

Figure 2-17 *Active/Standby Failover*

The standby device drops all transit traffic that it may receive and accepts only management connections. For a switchover to occur automatically, the active unit must become less operationally healthy than the standby. The failover event moves all transit traffic to the peer device, even if the actual impact on the previously active unit is localized. When running in multiple-context mode, all contexts switch over at the same time. Active/ standby failover is the only option when running in single-context mode.

What are these so-called security contexts? Security contexts enable a physical Cisco ASA to be partitioned into multiple standalone firewalls. Each context acts and behaves as an independent entity, with its own configuration, interfaces, security policies, routing table, and administrators. The following are some examples of scenarios in which security contexts are useful in network deployments:

- You act as a service provider and want to provide firewall services to customers; however, you do not want to purchase additional physical firewalls for each client.

- You manage an educational institution and want to segregate student networks from faculty networks for improved security while using one physical security appliance.

- You administer a large enterprise with different departmental groups, and each department wants to implement its own security policies.

- You have overlapping networks in your organization and want to provide firewall services to all those networks without changing the addressing scheme.

- You currently manage many physical firewalls, and you want to integrate security policies from all firewalls into one physical firewall.

- You manage a data center environment and want to provide end-to-end virtualization to reduce operational costs and increase efficiency.

The responsibilities of the active unit include the following items:

- Accept configuration commands from the user and replicate them to the standby peer. All management and monitoring of a failover pair should happen on the active unit because configuration replication is not a two-way process. Making any changes on the standby ASA causes configuration inconsistency that may prevent subsequent command synchronization and create issues after a switchover event. If you inadvertently made a change on the standby device, exit the configuration mode and issue the **write standby** command on the active unit to restore the proper state. This command completely overwrites the existing running configuration of the standby unit with the running configuration of the active ASA.

- Process all transit traffic, apply configured security policies, build and tear down connections, and synchronize the connection information to the standby unit, if configured for stateful failover.

- Send NetFlow Secure Event Logging (NSEL) and syslog messages to the configured event collectors. When necessary, you may configure the standby unit to transmit syslog messages with the **logging standby** command. Keep in mind that this command doubles the connection-related syslog traffic from the failover pair.

- Build and maintain dynamic routing adjacencies. The standby unit never participates in dynamic routing.

By default, failover operates in a stateless manner. In this configuration, the active unit only synchronizes its configuration to the standby device. All the stateful flow information remains local to the active ASA, so all connections must reestablish upon a failover event. While this configuration preserves ASA processing resources, most high-availability configurations require stateful failover. To pass state information to the standby ASA, you must configure a stateful failover link.

Stateful failover is not available on the Cisco ASA 5505 platform. When stateful replication is enabled, an active ASA synchronizes the following additional information to the standby peer:

■ Stateful table for TCP and UDP connections. To preserve processing resources, ASA does not synchronize certain short-lived connections by default. For example, HTTP connections over TCP port 80 remain stateless unless you configure the **failover replication http** command. Similarly, ICMP connections synchronize only in active/active failover with asymmetric routing (ASR) groups configured. Note that enabling stateful replication for all connections may cause up to a 30 percent reduction in the maximum connection setup rate supported by the particular ASA platform.

■ ARP table and bridge-group MAC mapping table when running in transparent mode.

■ Routing table, including any dynamically learned routes. All dynamic routing adjacencies must reestablish after a failover event, but the new active unit continues to forward traffic based on the previous routing table state until full reconvergence.

■ Certain application inspection data, such as General Packet Radio Service (GPRS), GPRS Tunneling Protocol (GTP), Packet Data Protocol (PDP), and Session Initiation Protocol (SIP) signaling tables. Keep in mind that most application inspection engines do not synchronize their databases because of resource constraints and complexity, so such connections switch over at the Layer 4 level only. As the result, some of these connections may have to reestablish after a failover event.

■ Most VPN data structures, including security associations (SA) for site-to-site tunnels and remote-access users. Only some clientless SSL VPN information remains stateless.

Stateful failover supports only Cisco ASA software features. The Cisco ASA FirePOWER module tracks connection state independently, and the Cisco ASAs do not synchronize their configuration or any other stateful data in failover. When a Cisco ASA switchover occurs, the Cisco ASA FirePOWER module typically recovers existing connections transparently to the user, but some advanced security checks may apply only to new flows that are established through the newly active Cisco ASA and its local application module.

In active/active failover, Cisco ASAs operate in multiple-context mode. In this configuration, the traffic load is split between members of the failover pair so that each unit is active for some set of security contexts. This way, both failover peers are passing traffic concurrently and fully utilizing their respective hardware resources.

Figure 2-18 illustrates active/active failover.

This separation is achieved by assigning specific application contexts to one of the two failover groups and then making each of the failover peers own one of these groups. As opposed to active/standby failover, where all contexts switch over to the peer on active unit failure, this model localizes the impact to the contexts in a particular failover group.

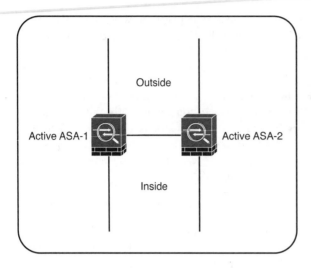

Figure 2-18   *Active/Active Failover*

In total, an ASA supports three failover groups when configured for active/active failover:

- **Group 0**: This is a hidden, nonconfigurable group that covers only the system context. It is always active on the same unit that is active for group 1.

- **Group 1**: All newly created contexts belong to this group by default. The admin context must always be a member of this group. By default, the primary unit owns this group, and you typically keep it this way.

- **Group 2**: Use this group to assign some contexts to be active on the secondary unit. The primary unit also owns this group by default, so you have to change its ownership to the secondary ASA after assigning all the desired contexts. Keep in mind that both groups have to be active on the same unit in order to move contexts between groups 1 and 2.

You should deploy active/active failover only when you can effectively separate the network traffic flows into these two independent groups. Keep in mind that interface sharing is not supported between contexts that belong to different failover groups.

Although active/active failover offers some load-sharing benefits, consider the following implications of this model:

- You must be able to separate the traffic flows into multiple contexts such that no interfaces are shared between contexts in different failover groups. Keep in mind that not all features are supported in multiple-context mode.

- If a switchover occurs, a single physical device must carry the full traffic load that was originally intended for two ASA units. This effectively reduces the benefits of load balancing because you should only plan the overall load on the failover pair for this worst-case scenario with a single remaining unit.

- When using stateful failover, the standby device requires as much processing power as the active one to create new connections; the only difference is that the standby unit does not have to accept transit traffic from the network. When you enable stateful replication with active/active failover, you significantly reduce the available processing capacity of each failover pair member.

Generally speaking, active/standby is the preferred deployment model for failover. Consider clustering instead of active/active failover when your ASA deployment scenario requires load sharing.

What Happens When the Cisco ASA FirePOWER Module Fails?

If the Cisco ASA FirePOWER module fails, you can configure it to do either of the following:

- Fail open
- Fail close

When the Cisco ASA FirePOWER module is configured to fail open, all traffic still passes through the Cisco ASA if the module fails. In contrast, when the Cisco ASA FirePOWER module is configured to fail close, all traffic stops through the Cisco ASA if the module fails.

Cisco ASA FirePOWER Services and Clustering

You can configure up to 16 identical Cisco ASA appliances in a cluster to act as a combined traffic-processing system. When clustering is enabled, the Cisco ASAs preserve the benefits of failover. In a cluster, virtual IP and MAC addresses are used for first-hop redundancy.

All cluster members must have identical hardware configuration, SSP types, application modules, and interface cards.

Figure 2-19 illustrates three Cisco ASAs configured in a cluster.

In a Cisco ASA cluster, the configuration is mirrored to all members, and connection state is preserved after a single member failure.

Clustered Cisco ASA provides flow symmetry and high availability to the Cisco ASA FirePOWER module. Packets and flows are not dropped by the Cisco ASA FirePOWER module but instead are marked for "drop" or "drop with TCP reset" and sent back to the corresponding Cisco ASA. This methodology allows the Cisco ASA to clear the connection from the state tables and send TCP resets, if needed.

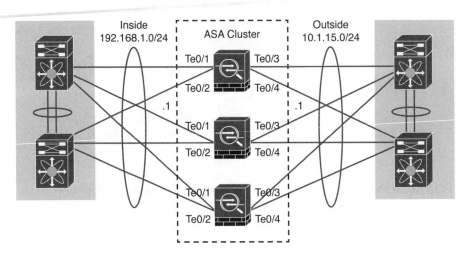

Figure 2-19   *Cisco ASA Cluster*

When clustering is configured, stateless load balancing is done via IP routing or spanned EtherChannel with the Link Aggregation Control Protocol (LACP). In addition, all Cisco ASA appliances are connected to the same subnet on each logical interface.

Figure 2-20 shows a Cisco ASA cluster configured with spanned EtherChannel.

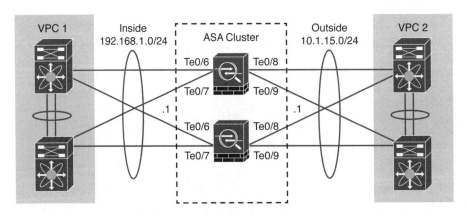

Figure 2-20   *Cisco ASA Cluster Configured with Spanned EtherChannel*

You can also configure a cluster in individual interface mode. Individual interface mode is supported in Cisco ASAs configured in routed (Layer 3) mode only. It is not supported in Cisco ASAs configured in transparent (Layer 2) mode.

Figure 2-21 shows a Cisco ASA cluster configured in individual interface mode.

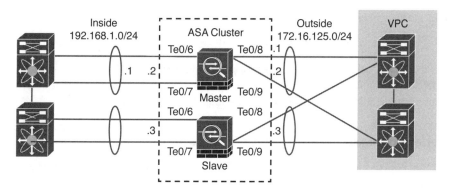

Figure 2-21   *Cisco ASA Cluster Configured in Individual Interface Mode*

In individual interface mode, the cluster master owns the virtual IP on data interfaces for management purposes only. All members get data interface IP addresses from IP address pools in the order in which they join the cluster.

Cluster Member Election

When Cisco ASAs are configured in a cluster, one member is elected as the master, and other Cisco ASAs are slaves. The master may be the first unit to join the cluster or may be based on a configured priority. A new master is elected only if the elected master fails. The master unit handles all management and centralized functions, and the configuration is locked on slaves.

Figure 2-22 illustrates the steps in the cluster master election process.

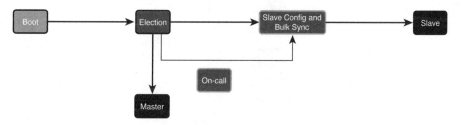

Figure 2-22   *Cisco ASA Cluster Master Election Process*

The following steps are illustrated in Figure 2-22:

Step 1.   A Cisco ASA with clustering enabled boots and immediately looks for a master within the cluster.

Step 2.   It waits 45 seconds before it receives a reply from a master. If no master is found, it assumes the role of master in the cluster.

Step 3.   If a master already exists, the Cisco ASA assumes the role of slave and synchronizes the configuration with the master Cisco ASA.

Step 4.   The master admits one unit at a time.

Step 5.   The cluster slave is ready to pass traffic.

There is a virtual IP address ownership for to-the-cluster connections, and the master and slaves process all regular transit connections equally. If a master fails, management traffic and other centralized connections must be reestablished upon master failure.

How Connections Are Established and Tracked in a Cluster

This section explains how connections are established and tracked in a Cisco ASA cluster configuration.

How a New TCP Connection Is Established and Tracked in a Cluster

Figure 2-23 illustrates how a new TCP connection is established and tracked within a cluster.

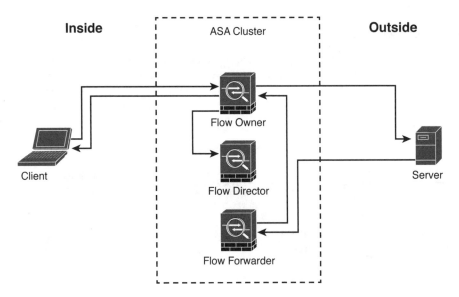

Figure 2-23   *A New TCP Connection in a Cisco ASA Cluster*

The following steps are illustrated in Figure 2-23:

Step 1.   A new TCP connection attempt is received from the client (TCP SYN packet).

Step 2.   The Cisco ASA that receives the TCP SYN (connection attempt) becomes the flow owner and adds the TCP SYN cookie. It then delivers the packet to the server.

Step 3.   The server may reply with a TCP SYN ACK (response) through another unit in the cluster.

Step 4.   If another Cisco ASA in the cluster receives the response, it forwards the packet to the flow owner and becomes the flow forwarder.

Step 5.   The flow owner delivers the TCP SYN to the client.

Step 6.   The flow owner updates the flow director with the connection information.

How a New UDP-Like Connection Is Established and Tracked in a Cluster

Figure 2-24 illustrates how a new UDP or another pseudo-stateful connection is established and tracked within a cluster.

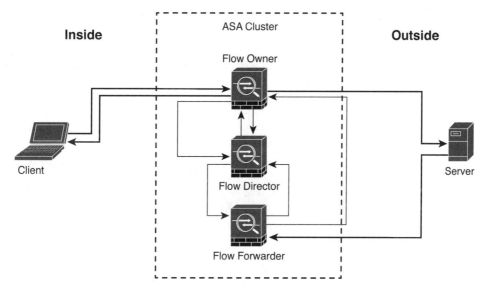

Figure 2-24   *A New UDP or Another Pseudo-stateful Connection in a Cisco ASA Cluster*

The following steps are illustrated in Figure 2-24:

Step 1.   A new UDP or another pseudo-stateful connection attempt is received from the client.

Step 2.   The Cisco ASA that receives the connection attempt queries the flow director to see if a connection already exists for that host.

Step 3.   The Cisco ASA that received the packet becomes the flow owner if no connection was found.

Step 4.   The packet is delivered to the server.

Step 5.   The flow owner updates the director with the new connection information.

Step 6.   The server responds to the client. If another Cisco ASA in the cluster receives the response, it forwards the packet to the flow owner and becomes the flow forwarder.

Step 7.   The flow forwarder queries the director to see what Cisco ASA is the flow owner.

Step 8.   The director updates the flow forwarder with the flow owner information.

Step 9.   The flow forwarder forwards the server response to the flow owner.

Step 10.   The server response is delivered to the client.

Centralized Connections in a Cluster

There are several Cisco ASA features where connections are centralized, such as VPN management, application inspection, and AAA for network access. If a feature is handled in a centralized way, the cluster master controls all the tasks.

Note   Packets for a nondistributed protocol inspection would have to all be forwarded to the cluster master for processing.

Centralized connections decrease overall cluster performance because they increase the processing and packet forwarding required to complete the given task.

Note   All features that are handled in a centralized way have flows always residing on the master unit in the cluster.

Figure 2-25 illustrates how a new centralized connection is established and tracked within a cluster.

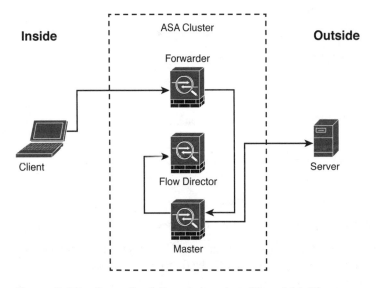

Figure 2-25   *Centralized Connections in a Cisco ASA Cluster*

The following steps are illustrated in Figure 2-25:

Step 1.   A new connection attempt is received from the client.

Step 2.   The Cisco ASA that receives the connection attempt recognizes the centralized feature and redirects the connection attempt to the master.

Step 3.   The master becomes the owner and delivers the packet to the server.

Step 4.   The master updates the director with the connection information.

What Happens When the Flow Owner Fails

The Cisco ASA clustering feature provides high availability and redundancy. Figure 2-26
illustrates what happens when a flow owner fails for some reason.

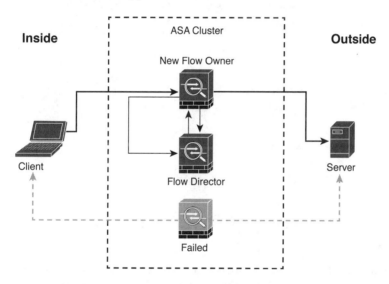

Figure 2-26   *Flow Owner Failure*

The following steps are illustrated in Figure 2-26:

Step 1.   A connection is already established between the client and the server.

Step 2.   The flow owner fails. This can be because of a power failure, hardware failure, or some other event, such as a system crash.

Step 3.   The client sends the next packet to the server, and another cluster member
receives the packet.

Step 4.   The Cisco ASA that receives the packet queries the director.

Step 5.   The director detects that the original flow owner failed and assigns a new
owner.

Step 6.   The packet is delivered to the server.

Step 7.   The new flow owner updates the flow director.

Deploying the Cisco ASA FirePOWER Services in the Internet Edge

The Cisco ASA FirePOWER module provides unprecedented capabilities to protect a corporate network from Internet threats. Many organizations of all sizes deploy the Cisco ASA FirePOWER module at their Internet edge. Figure 2-27 illustrates a pair of Cisco ASA with FirePOWER modules deployed in the Internet edge of a corporate office in Raleigh, North Carolina.

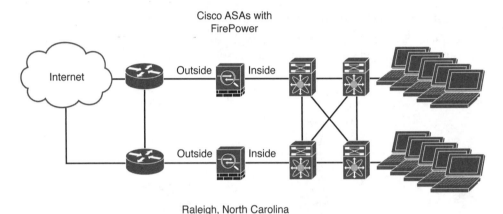

Figure 2-27   *Cisco ASA FirePOWER Module in the Internet Edge*

Deploying the Cisco ASA FirePOWER Services in VPN Scenarios

The Cisco ASA FirePOWER module can be deployed in site-to-site and remote-access VPN environments. As you learned earlier in this chapter, the decryption process takes place before the packets are sent to the Cisco ASA FirePOWER module by the Cisco ASA, and the packets are encrypted after they are inspected by the Cisco ASA FirePOWER module and sent back to the Cisco ASA.

Figure 2-28 illustrates how a Cisco ASA with the FirePOWER module is deployed in an office in New York, terminating SSL and IPsec (IKEv2) VPN tunnels from remote clients in the Internet.

In the example illustrated in Figure 2-28, the remote-access VPN clients are using the Cisco AnyConnect client; however, clientless SSL VPN is also supported.

Figure 2-29 illustrates how two Cisco ASAs with FirePOWER modules are deployed in the headquarters office in New York (ASA 1) and a branch office in Raleigh, North Carolina (ASA 2), establishing a site-to-site IPsec VPN tunnel. In addition, ASA 2 in New York is also terminating a site-to-site IPsec VPN tunnel to a router (R1) of a business partner in Las Vegas.

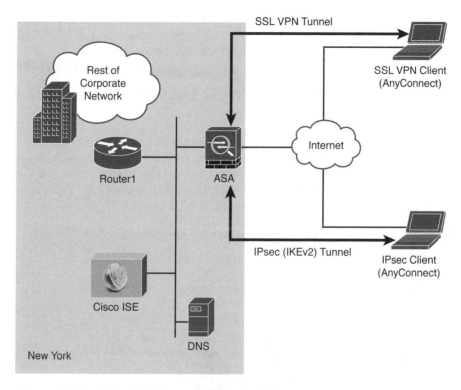

Figure 2-28 *Cisco ASA FirePOWER Module in a Remote-Access VPN Scenario*

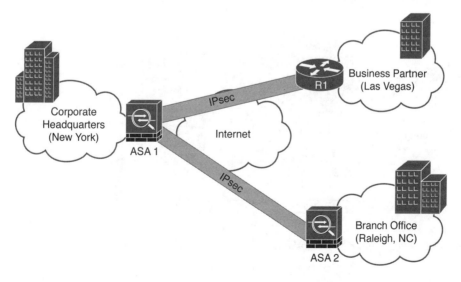

Figure 2-29 *Cisco ASA FirePOWER Module in a Site-to-Site IPsec VPN Scenario*

In the example illustrated in Figure 2-29, the Cisco ASA FirePOWER module not only protects against threats in the corporate network in the remote branch office but also protects against threats coming from an unmanaged business partner.

Deploying Cisco ASA FirePOWER Services in the Data Center

The data center can be a very complex world. It not only provides a rich set of services and architectures but also hosts the crown jewels of an organization. It is extremely important to maintain visibility of everything that is happening in the data center. The concept of "north-to-south" and "east-to-west" is often used in describing the types of communication (or flow) within and to the outside of the data center:

- North-to-south describes communication between end users and external entities.

- East-to-west describes communication between entities in the data center.

Figure 2-30 illustrates the concepts of north-to-south and east-to-west communication.

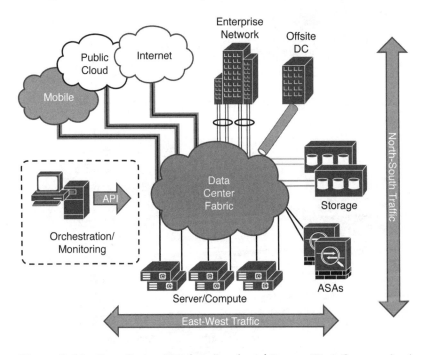

Figure 2-30   *Data Center North-to-South and East-to-West Communication*

The data center has many different high-throughput and low-latency requirements, in addition to increased high-availability requirements. In addition, automated provisioning and control with orchestration, monitoring, and management tools are crucial.

The data center architecture consists of three primary modular layers with hierarchical interdependencies:

- **Data center foundation:** This is the primary building block of the data center, on which all other services rely. Regardless of the size of the data center, the foundation must be resilient, scalable, and flexible to support data center services that add value, performance, and reliability. The data center foundation provides the computing necessary to support the applications that process information and the seamless transport between servers, storage, and the end users who access the applications.

- **Data center services:** These services include infrastructure components to enhance the security of the applications and access to critical data. They also include virtual switching services to extend the network control in a seamless manner from the foundation network into the hypervisor systems on servers to increase control and reduce operational costs (as well as other application resilience services).

- **User services:** These services include email, order processing, and file sharing or any other applications in the data center that rely on the data center foundation and services, like database applications, modeling, and transaction processing.

Figure 2-31 illustrates some of the components of the data center services architecture.

Examples of the data center service insertion components include the following:

- Firewalls (In the example illustrated in Figure 2-31, Cisco ASAs with FirePOWER modules are deployed.)

- Intrusion prevention systems (IPS)

- Application delivery features

- Server load balancing

- Network analysis tools (such as NetFlow)

- Virtualized services deployed in a distributed manner along with virtual machines

- Traffic direction with vPath and Nexus 1000v

- Application Centric Infrastructure (ACI) automated framework components for service insertion

In the case of virtualized environments, the Cisco ASAv (virtual machine) can be deployed to protect VM-to-VM communication. The Cisco ASA FirePOWER module in these environments is not supported, as the Cisco ASAv is just a virtual machine. Cisco FirePOWER virtual machines running network AMP can be deployed in those scenarios.

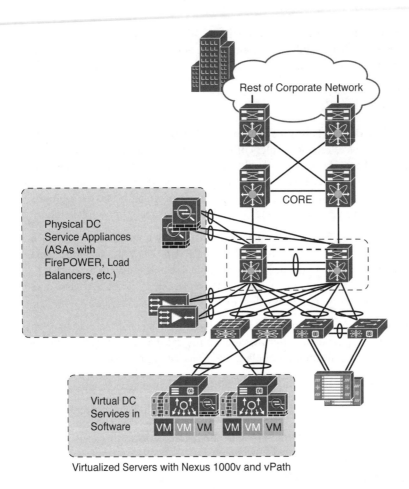

Figure 2-31 *The Data Center Services Architecture*

Note The Cisco ASAv supports both traditional tiered data center deployments and the fabric-based deployments of Cisco ACI environments. The Cisco ASAv can also be deployed in cloud environments like Amazon Web Services (AWS).

The Cisco ASA with FirePOWER modules can be deployed in geographically dispersed cluster environments.

Figure 2-32 shows an example in which four Cisco ASAs with FirePOWER modules are deployed in two separate sites (site A and site B).

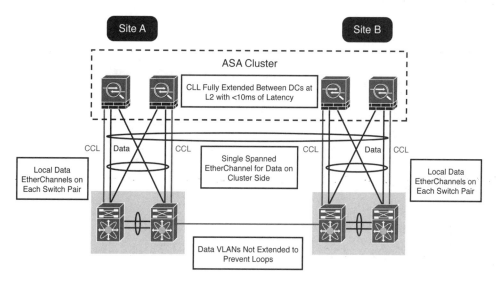

Figure 2-32 *Cisco ASA FirePOWER Module in a Geographically Dispersed Data Center*

In the example illustrated in Figure 2-32, the cluster of four Cisco ASAs is fully extended between the two data centers, using the cluster control links (CCL) operating at Layer 2 with a latency of less than 10 milliseconds. A single spanned EtherChannel for transient data is used on the cluster side. The local data links are also configured with EtherChannels at the switch pairs on each site.

Tip The data VLANs between the switches are not extended to prevent network loops.

Firepower Threat Defense (FTD)

In Chapter 1 you learned that Firepower Threat Defense software is unified software that provides next-generation firewall services, including the following:

- Stateful firewall capabilities

- Static and dynamic routing

- Next-generation intrusion prevention systems (NGIPS)

- Application visibility and control (AVC)

- URL filtering

- Advanced Malware Protection (AMP)

In the Cisco ASA, you can use FTD in single context mode and in routed or transparent mode. Multiple context mode is not supported at this writing.

The following are the Cisco ASA 5500-X models that support a reimage to run the FTD software:

- ASA 5506-X

- ASA 5506W-X

- ASA 5506H-X

- ASA 5508-X

- ASA 5512-X

- ASA 5515-X

- ASA 5516-X

- ASA 5525-X

- ASA 5545-X

- ASA 5555-X

To reimage one of the aforementioned Cisco ASA models, you must meet the following prerequisites:

- You must have a Cisco Smart Account. You can create one at Cisco Software Central (https://software.cisco.com).

- You need to review the FTD software version release notes to become familiar of the supported features, as Cisco continues to add features very regularly.

- Add at least a base FTD license to your Smart Account (for example, L-ASA5516T-BASE=).

- You must have access to an FMC (virtual or physical).

- You must have access to the console port of the Cisco 5500-X appliance on which FTD software will be installed, either directly from the computer being used for installing FTD software or through a terminal server.

- It is a best practice to back up your existing configuration.

- Understand that when you reimage and install FTD software on your Cisco ASA, all previous files and configurations saved on the ASA are lost.

- You need to have the required minimum free space (3 GB plus the size of the boot software) available on the flash (disk0).

- You must have an SSD in your Cisco ASA.

- You must have access to a TFTP server to host the FTD images.

In Chapter 3, you will learn how to reimage and install the FTD software in supported Cisco ASA models.

Summary

The Cisco ASA FirePOWER module provides network visibility, policy enforcement, and advanced threat protection across many organizations and the entire attack continuum. This chapter starts with an introduction to the Cisco ASA FirePOWER module. It explains the difference between inline and promiscuous (monitor-only) deployment modes. This chapter also covers the different Cisco ASA FirePOWER management options and provides guidance on what models to use, based on network size and demands. You have also learned about the Cisco ASA FirePOWER Services licensing and compatibility issues with other Cisco ASA features. This chapter also provides a deep dive into the Cisco ASA and the Cisco FirePOWER module packet-processing order of operations. You have learned how the Cisco ASA FirePOWER module behaves and is deployed in failover and clustering configurations. Several deployment scenarios are covered, including deploying Cisco ASA FirePOWER Services at the Internet Edge, in site-to-site and remote-access VPN scenarios, and in the data center. At the end of the chapter, you learned a few details about the FTD software and prerequisites prior to installation on a supported Cisco ASA model.

Chapter 3

Configuring Cisco ASA with FirePOWER Services

This chapter provides step-by-step guidance on how to set up and configure the Cisco ASA with FirePOWER Services module. The following topics are covered in this chapter:

- Setting up the Cisco ASA FirePOWER module in Cisco ASA 5585-X appliances

- Setting up the Cisco ASA FirePOWER module in Cisco ASA 5500-X appliances

- Configuring the Cisco ASA to redirect traffic to the Cisco ASA FirePOWER module

- Configuring the Cisco ASA FirePOWER services module for the FMC

- Configuring the Cisco ASA FirePOWER module using the Adaptive Security Device Manager (ASDM)

- Firepower Threat Defense (FTD)

Setting Up the Cisco ASA FirePOWER Module in Cisco ASA 5585-X Appliances

In Chapter 2, "Introduction to and Design of Cisco ASA with FirePOWER Services," you learned that in the Cisco ASA 5585-X, the Cisco ASA FirePOWER module includes a separate management interface. All management traffic to and from the Cisco ASA FirePOWER module must enter and exit this interface. You also learned that the Cisco ASA FirePOWER module needs Internet access to perform several operations.

Figure 3-1 shows an example of how you can physically connect the Cisco ASA FirePOWER module management interface to be able to reach the Internet by using the Cisco ASA interface.

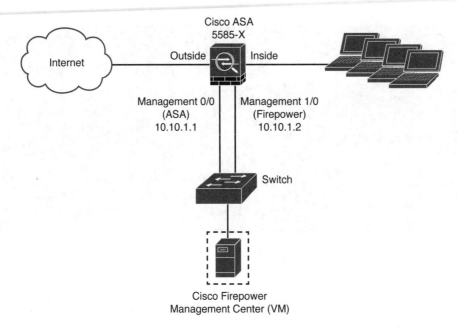

Figure 3-1 *Cisco ASA 5585-X Management Interfaces*

Figure 3-1 shows the Cisco ASA 5585-X with a module running Cisco ASA software and a module running FirePOWER Services. The Cisco ASA software is managed by using the interface named Management 0/0 in this example. This interface is configured with the IP address 10.10.1.1. The Cisco ASA FirePOWER module is managed by using the interface named Management 1/0, configured with the IP address 10.10.1.2.

You can access the Cisco ASA FirePOWER module command-line interface (CLI) by using the serial console port or Secure Shell (SSH).

Cisco ASA 5585-X appliances have a dedicated console port for the Cisco ASA FirePOWER module. You can use a DB-9 to RJ-45 serial cable or a USB serial adapter to connect to the console.

Note In all other Cisco ASA models, you connect to the Cisco ASA console and then you connect by using the backplane to the "module" or solid state drive (SSD) by using the **session sfr** command. The Cisco ASA 5506-X, Cisco ASA 5508-X, and Cisco ASA 5516-X also come with a mini-USB console port that you can use.

You can also connect to the Cisco ASA FirePOWER module by using SSH, with the default IP address.

Table 3-1 lists all the default parameters and credentials of the Cisco ASA FirePOWER module.

Table 3-1 *Cisco ASA FirePOWER Module Default Settings*

Option	Default Setting
Management IP address	Boot image: 192.168.8.8/24 System software image: 192.168.45.45/24
Gateway	Boot image: 192.168.8.1 System software image: No gateway
Username for SSH or session console	admin
Password for SSH or session console	Boot image: Admin123 System software image (legacy): Sourcefire System software image (6.0 and later): Admin123

Installing the Boot Image and Firepower System Software in the Cisco ASA 5585-X SSP

In order to have a fully functional Cisco ASA FirePOWER module in a Cisco ASA 5585-X, the boot image needs to first be installed, and then a system software package needs to be installed as well.

Note If you purchased a new Cisco ASA with FirePOWER Services, you do not need to reimage the system to install upgrade packages.

To install the boot image, you need to transfer the image from a TFTP server to the Management-0 port on the ASA Firepower SSP by logging in to the module's Console port.

Tip The Management-0 port is in the first slot on an SSP. This management port is also known as Management 1/0; however, it appears as Management-0 or Management 0/1 in ROMMON.

Figure 3-2 illustrates a topology with a Cisco ASA with a Firepower SSP and a TFTP server. The Cisco ASA Firepower SSP management interface is configured with IP address 10.10.1.1 and the TFTP server with 10.10.1.2.

Figure 3-2 *Firepower SSP TFTP Boot*

Follow these steps to install the boot image:

Step 1.   Place the boot image and a system software package on the TFTP server so that they can be accessed by the Cisco ASA FirePOWER module.

Step 2.   Connect to the Cisco ASA FirePOWER module through the Management 1/0 interface. You must use this interface to TFTP boot the boot image.

Step 3.   Reboot the system with the **system reboot** command.

Step 4.   As the system is booting, break out of the boot process by pressing **Esc** (the Escape key on your keyboard). If you see grub start to boot the system, you are too late, and you have to reboot the system again.

Step 5.   From the ROMMON prompt, configure the IP address for the Firepower SSP, the TFTP server address, the gateway, and the boot image path and file-name. The following example shows the configuration used in this example:

```
ADDRESS=10.10.1.1
SERVER=10.10.1.2
GATEWAY=10.1.1.2
IMAGE= asasfr-5500x-boot-6.0.0-1005.img
```

In this example, the IP address of the Firepower SSP is 10.10.1.1. The TFTP server address is 10.10.1.2, and the gateway is set to the TFTP server address, as well. The boot image is asasfr-5500x-boot-6.0.0-1005.img. After entering the preceding commands, issue the **set** command to apply the configuration.

Step 6.   Save the settings by using the **sync** command.

Step 7.   Start the download and boot process by using the **tftp** command.

Note   The boot takes several minutes. When it is finished, you see a login prompt.

Step 8.   Log in as **admin**, with the password **Admin123**, which is the default password.

Step 9.   Start configuring the system by issuing the **setup** command.

Step 10.   Configure the hostname, which can be up to 65 alphanumeric characters, with no spaces (though hyphens are allowed).

Step 11.   Configure the IP address. You can configure a static IPv4 or IPv6 address or use DHCP (for IPv4) or stateless autoconfiguration if you are configuring IPv6.

Step 12.   Identify at least one DNS server and set the domain name and search domain.

Note The management address, the gateway, and DNS information are the key settings to configure. Administrators often forget to set up the DNS server correctly, and this causes problems later in the configuration.

Step 13. Optionally, enable NTP and configure the NTP servers to set the system time.

Step 14. Install the system software image by using the **system install [noconfirm]** *url* command. Here is an example:

```
asasfr-boot> system install http://10.10.1.2/ asasfr-sys-6.0.0-1005.pkg
```

Note The **noconfirm** option skips all the confirmation messages.

The Cisco ASA FirePOWER module reboots when the installation is complete. This process can take more than 10 minutes. After the Cisco ASA FirePOWER module boots, you can log in as **admin** with the password **Sourcefire**. You can install the system software image from an HTTP, HTTPS, or FTP server that is accessible from the ASA SFR management interface.

Note Detailed step-by-step configuration options are provided later in this chapter.

Setting Up the Cisco ASA FirePOWER Module in Cisco ASA 5500-X Appliances

The following sections cover how to perform the initial setup of the Cisco ASA FirePOWER module in Cisco ASA 5500-X appliances.

Tip Cisco is always adding new models to its next-generation security appliances. Visit Cisco's Firepower compatibility guide to obtain the most recent information: www.cisco.com/c/en/us/td/docs/security/firepower/compatibility/ firepower-compatibility.html.

Installing the Boot Image and Firepower System Software in the SSD of Cisco ASA 5500-X Appliances

As you have already learned in this chapter, if you purchase a new Cisco ASA 5500-X appliance with the Cisco ASA FirePOWER module, the module software and required SSDs come preinstalled and ready to configure. However, you need to install the Cisco

ASA Firepower boot software, partition the SSD, and install the system software if you are adding a new Cisco ASA FirePOWER software module to an existing Cisco ASA or if the SSD needs to be replaced.

Tip   The flash (disk0) should have at least 3 GB of free space plus the space needed for the boot software in order to perform the reimaging process. If you are running the Cisco ASA in multi-context mode, you need to complete the reimaging steps in the system execution space. You also need to shut down any other modules from the Cisco ASA CLI, as shown in Example 3-1.

Example 3-1   *Shutting Down and Uninstalling the IPS Module*

```
sw-module module ips shutdown
sw-module module ips uninstall
reload
```

The commands in Example 3-1 shut down and uninstall the IPS software module (if installed on the Cisco ASA) and reboot the Cisco ASA. If you have a Cisco ASA CX module, you can use the same commands except use the **cxsc** keyword instead of **ips**.

Note   If you are just reimaging the Cisco ASA FirePOWER module, use the **sw-module module sfr shutdown** and **sw-module module sfr uninstall** commands.

Complete the following steps to install the boot image and the Firepower system software in the SSD of a Cisco ASA 5500-X appliance:

Step 1.   Download the Firepower boot image and system software packages from Cisco.com.

Step 2.   Transfer the boot image to the ASA. You can do this by using the CLI or the ASDM. If you select to install the image by using the ASDM, you can place the boot image on your workstation and upload it from there or you can place it on an FTP, TFTP, HTTP, HTTPS, SMB, or SCP server. In the ASDM, select **Tools > File Management** and choose the appropriate file transfer command, either **Between Local PC and Flash** or **Between Remote Server and Flash**. Figure 3-3 illustrates how to transfer the file between the remote server and flash.

If you choose to transfer the file by using the CLI, place the boot image on a TFTP, FTP, HTTP, or HTTPS server and then use the **copy** command to transfer it to the Cisco ASA flash. To transfer the file by using TFTP, enter the following command:

```
RTP-asa# copy tftp://10.10.1.2/asasfr-5500x-boot-5.4.1-69.img
disk0:/asasfr-5500x-boot-5.4.1-69.img
```

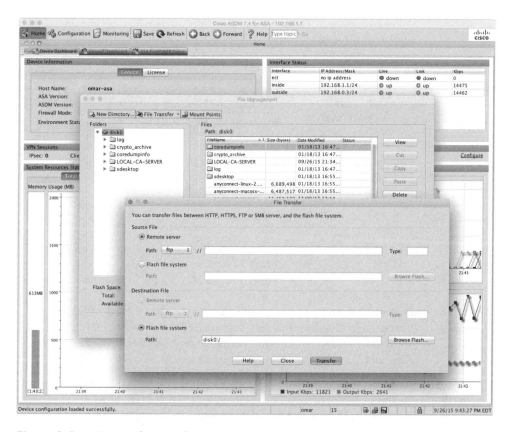

Figure 3-3 *ASDM File Transfer*

Step 3.   Transfer the boot software to disk0 on the ASA.

Step 4.   After the boot image is transferred to disk0 (flash), use **sw-module module sfr recover configure image disk0:** *file* to recover the Firepower module and install the boot image, as demonstrated here:

```
NY-asa# sw-module module sfr recover configure image
disk0:asasfr-5500x-boot-5.4.1-69.img
```

Step 5.   Use the **sw-module module sfr recover boot** command to load the Firepower boot image. This takes approximately 5 to 15 minutes.

Step 6.   Use the **session** command to connect to the Firepower module from the Cisco ASA, as demonstrated in the example that follows. The default username is **admin,** and the default password is **Admin123:**

```
RTP-asa# session sfr console
Opening console session with module sfr.
Connected to module sfr. Escape character sequence is 'CTRL-^X'.
```

```
Cisco ASA SFR Boot Image 5.4.1
asasfr login: admin
Password: Admin123
```

Note   The **session** command fails with a message about not being able to connect over ttyS1 if the module has not completed the boot process.

Step 7.   Configure the module so that you can install the system software package using the **setup** command, as shown here:

```
asasfr-boot> setup
```

```
                              Welcome to SFR Setup
                            [hit Ctrl-C to abort]
                          Default values are inside []
```

Enter the hostname, management address, gateway, DNS information, and, optionally, NTP server. It is very important to enter a correct DNS server to avoid name resolution problems during setup. You can also set the domain name and search domain.

Step 8.   Install the system software image by using the **system install [noconfirm]** *url* command. You can transfer the file using HTTP, HTTPS, or FTP. The following example demonstrates how to install the system software image by using HTTP:

```
asasfr-boot> system install http://10.10.1.3/asasfr-sys-5.4.1-211.pkg
Verifying
Downloading
Extracting
Package Detail
        Description:                Cisco ASA-Firepower 5.4.1-211
System Install
        Requires reboot:           Yes

Do you want to continue with upgrade? [y]: y
Warning: Please do not interrupt the process or turn off the system.
Doing so might leave system in unusable state.

Upgrading
Starting upgrade process ...
Populating new system image

Reboot is required to complete the upgrade. Press 'Enter' to reboot the
system.
```

```
(press Enter)
Broadcast message from root (ttyS1) (Mon Sep 28 12:12:48 2015):

The system is going down for reboot NOW!
Console session with module sfr terminated.
```

When the Firepower module reboots and you use the **session** command to access the module, you see a different login prompt, as shown in Example 3-2.

Example 3-2   *A Functional Firepower Module*

```
RTP-asa# session sfr console
Opening console session with module sfr.
Connected to module sfr. Escape character sequence is 'CTRL-^X'.

RTP-sfr login: admin
Password:
Last login: Sun Sep 27 02:02:28 UTC 2015 on ttyS1

Copyright 2001-2013, Sourcefire, Inc. All rights reserved. Sourcefire is
a registered trademark of Sourcefire, Inc. All other trademarks are
property of their respective owners.

Sourcefire Linux OS v5.4.1 (build 43)
Sourcefire ASA5512 v5.4.1 (build 211)

Last login: Sun Sep 27 02:02:28 on ttyS1

>
```

Configuring of Cisco ASA 5506-X, 5508-X, and 5516-X Appliances

When the Cisco ASA is booted with no configuration, it offers a setup menu that enables you to assign the initial parameters, such as the device name and an address for the management interface. You can choose to go through the initial setup menu for quick configuration. Example 3-3 shows the boot process (console output) for an ASA 5508.

Example 3-3   *Boot Process of the ASA 5508*

```
Rom image verified correctly
Cisco Systems ROMMON, Version 1.1.01, RELEASE SOFTWARE
Copyright (c) 1994-2014  by Cisco Systems, Inc.
Compiled Mon 10/20/2014 15:59:12.05 by builder
Current image running: Boot ROM0
Last reset cause: PowerCycleRequest
```

```
DIMM Slot 0 : Present
DIMM Slot 1 : Present


Platform ASA5508 with 8192 Mbytes of main memory
MAC Address: 18:8b:9d:ad:79:c1


Use BREAK or ESC to interrupt boot.
Use SPACE to begin boot immediately.


Boot in 10 seconds.
Located '.boot_string' @ cluster 840607.
#
 Attempt autoboot: "boot disk0:/asa951-lfbff-k8.SPA"


Located 'asa951-lfbff-k8.SPA' @ cluster 816328.


########################################################################
   ########################################################################
   ########################################################################
   ########################################################################
   ########################################################################
   ########################################################################
   ########################################################################
   ########################################################################
   ##################################################################


LFBFF signature verified.


INIT: version 2.88 booting
Starting udev
Configuring network interfaces... done.
Populating dev cache
dosfsck 2.11, 12 Mar 2005, FAT32, LFN
There are differences between boot sector and its backup.
Differences: (offset:original/backup)
  65:01/00
  Not automatically fixing this.
Starting check/repair pass.
Starting verification pass.
/dev/sdb1: 120 files, 838432/1918808 clusters
dosfsck(/dev/sdb1) returned 0
Processor memory 3754858905


Compiled on Wed 12-Aug-15 12:18 PDT by builders
```

```
Total NICs found: 13
i354 rev03 Gigabit Ethernet @ irq255 dev 20 index 08 MAC: 188b.9dad.79c1
ivshmem rev03 Backplane Data Interface     @ index 09 MAC: 0000.0001.0002
en_vtun rev00 Backplane Control Interface  @ index 10 MAC: 0000.0001.0001
en_vtun rev00 Backplane Int-Mgmt Interface    @ index 11 MAC: 0000.0001.0003
en_vtun rev00 Backplane Ext-Mgmt Interface    @ index 12 MAC: 0000.0000.0000
Verify the activation-key, it might take a while...
Running Permanent Activation Key: 0x7007c269 0x1098868c 0x54928558 0xa9987ca0
  0x081c04af


Licensed features for this platform:
Maximum Physical Interfaces      : Unlimited      perpetual
Maximum VLANs                    : 50            perpetual
Inside Hosts                     : Unlimited      perpetual
Failover                         : Active/Active  perpetual
Encryption-DES                   : Enabled        perpetual
Encryption-3DES-AES              : Enabled        perpetual
Security Contexts                : 2             perpetual
GTP/GPRS                         : Disabled       perpetual
AnyConnect Premium Peers         : 4             perpetual
AnyConnect Essentials            : Disabled       perpetual
Other VPN Peers                  : 100           perpetual
Total VPN Peers                  : 100           perpetual
Shared License                   : Disabled       perpetual
AnyConnect for Mobile            : Disabled       perpetual
AnyConnect for Cisco VPN Phone   : Disabled       perpetual
Advanced Endpoint Assessment     : Disabled       perpetual
Total UC Proxy Sessions          : 320           perpetual
Botnet Traffic Filter            : Disabled       perpetual
Cluster                          : Disabled       perpetual
VPN Load Balancing               : Enabled        perpetual


Encryption hardware device : Cisco ASA Crypto on-board accelerator (revision 0x1)


Cisco Adaptive Cisco ASA Software Version 9.5(1)


    ***************************** Warning ******************************
    This product contains cryptographic features and is
    subject to United States and local country laws
    governing, import, export, transfer, and use.
    Delivery of Cisco cryptographic products does not
    imply third-party authority to import, export,
    distribute, or use encryption. Importers, exporters,
    distributors and users are responsible for compliance
```

```
with U.S. and local country laws. By using this
product you agree to comply with applicable laws and
regulations. If you are unable to comply with U.S.
and local laws, return the enclosed items immediately.

A summary of U.S. laws governing Cisco cryptographic
products may be found at:
http://www.cisco.com/wwl/export/crypto/tool/stqrg.html

If you require further assistance please contact us by
sending email to export@cisco.com.
****************************** Warning *******************************

libgcc, version 4.8.1, Copyright (C) 2007 Free Software Foundation, Inc.
libgcc comes with ABSOLUTELY NO WARRANTY.
This is free software, and you are welcome to redistribute it under the General
Public License v.3 (http://www.gnu.org/licenses/gpl-3.0.html)
See User Manual (''Licensing'') for details.

libstdc++, version 4.8.23, Copyright (C) 2007 Free Software Foundation, Inc.
libstdc++ comes with ABSOLUTELY NO WARRANTY.
This is free software, and you are welcome to redistribute it under the General
Public License v.2 (http://www.gnu.org/licenses/gpl-2.0.html)
See User Manual (''Licensing'') for details.

Mdadm tools, version 3.2.6, Copyright (C) 1989, 1991 Free Software Foundation, Inc.
Copyright (C) 2002-2009 Neil Brown <neilb@suse.de>
mdadm comes with ABSOLUTELY NO WARRANTY.
This is free software, and you are welcome to redistribute it under the General
Public License v.2 (http://www.gnu.org/licenses/gpl-2.0.html)
See User Manual (''Licensing'') for details.

Cisco Adaptive Cisco ASA Software, version 9.5
Copyright (c) 1996-2015 by Cisco Systems, Inc.
For licenses and notices for open source software used in this product, please visit
http://www.cisco.com/go/asa-opensource

                    Restricted Rights Legend
Use, duplication, or disclosure by the Government is
subject to restrictions as set forth in subparagraph
(c) of the Commercial Computer Software - Restricted
Rights clause at FAR sec. 52.227-19 and subparagraph
(c) (1) (ii) of the Rights in Technical Data and Computer
Software clause at DFARS sec. 252.227-7013.
```

```
               Cisco Systems, Inc.
               170 West Tasman Drive
               San Jose, California 95134-1706

Reading from flash...
!!...
Cryptochecksum (unchanged): e7c1298c 7cf1ea71 242116d3 20270fcc

INFO: Power-On Self-Test in process.
................................................................
INFO: Power-On Self-Test complete.

INFO: Starting HW-DRBG health test...
INFO: HW-DRBG health test passed.

INFO: Starting SW-DRBG health test...
INFO: SW-DRBG health test passed.
Type help or '?' for a list of available commands.
ciscoasa>
```

In the first highlighted line in Example 3-3, the Cisco ASA starts loading the Cisco ASA software image and then verifies the activation key (license key), as you can see in the other highlighted lines. Then it lists all the open source licenses used in the software and performs system health checks. At the end of the boot process you get a prompt, which by default **is ciscoasa>**; this prompt changes, however, after you change the device hostname.

In Example 3-4, the Cisco ASA prompts you to specify whether you wish to go through the interactive menu to preconfigure the device. If you type **no**, the interactive menu is not shown, and the Cisco ASA shows the **ciscoasa>** prompt. If you type **yes**, the default option, the Cisco ASA walks you through the configuration of a number of parameters.

The Cisco ASA shows the default values in brackets ([]) before prompting you to accept or change them. To accept the default input, press Enter. After you go through the initial setup menu, the Cisco ASA displays the summary of the new configuration before prompting you to accept or reject it.

Example 3-4 *Cisco ASA Initial Setup Menu*

```
Pre-configure Firewall now through interactive prompts [yes]? yes
Firewall Mode [Routed]:
Enable password [<use current password>]: C1$c0123
Allow password recovery [yes]?
Clock (UTC):
  Year [2012]: 2016
```

```
    Month [Jul]: Jan
    Day [6]:6
    Time [01:08:57]: 21:27:00
Management IP address: 192.168.1.1
Management network mask: 255.255.255.0
Host name: NY-1
Domain name: securemeinc.org
IP address of host running Device Manager: 192.168.1.88

The following configuration will be used:
Enable password: <current password>
Allow password recovery: yes
Clock (UTC): 21:27:00 Jan 6 2016
Firewall Mode: Routed
Management IP address: 192.168.1.1
Management network mask: 255.255.255.0
Host name: NY-1
Domain name: securemeinc.org
IP address of host running Device Manager: 192.168.1.88

Use this configuration and write to flash? yes
Cryptochecksum: 629d6711 ccbe8923 5911d433 b6dfbe0c

182851 bytes copied in 1.190 secs (182851 bytes/sec)
NY-1>
```

You can assign the initial parameters and features by using either CLI commands or the ASDM.

Tip   You can rerun the interactive setup process by using the **setup** command in configuration mode.

Before you access the ASDM graphical console, you must install the ASDM software image on the local flash of the Cisco ASA if it is not present already. The ASDM interface only manages a local Cisco ASA. Therefore, if you need to manage multiple Cisco ASAs, you must install the ASDM software on all the Cisco ASAs. However, a single workstation can launch multiple instances of ASDM to manage more than one appliance.

Uploading ASDM

You can use the **dir** command to determine whether the ASDM software is installed. If the Cisco ASA does not have an ASDM image, your first step is to upload an image from an external file server, using one of the supported protocols. The appliance needs to be set up for basic configuration, including the following:

- Image interface names

- Image security levels

- Image IP addresses

- Image proper routes

After you set up basic information, use the **copy** command to transfer the image file, as shown in Example 3-5, where an ASDM file, named **asdm-751.bin**, is being copied from a TFTP server located at **172.18.82.10**. Verify the content of the local flash after the file is successfully uploaded.

Example 3-5   *Uploading the ASDM Image to the Local Flash*

```
NY-1# copy tftp flash
Address or name of remote host []? 172.18.82.10
Source filename []? asdm-751.bin
Destination filename [asdm-751.bin]? asdm-751.bin

Accessing tftp://172.18.82.10/asdm-715.bin...!!!!!!!!!!!!!!!!!!!
! Output omitted for brevity.
!!!!!!!!!!!!!!!!!!!!!!!!!!!!!!!!!!!!!!!!!!!!!
Writing file disk0:/asdm-715.bin...
!!!!!!!!!!!!!!!!!!!!!!!!!!!!!!!!!!!!!!!!!!!!!!!!!!!!!!!!!!!!!!!!!!!!!!!!!!!!!!!!!!!!
! Output omitted for brevity.
!!!!!!!!!!!!!!!!!!!!!!!!!!!!!!!!!!!!!!!!!!!!!!!!!!!!!!!!!!!!!!!!!!!!!!!!!!!!!!!
22658960 bytes copied in 51.30 secs (420298 bytes/sec)


NY-1# dir
Directory of disk0:/
135    -rwx  22834188     06:18:02 Jan 06 2016  asdm-715.bin
136    -rwx  37767168     06:22:46 Jan 06 2016  asa951-smp-k8.bin
4118732802 bytes total (3955822592 bytes free)
```

Setting Up the Cisco ASA to Allow ASDM Access

When the ASDM file is accessed, the Cisco ASA loads the first ASDM image that it finds from the local flash. If multiple ASDM images exist in the flash, use the **asdm image** command and specify the location of the ASDM image you want to load. This ensures that the appliance always loads the specified image when ASDM is launched. The following commands sets up the Cisco ASA to use **asdm-715.bin** as the ASDM image file:

```
NY-1(config)# asdm image disk0:/asdm-751.bin
```

The Cisco ASA uses the Secure Sockets Layer (SSL) protocol to communicate with the client. Consequently, the Cisco ASA acts as a web server to process the requests from the clients. You must enable the web server on the appliance by using the **http server enable** command.

The Cisco ASA discards the incoming requests until the ASDM client's IP address is in the trusted network to access the HTTP engine. To enable the HTTP engine and set up the appliance to trust the 192.168.1.0/24 network connected to the management interface, enter the following commands:

```
NY-1(config)# http server enable
NY-1(config)# http 192.168.1.0 255.255.255.0 management
```

Note The SSL VPN implementation on the Cisco ASA requires you to run the HTTP server on the appliance. Starting with Cisco ASA software version 8.0, you can set up the Cisco ASA to terminate both the SSL VPN and ASDM sessions on the same interface, using the default port 443. Use **https://<ASAipaddress>/admin** to access the GUI for administrative and management purposes.

Accessing the ASDM

You can access the ASDM interface from any workstation whose IP address is in the trusted network list. Before you establish the secure connection to the appliance, verify that IP connectivity exists between the workstation and the Cisco ASA.

To establish an SSL connection, launch a browser and point it to the appliance's IP address. In Figure 3-4, ASDM is accessed by entering **https://192.168.1.1/admin** as the URL. The URL is redirected to **https://192.168.1.1/admin/public/index.html**.

The Cisco ASA presents its self-signed certificate to the workstation so that a secure connection can be established. If the certificate is accepted, the Cisco ASA prompts you to present authentication credentials. If the ASDM authentication or enable password is not set up, there is no default username or password. If the enable password is defined, there is no default username, and you must use the enable password as the login password. If user authentication is enabled on the Cisco ASA through use of the **aaa authentication http console** command, then those login credentials must be provided. After a successful user authentication, the appliance presents two ways to launch ASDM:

- **Run Cisco ASDM as a local application:** The Cisco ASA offers a setup utility called asdm-launcher.msi, which can be saved to the workstation's local hard drive.

- **Run Cisco ASDM as a Java Web Start application:** The Cisco ASA launches ASDM in the client's browser as a Java applet. This option is not feasible if a firewall that filters out Java applets exists between the client and the Cisco ASA.

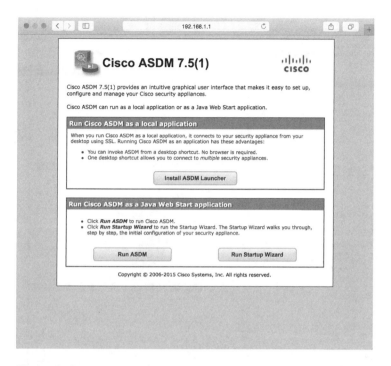

Figure 3-4 *Accessing the ASDM URL*

Note Running the ASDM as a local application is currently supported on Windows-based and OS X–based operating systems.

When the ASDM application is launched, it prompts for the IP address of the Cisco ASA to which you are trying to connect, as well as the user authentication credentials.

Note When you first launch the ASDM, the Cisco Smart Call Home functionality may prompt you to enable error and health information reporting either anonymously or by registering the product. You can choose not to enable if you are not interested.

If the user authentication is successful, the ASDM checks the current version of the installer application and downloads a new copy, if necessary. It loads the current configuration from the Cisco ASA and displays it in the GUI, as shown in Figure 3-5.

After you have established connectivity to the Cisco ASA, by using either the CLI or the ASDM, you are ready to start configuring the device. The following section guides you through basic setup of the Cisco ASA.

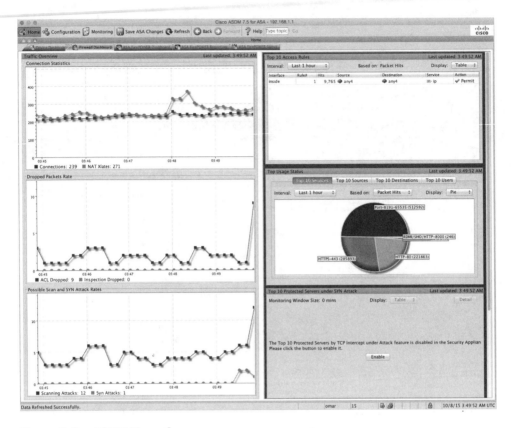

Figure 3-5   *ASDM Home Screen*

Setting Up a Device Name and Passwords

The default device name (also known as the hostname) of a Cisco ASA is **ciscoasa**. It is highly recommended that you set a unique device name to identify the Cisco ASA on the network. In addition, networking devices usually belong to a network domain. A domain name appends the unqualified hostnames with the configured domain name. For example, if the Cisco ASA tries to reach the host **secweb** by its hostname and the configured domain name on the Cisco ASA is **securemeinc.org**, the fully qualified domain name (FQDN) of the host is **secweb.securemeinc.org**.

In a new Cisco ASA, you can configure the Telnet and enable passwords. The Telnet password is used to authenticate remote sessions by using either the Telnet protocol or SSH. Prior to Cisco ASA software version 9.0(2), the default Telnet password was **cisco**. In version 9.0(2) and later, you must define a Telnet password using the **password** command. In addition, for an SSH connection, there is no default username or password in version 8.4(2) and later. You must configure the **aaa authentication ssh console** command to enable AAA authentication.

Example 3-6 shows the configuration you use in the CLI. The hostname is changed using the **hostname** command, the domain name is changed using the **domain-name** command, and the Telnet and enable passwords are changed using the **password** and **enable password** commands, respectively.

Example 3-6 *Setting Up the Hostname, Domain Name, and Passwords*

```
ciscoasa# configure terminal
ciscoasa(config)# hostname NY-1
NY-1(config)# domain-name secureminc.org
NY-1 (config)# password C1$c0123
NY-1 (config)# enable password C1$c0123
```

Tip If you view the configuration after adding the passwords, the Cisco ASA displays the encrypted passwords as follows:

```
NY-1# show running-config | include pass
enable password 9jNfZuG3TC5tCVH0 encrypted
passwd 2KFQnbNIdI.2KYOU encrypted
```

Configuring an Interface

Cisco ASA appliances come with a number of Fast Ethernet, Gigabit Ethernet, and 10-Gigabit Ethernet interfaces, depending on the platform. They also include one management interface (Management 0/0) in all one-rack unit (1 RU) models and two management interfaces (Management 0/0 and Management 0/1) in ASA 5580s and ASA 5585s. In addition, you can create one or more subinterfaces in each physical interface. The Fast Ethernet, Gigabit Ethernet, and 10-Gigabit Ethernet interfaces are used to route traffic from one interface to another, based on the configured policies, whereas the management interface is designed to establish out-of-band connections.

The Cisco ASA protects the internal network from external threats. Each interface is assigned a name to designate its role on the network. The most secure network is typically labeled as the inside network, whereas the least secure network is designated as the outside network. For semi-trusted networks, you can define them as demilitarized zones (DMZs) or any logical interface name. You must use the interface name to set up the configuration features that are linked to an interface.

The Cisco ASA also uses the concept of assigning security levels to the interfaces. The higher the security level, the more protected the interface. Consequently, the security level is used to reflect the level of trust of this interface with respect to the level of trust of another interface on the Cisco ASA. The security level can be between 0 and 100. Therefore, the most trusted network is placed behind the interface with a security level of 100, whereas the least protected network is placed behind an interface with a security level of 0. A DMZ interface should be assigned a security level between 0 and 100.

Note   When an interface is configured with a **nameif** command, the Cisco ASA automatically assigns a preconfigured security level. If an interface is configured with the name inside, the Cisco ASA assigns a security level of 100. For all the other interface names, the Cisco ASA assigns a security level of 0.

Cisco ASA enables you to assign the same security level to more than one interface. If communication is required between the hosts on interfaces at the same security level, use the **same-security-traffic permit inter-interface** global configuration command. In addition, if an interface is not assigned a security level, it does not respond at the network layer.

By default, you do not need to define an access control list (ACL) to permit traffic from a high security–level interface to a low security–level interface; however, if you want to restrict traffic flows from a high security–level interface destined to a low security–level interface, you can define an ACL. If you configure an ACL for traffic originating from a high security–level interface to a low security–level interface, it disables the implicit permit from that interface. All traffic is now subject to the entries defined in that ACL.

An ACL must explicitly permit traffic traversing the security appliance from a lower to a higher security–level interface of the firewall. The ACL must be applied to the lower security–level interface or globally.

The most important parameter under the interface configuration is the assignment of an IP address. This is required if an interface is to be used to pass traffic in a Layer 3 firewall, also known as routed mode. An address can be either statically or dynamically assigned. For a static IP address, you configure an IP address and its respective subnet mask.

The Cisco ASA also supports interface address assignment through a Dynamic Host Configuration Protocol (DHCP) server and by using PPPoE. Assigning an address by using DHCP is a preferred method if an ISP dynamically allocates an IP address to the outside interface. You can also inform the Cisco ASA to use the DHCP server's specified default gateway as the default route if the Obtain Default Route Using DHCP option is enabled in the ASDM. You can do this in the CLI by issuing the **ip address dhcp [setroute]** interface subcommand.

Note   If a Cisco ASA is deployed in transparent mode, the IP address is assigned in global configuration mode or on a bridge virtual interface (BVI) interface, depending of the version of code.

Assigning an interface address through DHCP is not supported if used with failover.

To configure a physical interface on a Cisco ASA by using ASDM, navigate to **Configuration > Device Setup > Interfaces**, select an interface, and click the **Edit** button.

Example 3-7 shows how to enable the GigabitEthernet0/0 interface as the outside interface and assigns a security level of 0. The IP address is 209.165.200.225 with a mask of 255.255.255.224.

Example 3-7 *Enabling an Interface*

```
NY-1# configure terminal
NY-1(config)# interface GigabitEthernet0/0
NY-1(config-if)# no shutdown
NY-1(config-if)# nameif outside
NY-1(config-if)# security-level 0
NY-1(config-if)# ip address 209.165.200.225 255.255.255.224
```

The ASDM enables you to configure the speed, duplex, and media type on an interface by opening the Edit Interface dialog box for the interface and clicking the Configure Hardware Properties button. By default, the speed and duplex are set to auto and can be changed to avoid link negotiations. If the speed and duplex settings do not match the speed and duplex settings on the other end of the Ethernet connection, you may see packet loss and experience performance degradation. The media type is either RJ-45 for copper-based interfaces or SFP for fiber-based interfaces. RJ-45 is the default media type.

Tip   The Ethernet-based interfaces on the Cisco ASA 5500 Series use the auto-MDI/ MDIX (media-dependent interface/media-dependent interface crossover) feature, which does not require a crossover cable when connecting interfaces of two similar types. These interfaces perform an internal crossover when a straight network cable connects two similar interfaces. This feature works only when both the speed and duplex parameters are set to auto-negotiate.

Example 3-8 shows the outside interface set up with a connection speed of 1000 Mbps, using full-duplex mode.

Example 3-8 *Configuring Speed and Duplex on an Interface*

```
NY-1# configure terminal
NY-1(config)# interface GigabitEthernet0/0
NY-1(config-if)# speed 1000
NY-1(config-if)# duplex full
```

The Cisco ASA shows the output of interface-related statistics when you issue the **show interface** command from the CLI. Example 3-9 shows GigabitEthernet0/0 set up as the outside interface and has an IP address of 209.165.200.225 and GigabitEthernet0/1 set up as the inside interface with an IP address of 192.168.10.1. This command also shows the packet rate and the total number of packets entering and leaving the interface.

Example 3-9 *show interface Command Output*

```
NY-1# show interface
Interface GigabitEthernet0/0 "outside", is up, line protocol is up
  Hardware is i82574L rev00, BW 1000 Mbps, DLY 10 usec
        Full-duplex, 1000 Mbps
        MAC address 000f.f775.4b53, MTU 1500
        IP address 209.165.200.225, subnet mask 255.255.255.224
        70068 packets input, 24068922 bytes, 0 no buffer
        Received 61712 broadcasts, 0 runts, 0 giants
        0 input errors, 0 CRC, 0 frame, 0 overrun, 0 ignored, 0 abort
        0 L2 decode drops
        13535 packets output, 7196865 bytes, 0 underruns
        0 output errors, 0 collisions, 0 interface resets
        0 babbles, 0 late collisions, 0 deferred
        0 lost carrier, 0 no carrier
        input queue (curr/max packets): hardware (0/1) software (0/11)
        output queue (curr/max packets): hardware (0/19) software (0/1)
  Traffic Statistics for "outside":
        70081 packets input, 23044675 bytes
        13540 packets output, 6992176 bytes
        49550 packets dropped
      1 minute input rate 1 pkts/sec,   362 bytes/sec
      1 minute output rate 1 pkts/sec,   362 bytes/sec
      1 minute drop rate, 0 pkts/sec
      5 minute input rate 1 pkts/sec,   342 bytes/sec
      5 minute output rate 1 pkts/sec,   362 bytes/sec
      5 minute drop rate, 0 pkts/sec
Interface GigabitEthernet0/1 "inside", is up, line protocol is up
  Hardware is i82546GB rev03, BW 1000 Mbps, DLY 10 usec
        Auto-Duplex(Full-duplex), Auto-Speed(1000 Mbps)
        MAC address 000f.f775.4b55, MTU 1500
        IP address 192.168.10.1, subnet mask 255.255.255.0
        1447094 packets input, 152644956 bytes, 0 no buffer
        Received 1203884 broadcasts, 0 runts, 0 giants
        0 input errors, 0 CRC, 0 frame, 0 overrun, 0 ignored, 0 abort
        20425 L2 decode drops
        332526 packets output, 151244141 bytes, 0 underruns
        0 output errors, 0 collisions, 0 interface resets
        0 babbles, 0 late collisions, 0 deferred
        0 lost carrier, 0 no carrier
        input queue (curr/max packets): hardware (0/1) software (0/14)
        output queue (curr/max packets): hardware (0/26) software (0/1)
  Traffic Statistics for "inside":
```

```
   777980 packets input, 80481496 bytes
   151736 packets output, 85309705 bytes
   395607 packets dropped
1 minute input rate 0 pkts/sec,  58 bytes/sec
1 minute output rate 0 pkts/sec,  0 bytes/sec
1 minute drop rate, 0 pkts/sec
5 minute input rate 0 pkts/sec,  66 bytes/sec
5 minute output rate 0 pkts/sec,  0 bytes/sec
5 minute drop rate, 0 pkts/sec
```

Configuring the Cisco ASA to Redirect Traffic to the Cisco ASA FirePOWER Module

As you learned in Chapter 2, you can configure the Cisco ASA FirePOWER module in inline mode or in monitor-only mode. Follow these steps to configure the Cisco ASA to redirect traffic to the Cisco ASA FirePOWER module in inline mode or monitor-only mode:

Step 1.   Log in to the ASDM.

Step 2.   Navigate to **Configuration > Firewall > Service Policy Rules**.

Note   If you previously had a legacy IPS module or CX module configured and an active service policy in the Cisco ASA, you must remove that policy before you configure the Cisco ASA FirePOWER Services policy. If your Cisco ASA is running in multiple context mode, you must configure the service policy within each security context.

Step 3.   Click the **Add** button to add a new service policy rule. The screen shown in Figure 3-6 appears.

Step 4.   Specify whether the policy will apply to a particular interface or globally and click **Next**. In this example, the policy will apply globally.

Step 5.   After you click **Next**, the screen shown in Figure 3-7 appears.

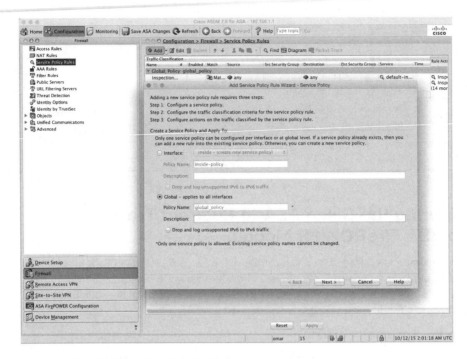

Figure 3-6 *Adding a New Service Policy*

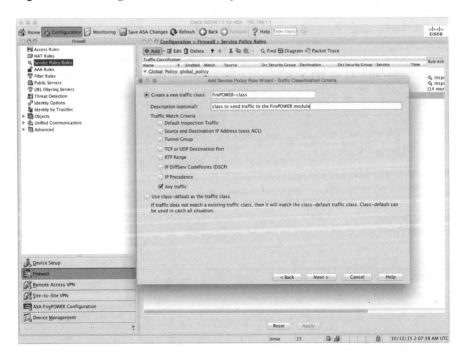

Figure 3-7 *Adding the New Traffic Class*

Step 6.   Enter the name of the new traffic class (for example, **firePOWER-class**).

Step 7.   Enter an optional description.

Step 8.   Optionally specify criteria for the traffic that will be matched and sent to the Cisco ASA FirePOWER module or use the default class (**class-default**). In this example, the class will match all traffic because the **Any traffic** checkbox is checked under the Traffic Match Criteria field.

Step 9.   Click **Next**. The Rule Actions page shown in Figure 3-8 appears.

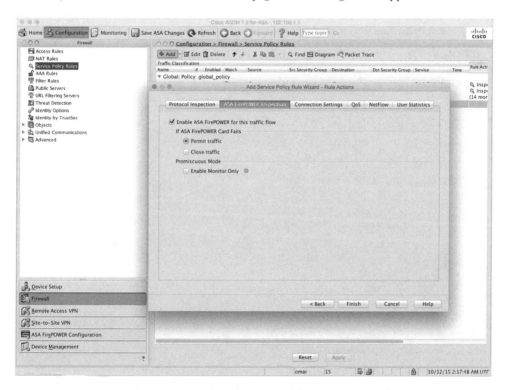

Figure 3-8   *The Rule Actions Page*

Step 10.   Navigate to the **ASA Firepower Inspection** tab and check the **Enable ASA Firepower for this traffic flow** checkbox, as shown in Figure 3-8.

Step 11.   Optionally configure the Cisco ASA to pass traffic if the Cisco ASA FirePOWER module fails (this is referred to as "fail open") or configure the Cisco ASA to stop all traffic (or "fail close"). In Figure 3-8, the Cisco ASA is configured to fail open because the **Permit traffic** option is selected in the **If ASA Firepower Card Fails** area.

Step 12.   Optionally check **Enable Monitor Only** to send a read-only copy of traffic to the module. This is also referred to as "inline tap mode." (By default, the Cisco ASA sends all traffic to the Cisco ASA FirePOWER module in inline mode.) In Figure 3-8, the Cisco ASA is configured to send all traffic to the Cisco ASA FirePOWER module, and the module is configure in inline mode.

Step 13.   Click **Finish.** The new service policy is shown on the Service Policy Rules page in ASDM, as shown in Figure 3-9.

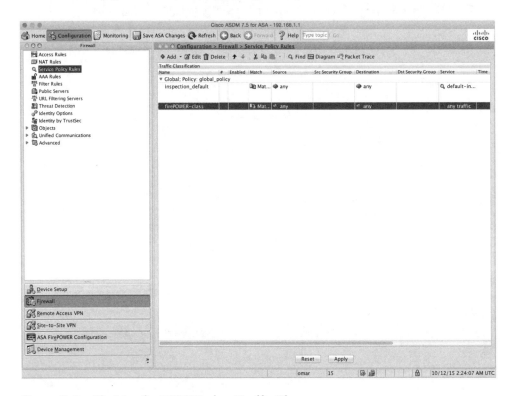

Figure 3-9   *The New firePOWER-class Traffic Class*

Example 3-10 shows the command-line interface (CLI) commands that were applied on the Cisco ASA by ASDM.

Example 3-10   *Configuring the Service Policy Using the CLI*

```
! The class map
class-map firePOWER-class
 description class to send all traffic to the Firepower module
! Matching all traffic to be sent to the Firepower module
 match any
!
```

```
! Applying the class to the policy map
policy-map global_policy
 class firePOWER-class
! The Firepower module configured to fail open
  sfr fail-open
!
! Applying the policy map to the service policy
service-policy global_policy global
```

Configuring the Cisco ASA FirePOWER Module for the FMC

You can register the Cisco ASA FirePOWER module to the Firepower Management Center (FMC). Chapter 12, "Reporting and Troubleshooting with Cisco Next-Generation IPS," covers the FMC in detail. Complete the following steps to register the Cisco ASA FirePOWER module to the FMC:

Step 1.   Log in to the Cisco ASA FirePOWER module.

Step 2.   Use the **configure manager** command as shown in the following example:

```
configure manager add 192.168.1.89 thisISaRegKey
```

In this example, the IP address of the FMC is **192.168.1.89.** You can also use the DNS hostname or an IPv6 address (if IPv6 is enabled in your network). If the FMC is not directly addressable, use the **DONTRESOLVE** keyword. In this example, the registration key is **thisISaRegKey**. The registration key is a unique alphanumeric registration key required to register a Cisco ASA FirePOWER module to the FMC. You can also enter an optional alphanumeric string (nat_id) that is used during the registration process between the FMC and the ASA FirePOWER module. This is required if the **DONTRESOLVE** keyword is used. In deployments where Network Address Translation (NAT) is configured, you must provide a hostname or an IP address either when you are configuring remote management or when you are adding the managed appliance. A self-generated alphanumeric registration key up to 37 characters in length identifies the connection. You can configure an optional unique alphanumeric NAT ID (nat_id) that can help the FMC establish communications in a NAT environment. The NAT ID must be unique among all NAT IDs used to register managed appliances.

Step 3.   Type **exit** to exit the configuration mode.

Configuring the Cisco ASA FirePOWER Module Using the ASDM

You can use the ASDM to configure the Cisco ASA FirePOWER module in only certain platforms, including the Cisco ASA 5506-X, 5506H-X, 5506W-X, 5508-X, and 5516-X appliances.

> **Note** For additional compatibility information, visit www.cisco.com/c/en/us/td/docs/security/asa/compatibility/asamatrx.html#48552.

The following sections covers how to configure the Cisco ASA FirePOWER module using the ASDM in supported platforms.

Configuring Access Control Policies

To view the access control policies that are applied in the Cisco ASA FirePOWER module, navigate to **Configuration > ASA FirePOWER Configuration > Policies > Access Control Policy**, as shown in Figure 3-10.

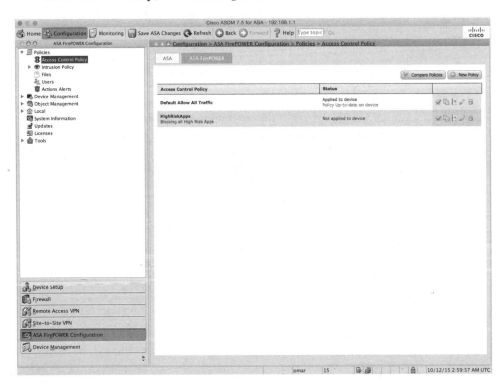

Figure 3-10 *Firepower Access Control Policy*

Creating a New Access Control Policy

Follow these steps to create a new access control policy in the Cisco ASA FirePOWER module:

Step 1.   Click the **New Policy** button. The dialog shown in Figure 3-11 appears.

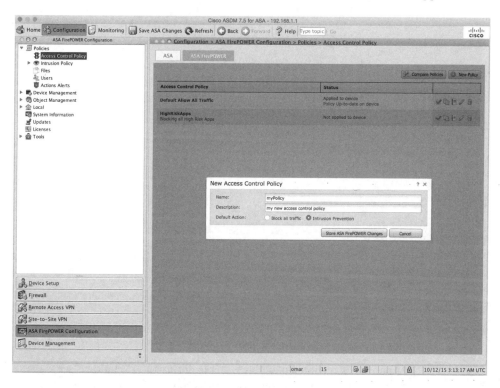

Figure 3-11   *Creating a New Access Control Policy*

Step 2.   Enter a name for the new access policy. In this example, the name of the new policy is **myPolicy**.

Step 3.   Enter an optional description for the policy.

Step 4.   Set Default Action to either **Block all traffic** or **Intrusion Prevention**. If you select the default action to **Block all traffic**, all traffic will be blocked without further inspection. In this example, the default action is set to **Intrusion Prevention**. When you first create an access control policy, you cannot choose to trust traffic as the default action. If you want to trust all traffic by default, change the default action after you create the policy. You can also use and modify the initial system-provided policy named **Default Trust All Traffic**. Figure 3-12 shows the Default Action dropdown menu options.

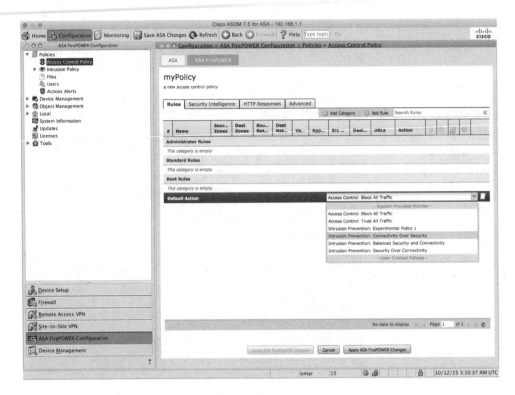

Figure 3-12 *Default Action Dropdown Menu Options*

You can also copy an existing policy from this ASA FirePOWER module or import a policy from another ASA FirePOWER module.

As previously mentioned, in this example, Intrusion Prevention is set as the default action. Therefore, the Cisco ASA FirePOWER module creates a policy with the **Intrusion Prevention: Balanced Security and Connectivity** default action.

Step 5.   Click **Store ASA Firepower Changes.**

Adding Rules to the Access Control Policy

You can more granularly control network traffic by adding rules to an access control policy. The rules within an access control policy are organized using a numbering scheme starting at 1. The Firepower system matches traffic to access control rules by ascending rule number. Typically, the Firepower system process network traffic according to the first access control rule, where all the rule's conditions match the traffic. These conditions include the following:

■ Security zone

■ Network or geographical location

- Ports

- Applications

- Requested URLs

- Users

To add a rule, click the **Add Rule** button, and the screen shown in Figure 3-13 appears.

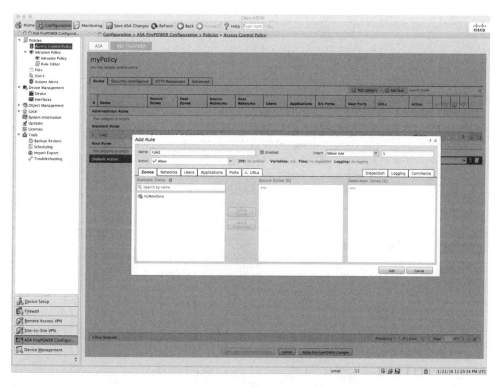

Figure 3-13 *Adding a New Rule*

Each rule also has an action that determines whether you monitor, trust, block, or allow matching traffic. When you allow traffic, you can specify that the system first inspect it with intrusion or file policies to block any exploits, malware, or prohibited files before they reach your assets or exit your network. On the other hand, after the system trusts or blocks traffic, it does not perform further inspection. Figure 3-14 shows the Action dropdown menu options.

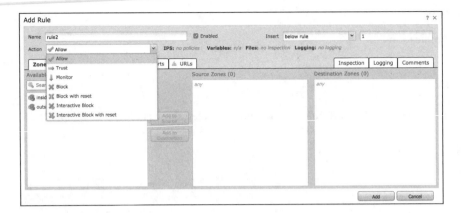

Figure 3-14 *Action Dropdown Menu Options*

To configure rules based on security zones, navigate to the **Zones** tab. You can also configure rule conditions to match network or geographical locations. Figure 3-15 shows
how to configure a rule condition based on geographical location of the source and destination networks. For instance, you can block or allow traffic that is sourced or destined
to a given geographical location. In Figure 3-15, the source networks are based in North
America (geolocation), and the destination networks are in Asia.

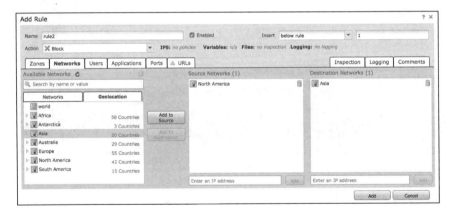

Figure 3-15 *Rules Based on Geolocation*

Cisco Security Intelligence–based traffic filtering and some decoding and preprocessing
occur before network traffic is evaluated by access control rules. The system matches
traffic to access control rules in the order you specify. In most cases, the system handles
network traffic according to the first access control rule where all the rule's conditions
match the traffic. Some of the filtering capabilities may rely on Layer 7 (application)
information, where the actual flow of the application may not be determined until a few
packets are analyzed in the communication between two or more hosts. Conditions can

be simple or complex; you can control traffic by security zone, network or geographical location, port, application, requested URL, and user.

You can also create rules based on the type and the risk of the application. Figure 3-16 shows how to create a rule based on application conditions, on the **Applications** tab.

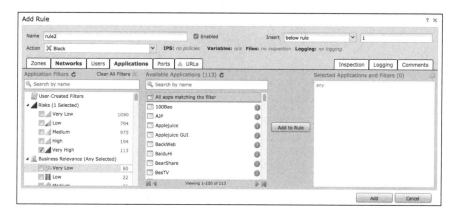

Figure 3-16   *Rules Based on Application Risk and Type*

Figure 3-17 shows how to use the **Ports** tab to create a rule based on given application ports. You can select predefined ports/applications such as FTP, Bittorrent, DNS over TCP or UDP, and so on.

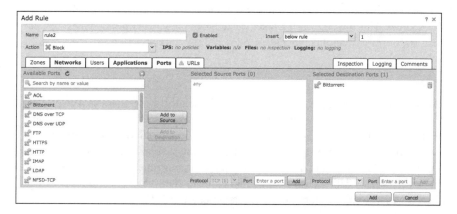

Figure 3-17   *Rules Based on Ports*

You can also create rules that match known URLs to sites known to be hosting pornography, drug content, dating sites, and many other categories. The URL filtering license is required in order to configure and enable rules based on URLs. Figure 3-18 shows how to use the **URLs** tab to configure a rule based on URL categories.

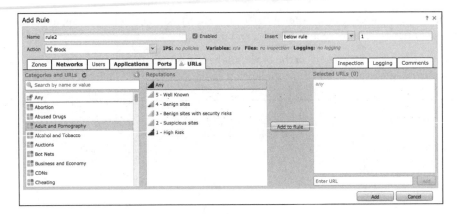

Figure 3-18 *Rules Based on URL Categories*

Security Intelligence

Security Intelligence from Cisco is available as a first line of defense against malicious
Internet sites and known malicious IP addresses. You can configure this feature to
instantly blacklist (block) connections based on the latest reputation intelligence from
Cisco Talos. You can configure access control policies with whitelists and blacklists,
based on Cisco Talos Security Intelligence by navigating to the Security Intelligence tab
under a given access policy, as shown in Figure 3-19.

You can override blacklists with custom whitelists in order to ensure continual access to
critical resources. This traffic filtering takes place before any other policy-based inspection, analysis, or traffic handling, including rules and the default action.

HTTP Responses

You can customize a web page for blocked URLs. When the system blocks a given
HTTP web request, you can customize what the user sees in a web browser depending
on how the session is blocked. For example, you can select **Block** or **Block with reset**
to deny the connection. A blocked session times out; the system resets Block with reset
connections. On the other hand, for both blocking actions, you can override the default
browser or server page with a custom page that explains that the connection was denied.
The Cisco ASA Firepower system calls this custom page an *HTTP response page*.

You can edit the block response page by navigating to the HTTP Responses tab under
the access control policy, as shown in Figure 3-20.

Figure 3-19 *Security Intelligence Tab*

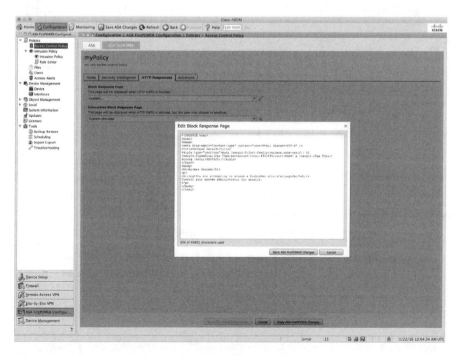

Figure 3-20 *Customizing Block Response Pages*

If you set the Cisco ASA FirePOWER module action to **Interactive Block** or **Interactive Block with reset**, you can configure an interactive HTTP response page that warns users but also allows them to click a button to continue or refresh the page to load the originally requested site. Users may have to refresh after bypassing the response page to load page elements that did not load. You can either display a generic system-provided response page or enter custom HTML, as shown in Figure 3-21.

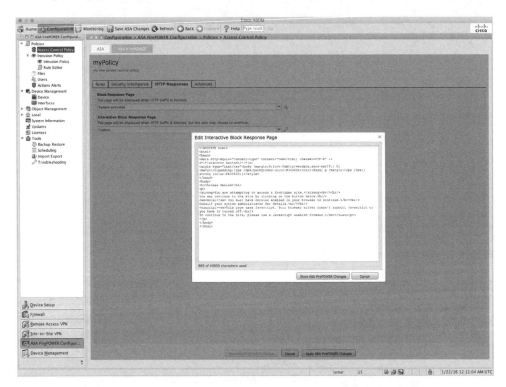

Figure 3-21 *Customizing Interactive Block Response Pages*

Access Control Policy Advanced Settings

The advanced access control policy settings typically require little or no modification because the default settings are appropriate for most deployments. However, you can also customize the following advanced settings (see Figure 3-22):

- **General Settings:** You can customize the number of characters you store in the Cisco ASA FirePOWER module database for each URL requested by users.

- **Network Analysis and Intrusion Policies:** You can change the access control policy's default intrusion policy and associated variable set, which are used to initially inspect traffic before the system can determine exactly how to inspect that traffic. You can also change the access control policy's default network analysis policy, which administers many preprocessing options. In addition, you can use custom network analysis rules and network analysis policies to tailor preprocessing options to specific security zones and networks.

- **File and Malware Settings:** You can set performance options for file control, file storage, and advanced malware protection.

- **Transport/Network Layer Preprocessor Settings:** You can create preprocessor settings that are applied globally to all networks, zones, and VLANs where you apply your access control policy.

- **Detection Enhancement Settings:** You can use adaptive profiles to improve reassembly of packet fragments and TCP streams in passive deployments, based on your network's host operating systems.

- **Performance Settings and Latency-Based Performance Settings:** You can tune and improve the performance of your system as it analyzes traffic for attempted intrusions.

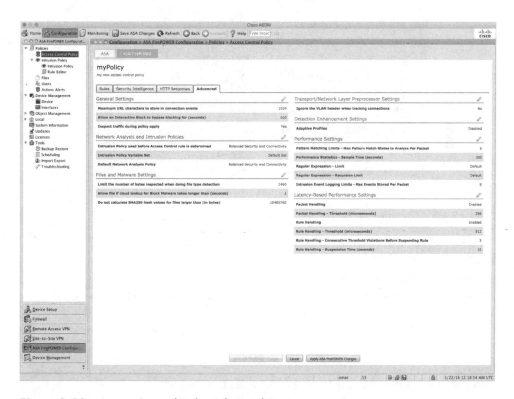

Figure 3-22 *Access Control Rules Advanced Settings*

Configuring Intrusion Policies

You can configure intrusion policies by navigating to **Configuration > ASA FirePOWER Configuration > Policies > Intrusion Policy**, where you can view your current custom intrusion policies, edit them, or create new ones. To create a new intrusion policy, click **Create Policy** to display the screen shown in Figure 3-23.

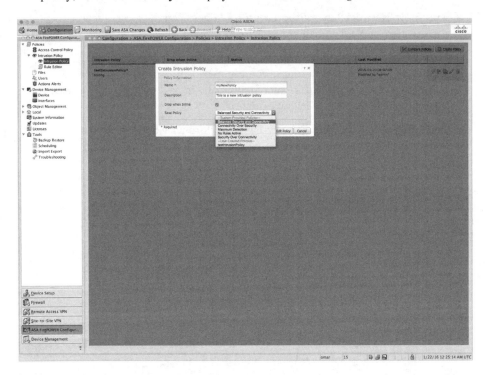

Figure 3-23   *Creating a New Intrusion Policy*

You must provide a name for the new intrusion policy, specify a base policy, and specify drop behavior.

The **Drop when Inline** setting defines how the Firepower module handles drop rules (intrusion or preprocessor rules whose rule state is set to **Drop and Generate Events**) and other intrusion policy configurations that affect traffic. You should enable drop behavior in inline deployments when you want to drop or replace malicious packets.

> **Note**   In Cisco ASA FirePOWER modules that are configured in passive mode, the system cannot affect traffic flow, regardless of the drop behavior.

The base policy sets the intrusion policy's default settings. You can use either a system-provided or custom policy as your base policy. Figure 3-23 shows the Base Policy drop-down menu options.

You can edit an intrusion policy by navigating to **Configuration > ASA FirePOWER Configuration > Policies > Intrusion Policy** and clicking the pencil (edit) button; the screen shown in Figure 3-24 appears.

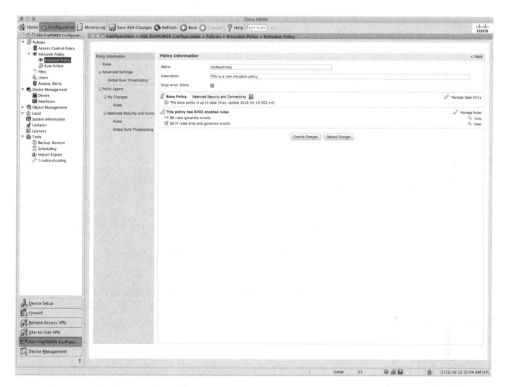

Figure 3-24   *Editing an Intrusion Policy*

To customize how rules are displayed in the intrusion policy or sort rules by several criteria, click **Manage Rules** to display the screen shown in Figure 3-25.

In the page shown in Figure 3-25, you can also display the details for a specific rule to see rule settings, rule documentation, and other rule settings. This page has four key categories:

- Filtering features
- Rule attribute menus
- Rules listing
- Rule details

Note   The column headers relate to the menus in the menu bar, where you access those configuration items.

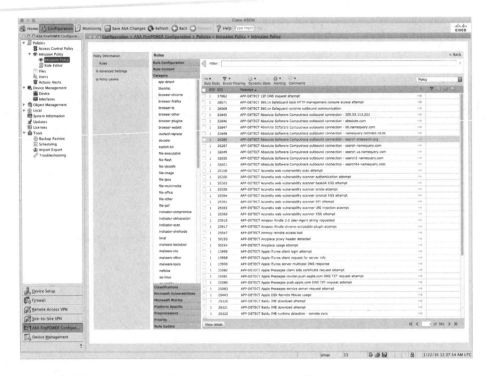

Figure 3-25 *Managing Rules Under an Intrusion Policy*

Custom Rules

You can create custom rules or edit or clone existing ones by navigating to **Configuration > ASA FirePOWER Configuration > Policies > Intrusion Policy > Rule Editor** (see Figure 3-26).

To modify an existing rule, click the pencil icon next to the specific rule. You can also import rules from another system by clicking the **Import Rules** button to display the screen shown in Figure 3-27.

New vulnerabilities are reported daily by many vendors in the industry. Cisco Talos releases rule updates that you can first import onto your Cisco ASA Firepower module and then implement by applying affected access control, network analysis, and intrusion policies.

Tip Rule updates are cumulative, and Cisco recommends that you always import the latest update. You cannot import a rule update that either matches or predates the version of the currently installed rules. Rule updates may contain new binaries, so make sure your process for downloading and installing them complies with your security policies. In addition, rule updates may be large, so import rules during periods of low network use.

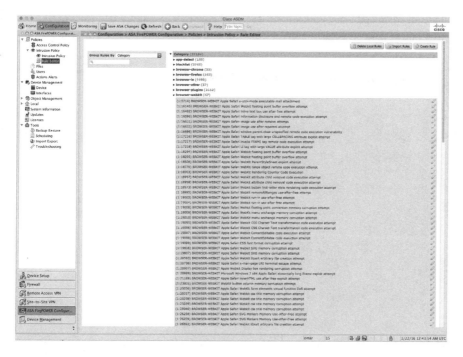

Figure 3-26 *The Rule Editor*

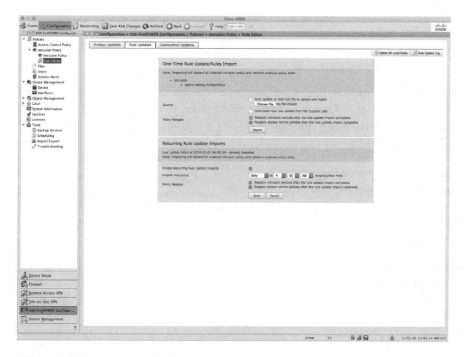

Figure 3-27 *Importing Rules*

If you are an advanced user, you can create a new rule by clicking **Create Rule** in the main **rule editor** page (refer to Figure 3-26). The screen shown in Figure 3-28 appears.

Figure 3-28   *Creating a Custom Rule*

When creating a custom standard text rule, you set the rule header settings and the rule keywords and arguments. After you create a custom rule, you can search for it by using the rule number. The format of the rule number is as follows:

> GID:SID:Rev

The rule number for all standard text rules starts with 1. The second part of the rule number, the Snort ID (SID), indicates whether the rule is a local rule or a rule provided by Cisco. Snort IDs for custom rules start at 1,000,000, and the SID for each new local rule is incremented by 1. The last part of the rule number is the revision number. Each time you edit a custom rule, the revision number increments by 1.

You enter the message you want displayed with the event in the **Message** field. The **Classification** dropdown menu allows you to select a classification to describe the type of event. Figure 3-29 shows examples of the options available in the **Classification** dropdown menu.

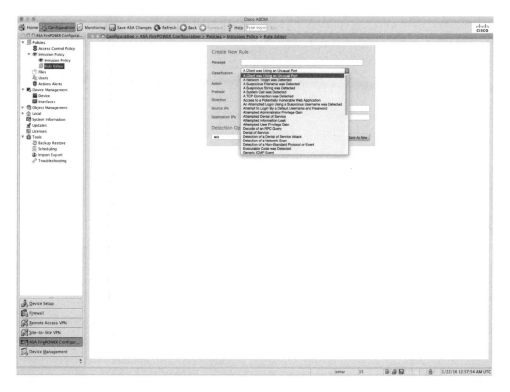

Figure 3-29 *Event Type Classification*

The **Action** list allows you to define the type of rule you are creating (**alert** to create an alert or **pass** to create a rule that ignores traffic that triggers the rule). You can select from the **Protocol** dropdown menu the traffic protocol (**tcp**, **udp**, **icmp**, or **ip**) of packets you want the rule to inspect.

The **Direction** dropdown menu allows you to select the operator that indicates which direction of traffic you want to trigger the rule.

You can also define the source and destination IP addresses and ports that should trigger the rule. Select **Directional** under the **Direction** dropdown menu to match traffic that moves from the source IP address to the destination IP address. Select **Bidirectional** to match traffic that moves in either direction.

You can select the detection options under the **Detection Options** dropdown menu and click the **Add Option** button. Figure 3-30 shows examples of the different detection options available.

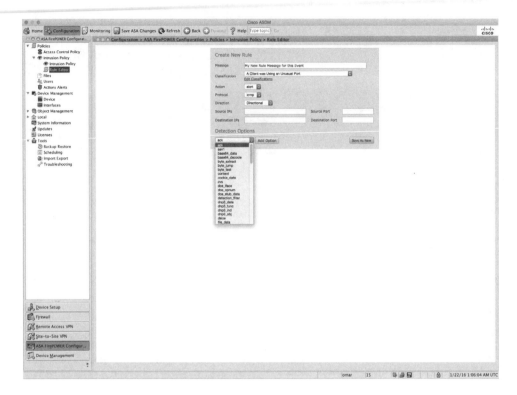

Figure 3-30   *New Rule Detection Option*

Configuring File Policies

You can configure file policies in a Cisco ASA FirePOWER module to perform advanced malware protection and file control. You can configure file policies by navigating to **Configuration > ASA FirePOWER Configuration > Policies > Files**. To create a new file policy, click the **New File Policy** button to open the dialog shown in Figure 3-31.

Enter the name of the new file policy and a description and then click the **Store ASA FirePOWER Changes** button. The screen shown in Figure 3-32 appears.

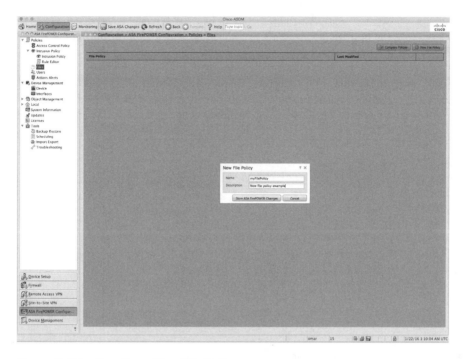

Figure 3-31 *Creating a New File Policy*

Figure 3-32 *The New File Policy*

The policy has two access control rules, both of which use the **Allow** action and are associated with file policies. The policy's default action is also to allow traffic, but without file policy inspection. A file policy, like its parent access control policy, contains rules that determine how the system handles files that match the conditions of each rule. You can configure file rules to take different actions for different file types, application protocols, or directions of transfer. To add a new file rule, click the **Add File Rule** button. The Add File Rule screen shown in Figure 3-33 appears.

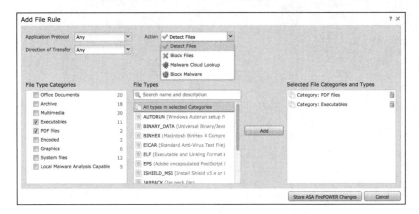

Figure 3-33   *Adding a New File Rule*

Note   Each file rule has an associated action that determines how the system handles traffic that matches the conditions of the rule.

You can set separate rules within a file policy to take different actions for different file types, application protocols, or directions of transfer.

The rule actions can be configured to the following:

- **Detect Files:** To log the detection of specific file types while still allowing their transmission

- **Block Files:** To block specific file types

- **Malware Cloud Lookup:** To log the malware disposition of files traversing the network based on a cloud lookup, while still allowing their transmission

- **Block Malware:** To calculate the SHA-256 hash value of specific file types, use a cloud lookup process to first determine whether files traversing the network contain malware, and block files that represent threats

You can select different file type categories in the **File Type Categories** section and select or search for specific file types under the **File Types** section (refer to Figure 3-33). Click the **Add** button to add file categories and file types.

Reusable Object Management

The Cisco ASA FirePOWER module allows you to create named objects, which are reusable configurations that associate a name with a value so that a named object is used instead. You can configure the following object types:

- Network-based objects that represent IP addresses and networks, port/protocol pairs, security zones, and origin/destination country (geographical location)

- Security Intelligence feeds and lists

- Application filters

- Ports

- URLs

- File lists

- Intrusion policy variable sets

You can use these objects in various places in the ASA FirePOWER module, including access control policies, network analysis policies, intrusion policies and rules, reports, dashboards, and so on. You can configure these objects by navigating to **Configuration > ASA FirePOWER Configuration > Object Management**.

Keeping the Cisco FirePOWER Module Up-to-Date

Cisco provides different types of updates for the Cisco ASA FirePOWER module, including the following:

- Major and minor updates to the module software itself (patches, feature updates, and major updates)

- Rule updates

- Geolocation database (GeoDB) updates

- Vulnerability database (VDB) updates

Patches include a limited range of fixes and usually change the fourth digit in the version number (for example, 5.4.2.1). Feature updates are more comprehensive than patches and generally include new features and usually change the third digit in the version number (for example, 5.4.3). Major updates include new features and functionality and may involve large-scale changes and usually change the first or second digit in the version number (for example, 5.4 or 5.5).

To apply and upload product updates, go to **Configuration > ASA FirePOWER Configuration > Updates**, navigate to the **Product Updates** tab, and click **Upload Update**, as shown in Figure 3-34.

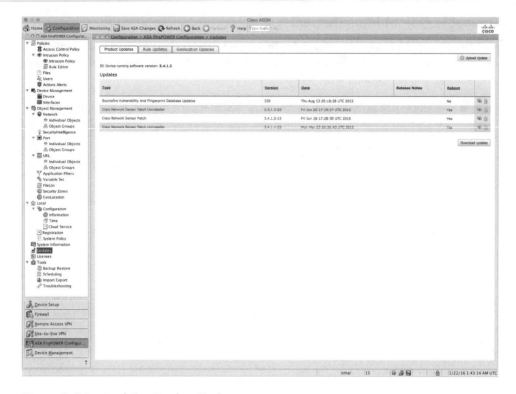

Figure 3-34   *Applying Product Updates*

VDB updates affect the database of known vulnerabilities to which hosts may be suscep-
tible. Intrusion rule updates provide new and updated intrusion rules and preprocessor
rules, modified states for existing rules, and modified default intrusion policy settings.

> **Tip**   Rule updates may also delete rules, provide new rule categories and default
> variables, and modify default variable values.

To configure or upload rule updates, go to **Configuration > ASA FirePOWER
Configuration > Updates** and navigate to the **Rule Updates** tab, as shown in
Figure 3-35.

Cisco recommends that you always import the latest update. You can apply one-time
rule updates or set the interval of recurring rule update imports.

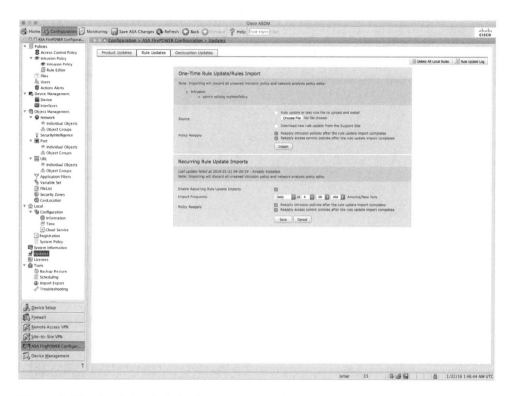

Figure 3-35 *Applying Rule Updates*

Note Rule updates are cumulative. You cannot import a rule update that either matches or predates the version of the currently installed rules.

Geolocation updates provide updated information on physical locations with detected routable IP addresses. As you learned earlier in this chapter, you can use geolocation data as a condition in access control rules. To configure or upload geolocation updates, go to **Configuration > ASA FirePOWER Configuration > Updates** and navigate to the **Geolocation Updates** tab, as shown in Figure 3-36.

You can import a one-time geolocation update or configure recurring updates, as shown in Figure 3-36.

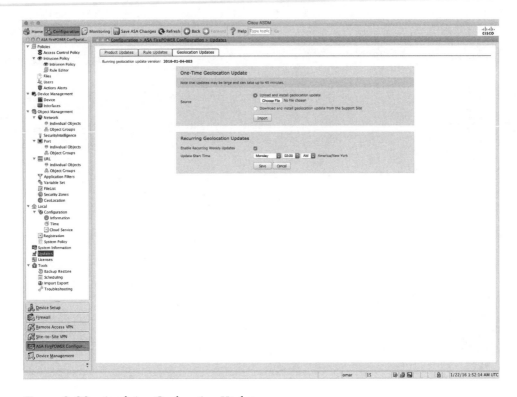

Figure 3-36   *Applying Geolocation Updates*

Firepower Threat Defense

As you learned in previous chapters, the Cisco Firepower Threat Defense (FTD) software can run on the following Cisco ASA models:

- Cisco ASA 5506-X

- Cisco ASA 5506H-X

- Cisco ASA 5506W-X

- Cisco ASA 5512-X

- Cisco ASA 5515-X

- Cisco ASA 5516-X

- Cisco ASA 5525-X

- Cisco ASA 5545-X

- Cisco ASA 5555-X

Note   Cisco is always adding new models to its next-generation security appliances. You should visit the Cisco Firepower compatibility guide to obtain the most recent information: www.cisco.com/c/en/us/td/docs/security/firepower/compatibility/firepower-compatibility.html.

Installing FTD Boot Image and Software

FTD provides next-generation firewall services, including stateful firewalling, dynamic routing, next-generation intrusion prevention systems (NGIPS), Application Visibility and Control (AVC), URL filtering, and Advanced Malware Protection (AMP) in a unified system image. You can use an FTD device in single-context mode and in routed or transparent mode.

If you are deploying a Cisco ASA 5506-X, Cisco ASA 5508-X, or Cisco ASA 5516-X, you must run ROMMON version 1.1.8 or later. You can transfer the new ROMMON image by using the **copy** command, as mentioned previously in this chapter. Once you copy the ROMMON image, you can use the **upgrade rommon disk0:** *rommon-image* command to upgrade the ROMMON in the system. The Cisco ASA then updates the ROMMON and reboots the system.

To install the FTD software in a supported Cisco ASA, you use the same procedure you learned earlier: You first install the boot image in ROMMON by pressing **Esc** during the boot process, and then, at the ROMMON prompt, enter **set** and configure the following parameters to establish temporary connectivity to the TFTP server:

- **ADDRESS:** The management IP address of the Cisco ASA.

- **SERVER:** The IP address of the TFTP server.

- **GATEWAY:** The gateway address to the TFTP server. If the TFTP server is directly attached to Management 1/0, use the IP address of the TFTP server. If the TFTP server and management address are on the same subnet, do not configure the gateway, or TFTP boot will fail.

- **IMAGE:** The boot image path and image name on the TFTP server. For example, if you place the file on the TFTP server in **/tftpboot/images/***filename*, the IMAGE value is **images/ftd-boot-***version*.**cdisk** or **ftd-boot-***version*.**lfbff**.

After you enter that information, use the **sync** command to save the settings and issue the **tftpdnld** command to initiate the download and boot process. The OS image should begin downloading through TFTP. When the OS download is complete, the system automatically boots with the image it just downloaded and stops at the boot CLI prompt.

After installing the boot image, use the **setup** command to enter the management IP address, subnet mask, and gateway and then use the **system install [noconfirm]** *url* command (as discussed earlier) to transfer and install the FTD software:

```
> system install http://10.10.10.123/ftd-6.0.1-123.pkg
```

After the FTD image is installed, choose **Yes** when the appliance reboot option is displayed. The Cisco ASA reboots, and the system prompts you for a username and password when the reboot is complete. At this point, the OS and package installation is complete.

FTD Firewall Mode

The FTD software supports routed and transparent firewall modes, just like the legacy Cisco ASA software. The default is routed. In transparent mode you can create up to 250 bridge groups, with 4 interfaces per bridge group. In devices configured in transparent mode, the diagnostic interface updates the MAC address table in the same manner as a data interface; therefore, you should not connect both a diagnostic interface and a data interface to the same switch unless you configure one of the switch ports as a routed port. Otherwise, if traffic arrives on the diagnostic interface from the physically connected switch, FTD updates the MAC address table to use the diagnostic interface, instead of the data interface, to access the switch. This action causes a temporary traffic interruption; the FTD device does not re-update the MAC address table for packets from the switch to the data interface for at least 30 seconds for security reasons.

To change the firewall mode in FTD, you can use the **configure firewall [routed | transparent]** command, as demonstrated here:

```
> configure firewall transparent
This will destroy the current interface configurations, are you sure that you want
to proceed? [y/N] y
The firewall mode was changed successfully.
```

FTD Interface Types

There are three general types of interfaces in FTD:

- Management interface
- Diagnostic interface
- Routed mode deployment

The management interface is a dedicated interface for management tasks and registering the device to the FMC. It runs a separate SSH server and uses its own local authentication, IP address, and static routing. To configure its settings by using the CLI, you can use the **configure network** command or change the IP address in the FMC by navigating to **Devices > Device Management > Devices > Management.**

The diagnostic interface only allows management traffic and does not allow through traffic. You can configure the diagnostic logical interface along with the rest of the data interfaces in the FMC by navigating to **Devices > Device Management > Interfaces.** Using the diagnostic interface is optional. The diagnostic interface and data interfaces can be used to communicate with external LDAP or RADIUS servers for authentication.

Tip   Cisco recommends that you not configure the diagnostic interface and, in fact, suggests that you remove the name for this interface if you do not have an inside router. The major benefit of disabling the diagnostic interface is that you can place the management interface on the same network as any other data interfaces. If you leave the diagnostic interface configured, its IP address must be on the same network as the management IP address, and it counts as a regular interface that cannot be on the same network as any other data interfaces. Because the management interface requires Internet access for updates, putting the management interface on the same network as an inside interface means you can deploy the FTD device with only a switch on the inside and point to the inside interface as its gateway.

FTD Security Zones

Each interface must be assigned to a single security zone. This is the same principle you learned earlier, with Cisco ASA running Firepower Services. You apply security policy based on zones. For instance, you can configure your access control policy to enable traffic to go from inside to outside but not from outside to inside, for example. You can create security zones in the FMC by navigating to the **Objects** page.

You can also add a security zone can when you are configuring an interface. You can only add interfaces to the correct zone type for your interface—either Passive, Inline, Routed, or Transparent zone types.

Note   The diagnostic and management interfaces cannot belong to a security zone.

Static and Dynamic Routing in FTD

FTD supports static routes and the following dynamic routing protocols:

- OSPF
- BGP
- RIP

To add a static route, follow these steps:

Step 1.   Log in to the FMC, navigate to **Devices > Device Management**, and edit the FTD device. Then select the **Routing** tab.

Step 2.   Select **Static Route** from the table of contents and click **Add Routes**.

Step 3.   Select **IPv4** or **IPv6**.

Step 4.   Enter or select the **Interface** to which this static route applies. In the **Available Network** list, enter or select the destination network. If you are adding a default route, create an object with the address **0.0.0.0/0** and select it there.

Step 5.   Enter or select the gateway router in the **Gateway** or **IPv6 Gateway** field.

Step 6.   Enter the number of hops to the destination network in the Metric field. Valid values range from 1 to 255, and the default value is 1.

Step 7.   If you want to monitor route availability, in the **Route Tracking** field enter or select the name of a service level agreement (SLA) **Monitor** object that defines the monitoring policy. This is only supported in IPv4 and not in IPv6.

Step 8.   Click **OK**.

To configure OSPF, RIP, or BGP, navigate to **Devices > Device Management** and edit the FTD device and then select the routing protocol in the **Routing** area.

Note   OSPF, RIP, and BGP routing protocol configuration is very similar to the legacy Cisco ASA software configuration.

The access policy, IPS, AMP, URL filtering, and other configurations in FTD are the same as the Firepower software options you learned previously in this chapter.

Summary

In this chapter you have learned how to configure the Cisco ASA and the Cisco ASA FirePOWER module. You have seen step-by-step examples of how to set up the Cisco ASA FirePOWER module in Cisco ASA 5585-X and in Cisco ASA 5500-X appliances. You have also learned how to configure the Cisco ASA to redirect traffic to the Cisco ASA FirePOWER module. The Cisco ASA FirePOWER module can be managed and configured with the FMC. In addition, you have learned how to configure the Cisco ASA FirePOWER module for the FMC. The Cisco ASA FirePOWER module can be configured using ASDM in certain platforms only—the Cisco ASA 5506-X, 5506H-X, 5506W-X, 5508-X, and 5516-X appliances. In this chapter you have learned how to configure the Cisco ASA FirePOWER module using the ASDM in the supported platforms. You have learned how to configure access control, intrusion and file policies, and custom rules. In addition, you have learned how to configure reusable objects to ease configuration tasks. You have also learned how to apply product updates and how to import and schedule rule and geolocation database updates. Finally, you have gotten an overview of how to install the FTD software on a Cisco ASA as well as how to configure interfaces, security zones, and dynamic routing.

Chapter 4

Troubleshooting Cisco ASA with FirePOWER Services and Firepower Threat Defense (FTD)

This chapter provides step-by-step guidance on how to troubleshoot common problems you may encounter when deploying the Cisco ASA with FirePOWER Services module and the Firepower Threat Defense software. The following topics are covered in this chapter:

- Useful **show** commands

- Access control policy details

- Network configuration details

- Storage usage monitoring

- Running process analysis

- System log (Syslog)

- System task monitoring and troubleshooting

- Advanced troubleshooting logs

- Useful ASA debugging commands

Useful show Commands

Several **show** commands can be very helpful when troubleshooting problems in the Cisco ASA with FirePOWER Services module. These **show** commands also apply to Cisco Firepower Threat Defense (FTD).

If you are running the Cisco ASA with FirePOWER Services module, connect to the module using the **session** command. Alternatively, you can connect directly to the module management interface using secure shell (SSH). Once you are in the module, to get an overview of all the **show** commands that are available, log in to the command-line interface (CLI) of the Cisco ASA with FirePOWER Services module and enter the **show** command as demonstrated in Example 4-1.

Example 4-1 *Available show Commands*

```
ASA-1# session sfr console
Opening console session with module sfr.
Connected to module sfr. Escape character sequence is 'CTRL-^X'.RTP-SF login: admin
Password:
Last login: Fri Jan 22 04:34:20 UTC 2016 on ttyS1
Copyright 2004-2015, Cisco and/or its affiliates. All rights reserved.
Cisco is a registered trademark of Cisco Systems, Inc.
All other trademarks are property of their respective owners.
Cisco Linux OS v5.4.1 (build 12)
Cisco ASA5508 v5.4.1.2 (build 23)
> show
Show>
access-control-config  Show Current Access-Control Configuration
audit-log              Show audit log
configure              Change to Configuration mode
cpu                    Show CPU utilization
database               Change to Show Database Mode
device-settings        Show device settings
disk                   Show disk usage
disk-manager           Display current status of local disk(s)
dns                    Show DNS configuration
end                    Return to the default mode
exit                   Exit Show Mode
expert                 Invoke a shell
help                   Display an overview of theLI syntax
history                Display the current session's command line history
hostname               Show hostname
hosts                  Show hosts
ifconfig               Show currently configured interfaces
interfaces             Show interface configuration
kdump               Display status of kernel crash dump feature
log-ips-connection   Display Logging of Connection Events setting
logout                 Logout of the current CLI session
managers               Show managing Defense Centers
memory                 Show available memory
model               Show model
netstat                Show network connections
network                Show configuration of management interface
network-static-routes  Show static routes for management interfaces
```

```
ntp                     Show NTP configuration
perfstats               Shoperfstats
process-tree            Show processes in tree format
processes               Show processes
route                   Show configured routes
serial-number           Show serial number
show                    Change to Show Mode
summary                 Show summary
system             Change to System Mode
time                    Show time
traffic-statistics      Show traffic statistics
user                    Show specified users
users                   Show all users
version                 Show versions
```

The following sections cover some of the most useful **show** commands and when to use them.

Displaying the Access Control Policy Details

In Chapter 3, "Configuring Cisco ASA with FirePOWER Services," you learned about the access control policies in the Cisco ASA FirePOWER module. You may encounter problems related to the configuration of those policies and perhaps configuration errors in Cisco's Adaptive Security Device Manager (ASDM). An alternative way to view the access control policy configuration is by using the **show access-control-config** command, whose output can be useful when you're troubleshooting configuration issues related to access control policies. Example 4-2 shows an example of output from the **show access-control-config** command.

Example 4-2 *show access-control-config Command Output*

```
Show> show access-control-config
! The following is the policy we already had configured in the system (myPolicy).
====================[ myPolicy ]====================
Description             : my new access control policy
HTTP Block Response     : Default
Interactive Block Response: Default
=================[ Default Action ]=================
! In this case, the default action is set to allow the traffic through the device.
Default Action          : Allow
Default Policy          : Balanced Security and Connectivity
Logging Configuration
    DC                  : Disabled
    Beginning           : Disabled
```

```
      End                 : Disabled
Rule Hits               : 45894
Variable Set            : Default Set
! The following two sections are the whitelist and blacklist from the global threat
  intelligence coming from Cisco.
=======[ Security Intelligence - Whitelist ]========
    Name                 : Global Whitelist (List)
    Zone                 : any
=======[ Security Intelligence - Blacklist ]========
Logging Configuration   : Enabled
    DC                   : Enabled
--------------------[ Block ]----------------------
    Name                 : Malware (Feed)
    Zone                 : any
    Name                 : Tor_exit_node (Feed)
    Zone                 : any
    Name                 : Bogon (Feed)
    Zone                 : any
    Name                 : CnC (Feed)
    Zone                : any
    Name                 : Global Blacklist (List)
    Zone                 : any
    Name                 : Phishing (Feed)
    Zone                 : any
! The following two main categories (admin_category and root_category) are default
  built-in rules
======[ Category: admin_category (Built-in) ]=======
=====[ Category: standard_category (Built-in) ]=====
------------------[ Rule: rule1 ]-------------------
    Action               : Block
    Source Zones         : myNewZone
    Destination Zones    : myNewZone
    Logging Configuration
      DC                 : Disabled
      Beginning          : Disabled
      End                : Disabled
      Files              : Disabled
    Rule Hits            : 0
=======[ Category: root_category (Built-in) ]=======
===============[ Advanced Settings ]===============
General Settings
  Maximum URL Length             : 1024
  Interactive Block Bypass Timeout   : 600
Network Analysis and Intrusion Policies
```

```
    Initial Intrusion Policy            : Balanced Severity and Connectivity
  Initial Variable Set              : Default Set
    Default Network Analysis Policy     : Balanced Security and Connectivity
  Files and Malware Settings
    File Type Inspect Limit           : 1460
    Cloud Lookup Timeout              : 2
    Minimum File Capture Size         : 6144
    Maximum File Capture Size         : 1048576
    Min Dynamic Analysis Size         : 15360
    Max Dynamic Analysis Size         : 2097152
    Malware Detection Limit           : 10485760
  Transport/Network Layer Preprocessor Settings
    Detection Settings
      Ignore VLAN Tracking Connections : False
    Maximum Active Responses          : No Maximum
    Minimum Response Seconds          : No Minimum
    Session Termination Log Threshold  : 1048576
  Detection Enhancement Settings
    Adaptive Profile                  : Disabled
  Performance Settings
    Event Queue
      Maximum Queued Events           : 5
      Disable Reassembled Content Checks: False
  Performance Statistics
      Sample time (seconds)           : 300
      Minimum number of packets       : 10000
      Summary                         : False
      Log Session/Protocol Distribution : False
    Regular Expression Limits
      Match Recursion Limit           : Default
      Match Limit                     : Default
    Rule Processing Configuration
      Logged Events                   : 5
      Maximum Queued Eve          : 8
      Events Ordered By               : Content Length
  Latency-Based Performance Settings
    Packet Handling
      Threshold (microseconds)        : 256
    Rule Handling
      Violations Before Suspending Rule : 3
      Threshold (microseconds)        : 512
      Session Time                : 10
! The following is the HTML code for the block response after a website or web
  resource is blocked.
```

```
============[ HTTP Block Response HTML ]============
HTTP/1.1 403 Forbidden
Connection: close
Content-Length: 506
Content-Type: text/html; charset=UTF-8
<!DOCTYPE html>
<html>
<head>
<meta http-equiv="content-type" content="text/html; charset=UTF-8" />
<title>Access Denied</title>
<style type="text/css">body {margin:0;font-family:verdana,sans-serif;} h1 {margi
n:0;padding:12px 25px;background-color:#343434;color:#ddd} p {margin:12px 25px;}
 strong {color:#E0042D;}</style>
</head>
<body>
<h1>Access Denied<1>
<p>
<strong>You are attempting to access a forbidden site.</strong><br/><br/>
Consult your system administrator for details.
</p>
</body>
</html>
============[ Interactive Block HTML ]=============
HTTP/1.1 200 OK
Connection: close
Content-Length: 869
Content-Type: text/html; charset=UTF-8
<!DOCTYPE html>
<html>
<head>
<meta http-equiv="content-type" content="text/html; charset=UTF-8" />
<title>Access Denied</title>
<style type="text/css">body {margin:0;font-family:verdana,sans-serif;} h1 {margi
n:0;padding:12px 25px;background-color:#343434;color:#ddd} p {margin:12px 25px;}
/head>g {color:#E0042D;}</style>
<body>
<h1>Access Denied</h1>
<p>
<strong>You are attempting to access a forbidden site.</strong><br/><br/>
You may continue to the site by clicking on the button below.<br/>
<em>Note:</em> You must have cookies enabled in your browser to continue.</br><b
r/>
Consult your system administrator for details.<br/><br/>
```

```
<noscript><em>This page uses JavaScript. Your browser either doesn't support
  JavaScript or you have it turned off.<br/>
To continue to the site, please use a Javascript enabled browser.</em></noscript>
>
</p>
</body>
</html>
```

Displaying the Network Configuration

A good way to display the network configuration in the Cisco ASA FirePOWER module is by using the **show network** command, as shown in Example 4-3.

Example 4-3 *show network Command Output*

```
Show> show network
===============[ System Information ]===============
Hostname                : RTP-SF
Domains                 : cisco.com
DNS Servers             : 208.67.222.222
Management port         : 8305
IPv4 Default route
  Gateway               : 192.168.78.1
=====================[ eth0 ]=====================
State                   : Enabled
Channels                : Management & Events
Mode                    :
MDI/MDIX                : Auto/MDIX
MTU                     : 1500
MAC Address             : 18:8B:9D:AD:79:C0
--------------------[ IPv4 ]--------------------
Configuration           : Manual
Address                 : 192.168.78.2
Netmask                 : 255.255.255.0
Broadst                 : 192.168.78.255
--------------------[ IPv6 ]--------------------
Configuration           : Disabled
===============[ Proxy Information ]===============
State                   : Disabled
Authentication          : Disabled
```

The **show network** command displays the system information, including the module host name, configured domain name, DNS servers, management port, and default gateway. It also provides the configured IPv4 and IPv6, netmask, and broadcast addresses. It shows whether the management port is enabled or disabled, as well as the interface MAC address, configured MTU size, and other information.

To display the IPv4 and IPv6 routing table, you can use the **show route** command, as shown in Example 4-4.

Example 4-4   *Displaying the Routing Table*

```
Show> show route
Kernel IP routing table
Destination      Gateway          Netmask          Flags Metric Ref     Use Iface
192.168.78.0     0.0.0.0          255.255.255.0    U     0      0         0 eth0
127.0.0.0        0.0.0.0          255.255.0.0      U     0      0         0 cplane
0.0.0.0          192.168.78.1     0.0.0.0          UG    0      0         0 eth0


Kernel IPv6 routing table
Destination                  Next Hop     Flags  Metric  Ref    Use  Iface
::1/128                      ::           U      0       16     1    lo
fe80::200:ff:fe02:1/128      ::           U      0       0      1    lo
fe80::1a8b:9dff:fead:79c0/128  ::         U      0       0      1    lo
fe80::/64                    ::           U      256     0      0    cplane
fe80::/64                    ::           U      256     0      0    eth0
ff00::/8                     ::           U      256     0      0    cplane
ff00::/8                     ::           U      256     0      0    eth0
```

In Example 4-4 you can see that the IPv4 default gateway is set to 192.168.78.1, and the other two routes are the local networks assigned to the management interface (eth0) and loopback address. In this example, IPv6 is disabled, and you see only locally specific IPv6 information.

To display configured static routes, you can use the **show network-static-routes** command.

The **show ifconfig** command provides similar output to the Linux **ifconfig** command, as shown in Example 4-5.

Example 4-5   *show ifconfig Command Output*

```
Show> show ifconfig
cplane     Link encap:Ethernet   HWaddr 00:00:00:02:00:01
           inet addr:127.0.2.1  Bcast:127.0.255.255  Mask:255.255.0.0
           inet6 addr: fe80::200:ff:fe02:1/64 Scope:Link
           UP BROADCAST RUNNING MULTICAST  MTU:1500  Metric:1
           RX packets:1480872 errors:0 dropped:0 overruns:0 frame:0
```

```
                TX packets:248543 errors:0 dropped:0 overruns:0 carrier:0

                collisions:0 txqueuelen:1000

                RX bytes:88914526 (84.7 Mb)  TX bytes:22370811 (21.3 Mb)


eth0      Link encap:Ethernet  HWaddr 18:8B:9D:AD:79:C0

                inet addr:192.168.78.2  Bcast:192.168.78.255  Mask:255.255.255.0

              inet6 addr: fe80::1a8b:9dff:fead:79c0/64 Scope:Link

                UP BROADCAST RUNNING MULTICAST  MTU:1500  Metric:1

                RX packets:2562033 errors:0 dropped:0 overruns:0 frame:0

                TX packets:284558 errors:0 dropped:0 overruns:0 carrier:0

                collisions:0 txqueuele1000

                RX bytes:1123651792 (1071.5 Mb)  TX bytes:102970664 (98.2 Mb)


lo        Link encap:Local Loopback

                inet addr:127.0.0.1  Mask:255.255.255.0

                inet6 addr: ::1/128 Scope:Host

                UP LOOPBACK RUNNING  MTU:16436  Metric:1

                RX pack:147207 errors:0 dropped:0 overruns:0 frame:0

                TX packets:147207 errors:0 dropped:0 overruns:0 carrier:0

                collisions:0 txqueuelen:0

                RX bytes:59089295 (56.3 Mb)  TX bytes:59089295 (56.3 Mb)
```

The output shown in Example 4-5 is very similar to the output of the **ifconfig** command in most Linux operating systems. The highlighted lines show the network configuration of eth0, which is the management interface. A better way to display the interface configuration is to use the **show interfaces** command, as demonstrated in Example 4-6.

Example 4-6 *show interfaces Command Output*

```
Show> show interfaces
! This is the outside interface of the ASA. It is associated with the "Internet"
  security zone.
--------------------[ outside ]--------------------
Physical Interface        : GigabitEthernet1/1
Type                      : ASA
Security Zone             : Internet
Status                    : Enabled
Load Balancing Mode       : N/A
! This is the inside interface of the ASA. It is associated with the "myNewZone"
  security zone.
--------------------[ inside ]--------------------
Physical Interface        : GigabitEthernet1/2
Type                      : ASA
Security Zone             : myNewZone
Status                    : Enabled
```

```
Load Balancing Mode      : N/A
--------------------[ cplane ]--------------------
IPv4 Address             : 127.0.2.1
! Ethernet 0 (eth0) is the management interface.
--------------------[ eth0 ]--------------------
Physical Interface       : ethType                    : Management
Status                   : Enabled
MDI/MDIX                 : Auto
MTU                      : 1500
MAC Address              : 18:8B:9D:AD:79:C0
IPv4 Address             : 192.168.78.2
--------------------[ tun10 ]--------------------
--------------------------------------------------
```

Monitoring Storage Usage

It is very important to monitor disk/storage usage by module to understand the available resources. A good CLI command to use to monitor storage usage and health is the **show disk** command. Example 4-7 shows an example of the output generated by this command.

Example 4-7   *show disk Command Output*

```
Show> show disk
Filesystem     Size   Used  Avail  Use%  Mounted on
/dev/root      3.7G   692M  2.9G    20%  /
devtmpfs       1.7G    60K  1.7G     1%  /dev
/dev/sda1       92M    35M   53M    40%  /boot
/dev/vda7       65G   9.4G   53G    16%  /var
none           1.7G   7.0M  1.7G     1%  /dev/shm
```

The output shown in Example 4-7 includes a few columns: Filesystem (partition), Used, Avail, Use%, and Mounted on. This is very similar to the output of the **df** command in Linux.

You can run out of disk space on the Firepower Management Center, the Firepower appliances, or the Cisco ASA FirePOWER Services module for many different reasons. When this happens, the high disk utilization may trigger a health alert or the system may fail a software update attempt.

Storing large volumes of old backup files on the system can take excessive space on your disk. In order to correct this, delete the old backup files using the web management interface under **System > Tools > Backup/Restore**.

Note As a best practice, you can configure remote storage to store large backup files.

The system may also run out of space if you always keep the previous software update, upgrade, and patch files. To correct this, delete the older update and patch files that are no longer necessary under **System > Updates**.

You have to be careful not to oversubscribe the FMC—for instance, if the module or any other managed device has stopped sending events to the FMC or if a device is generating more events than the FMC is designed to receive (per second). Also, if the FMC is unable to receive new IPS events, you should check to see if there are any communication issues between the managed device and the management center.

The root (/) partition is a fixed size and is not intended for personal storage. If the root (/) partition is full, you should check for unnecessary files in the /root, /home, and /tmp folders. Because these folders are not meant for personal storage, you can delete any personal files in them by using the **rm** command.

In ASDM, you can monitor the disk usage by navigating to **Monitoring > ASA FirePOWER Monitoring > Statistics**, as shown in Figure 4-1.

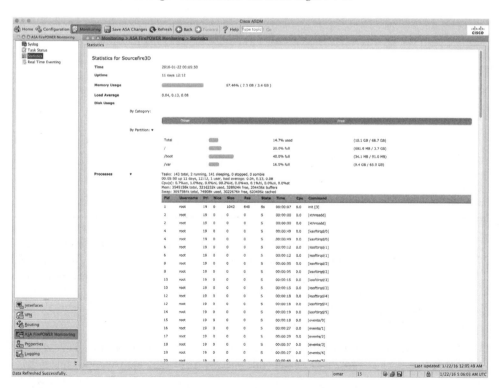

Figure 4-1 *ASDM FirePOWER Monitoring Statistics*

Analyzing Running Processes

In ASDM, you can display and analyze all running processes much the way you display process information in Linux: just navigate to **Monitoring > ASA FirePOWER Monitoring > Statistics**, as shown in Figure 4-1. You can obtain similar output by using the **show processes** command in the CLI, as shown in Example 4-8.

Example 4-8 *Displaying the Running Processes in the CLI*

```
Show> show processes
  PID USER       PR  NI   VIRT   RES   SHR S %CPU %MEM    TIME+   COMMAND
 4203 root       20   0   7964  2120 1024 S    4  0.1   5:02.35 pmmon.sh
 4280 root       20   0   140m  7640 1260 S    4  0.2 293:38.98 diskmanager
 4281 root       20   0   9388   952  700 S    4  0.0 269:27.89 UEChanneld
25195 sfsnort     1 -19  1042m  402m  20m S    4 11.6  15:03.18 snort
 4323 root        0 -20      0     0    0 S    2  0.0 254:39.37 kvm_ivshmem_rxt
24135 admin      20   0  17376  1364  984 R    2  0.0   0:00.01 top
25194 sfsnort     1 -19   970m  387m  13m S    2 11   17:52.33 snort
    1 root       20   0   4168   640  588 S    0  0.0   0:07.31 init
    2 root       20   0      0     0    0 S    0  0.0   0:00.00 kthreadd
    3 root       RT   0      0     0    0 S    0  0.0   0:00.06 migration/0
    4 root       20   0      0     0    0 S    0  0.0   0:.54 ksoftirqd/0
    5 root       RT   0      0     0    0 S    0  0.0   0:00.03 migration/1
    6 root       20   0      0     0    0 S    0  0.0   0:12.69 ksoftirqd/1
    7 root       RT   0      0     0    0 S    0  0.0   0:00.06 migration/2
    8 root       20   0      0     0    0 S  0.0    0:05.53 ksoftirqd/2
    9 root       RT   0      0     0    0 S    0  0.0   0:09.59 migration/3
   10 root       20   0      0     0    0 S    0  0.0   0:15.40 ksoftirqd/3
   11 root       RT   0      0     0    0 S    0  0.0   0:11.04 migration/4
   12 root       20   0      0     0    0    0  0.0   0:18.08 ksoftirqd/4
   13 root       RT   0      0     0    0 S    0  0.0   0:12.15 migration/5
   14 root       20   0      0     0    0 S    0  0.0   0:19.53 ksoftirqd/5
<output omitted for brevity>
```

The **show process** command output shown in Example 4-8 is very similar to the output of the **ps** command in Linux. Understanding what processes are running on your system and what they are doing is important. You need to know which processes are using the most memory and which ones are using the most CPU. You also need to know how to find a particular process. A key process is the snort process (highlighted in Example 4-8), which is the IPS engine of the system.

You can also use the **show process-tree** command to show the processes in a tree format that indicates which processes are dependent of each other, as shown in Example 4-9.

Example 4-9 *show process-tree Command Output*

```
Show> show process-tree
init(1)-+-agetty(4199)
        |-agetty(4200)
        |-agetty(4201)
        |-crond(2661)
        |-klogd(2651)
        |-login(20653)---clish(20656)-+-sh(24269)-+-more(24271)
        |                             |           '-pstree(24270)
        |                             '-{clish}(20659)
        |-nscd(14774)-+-{nscd}(14777)
        |             |-{nscd}(14778)
        |             |-{nscd}(14779)
        |             |-{nscd}(14780)
        |             |-{nscd(14781)
        |             '-{nscd}(14782)
        |-pm(4214)-+-ASAConfig.pl(4269)
        |          |-ActionQueueScra(4277)
        |          |-CloudAgent(4289)-+-{CloudAgent}(4316)
        |          |                  |-{CloudAgent}(4317)
        |          |                  |-{CloudAgent}(4318)
        |          |                  '-{CloudAgent}(4319)
        |          |-Pruner.pl(4276)
        |          |-SFDataCorrelato(4272)-+-{SFDataCorrelato}(4375)
        |          |                       |-{SFDataCorrelato}(4376)
        |          |                       |-{SFDataCorrelato}(4377)
        |          |                       |-{SFDataCorrelato}(4380)
        |          |                       |-{SFDataCorrelato}(4382)
        |          |                       |-{SFDataCorrelato}(4384)
        |          |                       |-{SFDataCorrelato}(4387)
        |          |                       |-{SFDataCorrelato}(4469)
        |          |                       |-{SFDataCorrelato}(4470)
<output omitted for brevity>
```

The output shown in Example 4-9 is very similar to the output of the **pstree** command in Linux. Example 4-9 shows running processes as a tree so that you can see what processes are related to each other.

Using the System Log (Syslog)

The syslog is one of the most useful tools for troubleshooting problems you might encounter in the Cisco ASA FirePOWER module. You can view the syslog in ASDM by navigating to **Monitoring > ASA FirePOWER Monitoring > Syslog,** as shown in Figure 4-2.

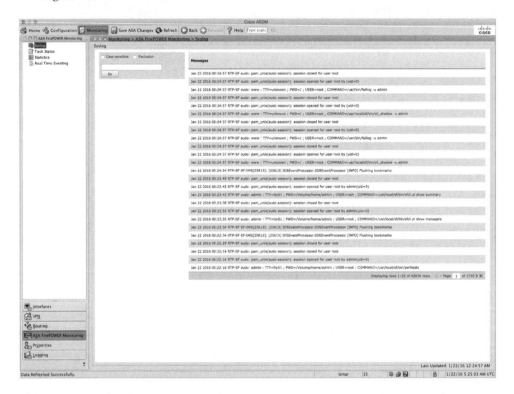

Figure 4-2 *ASDM FirePOWER Syslog*

You can also view real-time event information of all functions of the Cisco ASA FirePOWER module by navigating to **Monitoring > ASA FirePOWER Monitoring > Real Time Eventing,** as shown in Figure 4-3. You can see all ASA FirePOWER events by selecting the All ASA FirePOWER Events tab, as shown in Figure 4-3. You can also see events related to connections passing through the module, intrusion, file inspection, or malware file events and security intelligence events by selecting the corresponding tabs. This screen also allows you to filter by many different criteria.

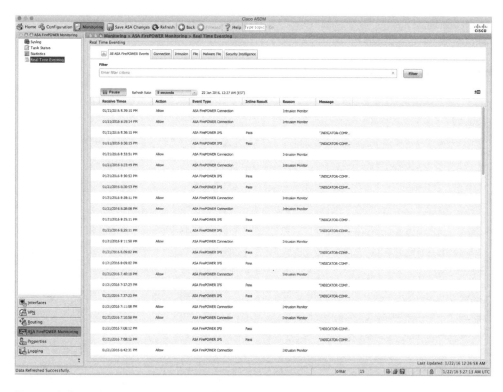

Figure 4-3 *ASDM FirePOWER Real Time Eventing*

You can access very detailed logs by using the **expert** command to go into the "expert" mode. This command brings you to a Linux prompt, as shown in Example 4-10.

Example 4-10 *Generating Detailed Logs with Expert Mode*

```
Show> expert
admin@RTP-SF:~$ cd /
admin@RTP-SF:/$ ls
DBCheck.log   boot    dyn-preproc-upgrade-log   lib         mnt    sbin   upgraded
Volume        cisco   etc                       lib64       proc   sys    usr
Bin           dev     home                      lost+found  root   tmp    var
```

While in expert mode, you can access many logs by changing directories to **/var/log/**, as shown in Example 4-11.

Example 4-11 *Accessing Detailed Logs in Expert Mode*

```
admin@RTP-SF:~$ cd /var/log
admin@RTP-SF:/var/log$ ls
SMART_STATUS_sda_20160119050740.txt
```

```
action_queue.log
action_queue.log.1.gz
action_queue.log.2.gz
action_queue.log.3.gz
action_queue.log.4.gz
asacx_init.log
audit
btmp
cisco
configure-model.log
configure.log
configure.log.old
cron
cron.1.gz
cron.2.gz
cron.3.gz
cron.4.gz
diskmanager.log
dmesg
eth0.down.log
eth0.down.log.old
th0.up.log.old
faillog
firesight-query.log
firesight-query.log.1.gz
firesight-query.log.2.gz
firesight-query.log.3.gz
firesight-query.log.4.gz
firstboot.S01reset_failopen_if
firstboot.S03install-math-pari.sh
firstboot.S04fix-httpd.sh
firstboot.S05set-mgmnt-port
firstboot.6addusers
firstboot.S07uuid-init
firstboot.S09configure_mysql
firstboot.S10database
firstboot.S10database.15vulndb-init.log
firstboot.S12install_infodb
firstboot.S15set-locale.sh
<output omitted for brevity>
```

You can view each log by using the **cat** command. For example, to view the scheduled tasks log, you can use the **cat schedule_tasks.log** command, as shown in Example 4-12.

Instead of using the **cat** command, you can use the **tail** command, which is basically the same as the Linux **tail** command. To view new log lines as they are generated, you can use the **tail -f** command.

Example 4-12 *Viewing the Scheduled Tasks Log*

```
admin@RTP-SF:/var/log$ cat schedule_tasks.log
Jan 17 08:00:01 RTP-SF schedule_wrapper.pl[31159]: Starting run of task 2...
Jan 17 08:00:02 RTP-SF schedule_wrapper.pl[31159]: Task 2 should not be run now. at
  /usr/local/sf/bin/schedule_wrapper.pl line 217.
Jan 17 08:00:02 RTP-SF schedule_wrapper.pl[31159]: Ending run of task 2 ().
Jan 17 08:00:02 RTP-SF schedule_wrapper.pl[31159]:
Jan 17 08:00:02 RTP-SF schedule_wrapper.pl[31159]:
Jan 17 09:00:02 RTP-SF schedule_wrapper.pl[2879]: Starting run of task 2...
Jan 17 09:00:03 RTP-SF schedule_wrapper.pl[2879]: Validating task 2...
Jan 17 0:00:03 RTP-SF schedule_wrapper.pl[2879]: VALIDATING 1 1 on on at /usr/local/
  sf/lib/perl/5.10.1/SF/ScheduleTask/UpdateSRU.pm line 47.
Jan 17 09:00:03 RTP-SF schedule_wrapper.pl[2879]: Task 2 was validated successfully.
Jan 17 09:00:03 RTP-SF schedule_wrapper.pl[2879]: Executing task ..
Jan 17 09:00:03 RTP-SF schedule_wrapper.pl[2879]: RUN UpdateSRU task...
Jan 17 09:00:03 RTP-SF schedule_wrapper.pl[2879]: ---------------
Jan 17 09:00:03 RTP-SF schedule_wrapper.pl[2879]:
Jan 17 09:00:03 RTP-SF schedule_wrapper.pl[2879]: https://support.sourcefire.com/
  auto-upde/auto-dl.cgi/72:18:8B:9D:AD:79:C0/
Jan 17 09:00:03 RTP-SF schedule_wrapper.pl[2879]:
Jan 17 09:00:03 RTP-SF schedule_wrapper.pl[2879]: https://support.sourcefire.com/
  auto-update/auto-dl.cgi/72:18:8B:9D:AD:79:C0/GetCurrent/sf.xml-----------------
Jan 17 09:00:03 RTP-SF schedule_wpper.pl[2879]:
Jan 17 09:00:03 RTP-SF schedule_wrapper.pl[2879]:
Jan 17 09:00:05 RTP-SF schedule_wrapper.pl[2879]: We have SF::System::Md5Sum
  --a8ebe509a002cbe7f26a3879eb553d85   ./Sourcefire_Rule_Update-2016-01-13-002-vrt.
  sh.
Jan 17 09:00:16 RTP-SF schedule_wrapper.pl[2879]: CaughSFSystem Exception!
Jan 17 09:00:16 RTP-SF schedule_wrapper.pl[2879]:   System (/usr/local/sf/bin/
  install_rule.pl /var/sf/SRU/Sourcefire_Rule_Update-2016-01-13-002-vrt.sh) Failed
  at /usr/local/sf/lib/perl/5.10.1/SF/System/Privileged.pm line 2636.
Jan 17 09:00:16 RTP-SF schedule_wrapr.pl[2879]:
Jan 17 09:00:16 RTP-SF schedule_wrapper.pl[2879]: Request stdout!
Jan 17 09:00:16 RTP-SF schedule_wrapper.pl[2879]: The package is /var/sf/SRU//var/
  sf/SRU/Sourcefire_Rule_Update-2016-01-13-002-vrt.sh
Jan 17 09:00:16 RTP-SF schedule_wrapper.pl[2879]: Verifying archive egrity... All
  good.
<output omitted for brevity>
```

Monitoring and Troubleshooting System Tasks

You can display complete, pending, or failed jobs (system tasks) by navigating to
Monitoring > ASA FirePOWER Monitoring > Task Status, as shown in Figure 4-4.

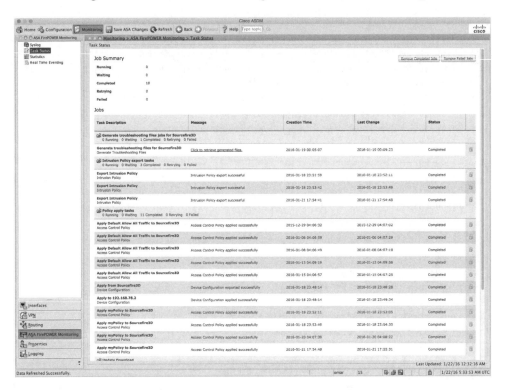

Figure 4-4   *ASDM FirePOWER Task Status*

This screen is useful for viewing and troubleshooting problems with specific tasks, such
as intrusion policy tasks, access policies, device update downloads and installations,
and more.

Generating Advanced Troubleshooting Logs

You can use the **system generate-troubleshoot** command to generate very advanced and
detailed logs that can be used for troubleshooting, as shown in Example 4-13.

Example 4-13   *The system generate-troubleshoot Command*

```
> system generate-troubleshoot
One or more subset options required.  Displaying list of options:
ALL - Run ALL Of The Following Options
SNT - Snort Performance and Configuration
```

```
PER - Hardware Performance and Logs
SYS - System Configuration, Policy, and Logs
DES - Detection Configuration, Policy, and Logs
NET - Interface and Network Related Data
VDB - Discovery,wareness, VDB Data, and Logs
UPG - Upgrade Data and Logs
DBO - All Database Data
LOG - All Log Data
NMP - Network Map Information
```

Example 4-14 demonstrates the use of the **all** keyword to generate logs for all the aforementioned options.

Example 4-14   *system generate-troubleshoot all Command Output*

```
> system generate-troubleshoot all
Starting /usr/local/sf/bin/sf_troubleshoot.pl...
Please, be patient.  This may take several minutes.
The troubleshoot option code specified is ALL.
Troubleshooting information successfully created at /var/common/
  results-01-22-2016--184950.tar.gz
```

The **system generate-troubleshoot all** command can take several minutes to run, as the warning message in Example 4-14 indicates. This command generates and collects an incredible number of logs that are extremely useful for troubleshooting many problems.

After the command finishes and stores all the logs, you can then transfer the archive to your local machine or to an admin server using secure copy (SCP), as shown in Example 4-15.

Example 4-15   *Transferring Troubleshooting Logs to a Local Machine/Admin Server*

```
System> system file secure-copy omar.cisco.com omar dest_dir /var/common/
  results-01-22-2016--184950.tar.gz
The authenticity of host 'omar.cisco.com (172.18.104.139)' can't be established.
ECDSA key fingerprint is 9b:f1:b2:62:04:65:be:29:94:af:09:9a:04:50:2c:0a.
Are you sure you want to continue connecting (yes/no)? yes
omar@omar.cisco.com's password:********************
copy successful.
```

You can also generate the troubleshooting files in ASDM by navigating to **Configuration > ASA FirePOWER Configuration > Tools > Troubleshooting,** as shown in Figure 4-5.

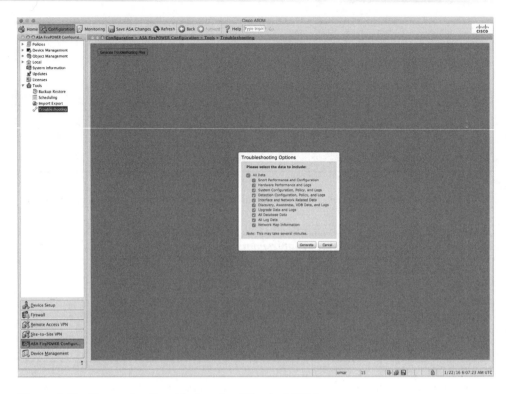

Figure 4-5   *Generating Troubleshooting Files in ASDM*

Sometimes you may run into trouble when trying to determine what access control rule is blocking or allowing traffic. The restricted shell in the Firepower software provides a utility that can help you determine the status of each flow as the system receives packets in real time. You can invoke this utility by using the **system support firewall-engine-debug** command, which prompts you to enter the following information:

- IP protocol, either TCP or UDP

- Client IP

- Client port

- Server IP

- Server port

Example 4-16 shows output from the **system support firewall-engine-debug** command after you enter the required information.

Example 4-16 *system support firewall-engine-debug Command Output*

```
10.10.10.123-33533 and 10.20.20.21-80 6 Starting VLan first with intfs 2 -> 1, vlan
  0, svc 0, payload 0, client 0, misc 0, user 0, url
10.10.10.123-33533 and 10.20.20.21-80 6 pending rule order 1, 'Block social media',
  URL
10.10.10.123-33533 and 10.20.20.21-80 6 Starting VLan first with intfs 2 -> 1, vlan
  0, svc 0, payload 0, client 0, misc 0, user 0, url
10.10.10.123-33533 and 10.20.20.21-80 6 pending rule order 1, 'Block social media',
  URL
10.10.10.123-33533 and 10.20.20.21-80 6 Starting VLan first with intfs 2 -> 1, vlan
  0, svc 0, payload 0, client 0, misc 0, user 0, url
10.10.10.123-33533 and 10.20.20.21-80 6 pending rule order 1, 'Block social media',
  URL
10.10.10.123-33533 and 10.20.20.21-80 6 Starting VLan first with intfs 2 -> 1, vlan
  0, svc 676, payload 629, client 638, misc 0, user 0, url http://cisco.com/
10.10.10.123-33533 and 10.20.20.21-80 6 match rule order 1, 'Block social media',
  action Block
```

The Cisco ASA drops packets if they are not compliant with the enterprise's configured
security policy or if something is wrong in the system. These drops could be related to
the deny statements in the ACLs, illegitimate VPN packets, a malformed TCP segment,
or a packet with invalid header information. In some cases, you will want to get the sta-
tistical information about the packets or connections dropped by the security appliance
within its accelerated security path (ASP). You can use the **show asp drop** ASA command to view the reasons that a packet was dropped, as shown in Example 4-17.

Example 4-17 *show asp drop Command Output*

```
ASA# show asp drop
Frame drop:
No route to host (no-route) 618
  Interface is down (interface-down) 4
Last clearing: Never
Flow drop:
Last clearing: Never
```

The highlighted lines in Example 4-17 shows that the frame was dropped because
there was no route to the destination. In this case, it was because the egress interface
was down.

Useful ASA Debugging Commands

A few debugging commands in the Cisco ASA are useful when you're troubleshooting problems with the module. The following are the most popular ones:

- **debug sfr error:** Used to display errors related to the Cisco ASA FirePOWER module

- **debug sfr event:** Used to display general events related to the Cisco ASA FirePOWER module

- **debug sfr message:** Used to display hardware messages between the Cisco ASA and the module

Example 4-18 shows the output of the **debug sfr event** command.

Example 4-18   *Debugging Module Events*

```
ASA-1# debug sfr event
debug sfr event enabled at level 1
ASA-1# debug sfr event
DP SFR Event: Sending Conn Unique ID (3790083) TLV for 192.168.78.2/123 -
    184.105.192.247/123
DP SFR Event: Sending Conn Unique ID (3790084) TLV for 192.168.78.138/59782 -
    204.141.57.101/443
DP SFR Event: Sending Conn Unique ID (3790085) TLV for 192.168.78.132/27646 -
    208.67.222.222/53
DP SFR Event: Sending Conn Unique ID (3790086) TLV for 192.168.78.132/49148 -
    173.194.206.95/443
DP SFR Event: Sending Conn Unique ID (3790089) TLV for 192.168.78.132/12363 -
    208.67.222.222/53
DP SFR Event: Sending Conn Unique ID (3790090) TLV for 192.168.78.132/37421 -
    74.125.228.243/443
DP SFR Event: Sending Conn Unique ID (3790093) TLV for 192.168.78.135/777 -
    8.8.8.8/0
<output omitted for brevity>
```

Summary

In this chapter, you have learned about several commands and utilities that are useful when troubleshooting problems in the Cisco ASA FirePOWER module. These commands are also useful when you're troubleshooting problem in FTD software. You have learned how to perform basic monitoring, and you have learned how to use expert-level commands to view and analyze detailed logs in the module. You have also learned how to generate detailed troubleshooting files in the CLI and in ASDM. You have also learned about the available debugging commands in the ASA for troubleshooting problems in the module.

Chapter 5

Introduction to and Architecture of Cisco AMP

This chapter covers the following topics:

- The architecture, components, and types of AMP

- The AMP public cloud architecture

- The AMP private cloud architecture

- AMP private cloud air gap mode

This chapter provides an introduction to the Cisco Advanced Malware Protection (AMP) solution, the AMP architecture, and AMP cloud types.

Introduction to Advanced Malware Protection (AMP)

In Chapter 1, "Fundamentals of Cisco Next-Generation Security," you learned about the different Cisco next-generation security products and technologies. You learned that those security technologies and processes should not only focus on detection but also should provide the capability to mitigate the impact of an attack. Organizations must maintain visibility and control across the extended network during the full attack continuum:

- Before an attack takes place

- During an active attack

- After an attacker starts to damage systems or steal information

In Chapter 1 you also learned about the many different types of malicious software (malware). The AMP solution enables you to detect and block malware, continuously analyze for malware, and get retrospective alerts. It has the following features:

- **File reputation:** AMP allows you to analyze files inline and block or apply policies.

- **File sandboxing:** AMP allows you to analyze unknown files to understand true file behavior.

- **File retrospection:** AMP allows you to continue to analyze files for changing threat levels.

There are major architectural benefits to the AMP solution, which leverages a cloud infrastructure for the heavy lifting.

The architecture of AMP can be broken down into three main components: the AMP cloud, AMP client connectors, and intelligence sources. AMP client connectors include AMP for Networks, AMP for Endpoints, and AMP for Content Security.

Figure 5-1 illustrates the cloud architecture, showing how AMP receives intelligence from many sources and a variety of client connectors.

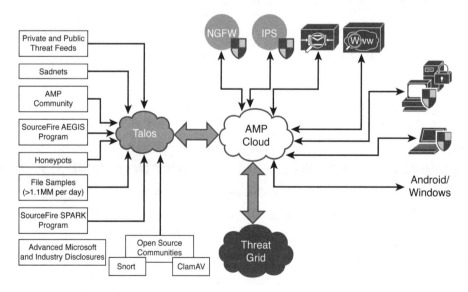

Figure 5-1   *AMP Architecture*

The AMP cloud contains many different analysis tools and technologies to detect malware in files, including the Threat Grid analysis solution. Cisco's research teams, including the Cisco Talos security intelligence and research group, feed information about malware into the AMP cloud. Threat intelligence from Cisco products, services, and third-party relationships is also sent to the AMP cloud. The following are some examples:

- **Snort, ClamAV, and Immunet AV open source communities:** Users of these open source projects contribute threat information daily.

- **Talos:** The Cisco Talos security intelligence and research group is a team of leading threat researchers that contributes to the threat information ecosystem of Cisco security products. Talos team members get threat information from a variety of sources and their own internal research efforts. Talos maintains the official rule sets of Snort.org, ClamAV, SenderBase.org, and SpamCop. Talos is also the primary team that contributes to the Cisco Collective Security Intelligence (CSI) ecosystem. You can follow Talos on Twitter @talos and subscribe to the official Talos blog at http://blogs.cisco.com/author/talos.

- **Threat Grid:** This deep threat analysis solution leverages many identification techniques, including sandboxing. Threat Grid is built as a cloud architecture and is used to do deep analysis of file samples submitted to the AMP Threat Grid cloud. The analysis results are fed into the AMP cloud and can be used to update file disposition (the result).

- **Over 100 TB of threat intelligence data daily:** A variety of sources contribute to the vast amount of data provided to Cisco through submitted malware samples, data from the web, and email traffic monitored by Cisco products and other third-party sources.

- **1.6 million global sensors:** Cisco has programs designed to foster cooperation and information sharing of threat intelligence data. Cisco therefore has access to data from more than 1.6 million sensors worldwide.

- **Advanced Microsoft and industry disclosures:** Cisco has cooperative relationships with many industry-leading vendors of software products that yield advanced information about vulnerabilities and threats. AMP customers benefit from access to the vast amount of information gathered by Cisco through quick release of signature updates and threat protection.

Role of the AMP Cloud

The most critical item of the Cisco AMP architecture is the AMP cloud itself. The AMP cloud has two deployment methods—public and private—and regardless of the deployment chosen, the role of the cloud is the same.

The AMP cloud houses all the detection signatures. A major benefit of storing these signatures in the cloud is that it reduces the client connector size and reduces the processing requirements on the client, since the bulk of the work is handled in the cloud.

An interesting and fairly unique feature is that AMP administrators can create custom signatures in the cloud, and then those custom signatures are pushed to the connectors.

In addition, the cross-referencing of files and signatures is done in the AMP cloud, so the cloud can be self-updating, without having to constantly communicate updates to the connectors.

The AMP cloud is also responsible for large-scale data processing, or big data. The data comes to the AMP cloud from multiple sources, including honeypots, threat feeds, open source communities, AV solutions such as Immunet AV and ClamAV, and more. File samples are provided to the AMP cloud, where they are processed. If the disposition of a sample file is deemed to be malicious, it is stored in the cloud and reported to the client connectors that see the same file.

Note AMP customer data is never shared with any other entity.

Advanced analytic engines, including Threat Grid, are part of the AMP cloud and are constantly correlating the incoming data. The analytical results are used to update the AMP signatures. In addition to the advanced analytics, machine-learning engines are employed to further refine signatures and reevaluate detections that have already been performed. The cloud is not just a repository of signatures; the decision making is performed in real time, evolving constantly based on the data received.

Doing Security Differently

There is this brilliant engineer from Cisco SourceFire named Eric Howard. Eric is one of the world's foremost experts in AMP, and he presents security, particularly the AMP solution, in a unique way that brings tremendous clarity. This section of the book is designed to mirror his presentation style.

Eric talks about the need to "do security differently." He says that companies need two security plans: Security Plan A is prevention, and Security Plan B is retrospection.

The Prevention Framework

Prevention involves keeping malware at bay. With prevention, speed is critical. It requires real-time, dynamic decisions to be made from real-world data. The data must have high accuracy, with low false positives and false negatives. Prevention could also be viewed as the "security control mode."

As illustrated in Figure 5-2, the AMP cloud's prevention framework is made up of seven core components: 1-to-1 signatures, Ethos, Spero, indicators of compromise (IOCs), device flow correlation, advanced analytics, and dynamic analysis.

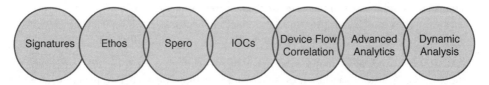

Figure 5-2 *The Protection Framework*

1-to-1 Signatures

1-to-1 signatures are a traditional technology that is used all over the security industry in various forms. With these signatures, a hash is created of a file, and that hash is compared to a database. If a match is found, the specific file is known, and a verdict—clean or malicious—is returned. If the hash has not been seen before, the cloud returns a verdict of unknown. The benefit of this method is that it can quickly identify and block malicious files. The downside is that a simple change to a file also changes the hash, thereby evading the signature.

AMP differentiates itself from other 1-to-1 signature solutions by storing the signature database in the cloud instead of on the client. The database is quite large, and many solutions cut corners by including only a subset of the signatures in the full database. Storing the database in the cloud allows AMP to leverage the entire database. Comparing the files to the database can be quite resource intensive. AMP does the comparison in the cloud, freeing those resources from the client connector. AMP is also able to collect, process, and detect in near real time.

Ethos Engine

The next component of the protection framework is the Ethos engine. Ethos is a "fuzzy fingerprinting" engine that uses static or passive heuristics. The engine creates generic file signatures that can match polymorphic variants of a threat. This is useful because when a threat morphs or a file is changed, the structural properties of that file often remain the same, even though the content has changed.

Unlike most other signature tools, Ethos uses distributed data mining to identify suitable files. It uses in-field data for sources, which provides a highly relevant collection from which to generate the signatures. Ethos is completely automated and provides rapid generation of the generic signatures that are based on in-field data instead of relying on individual "rockstar" engineers to generate a limited number of generic signatures.

Note   At this writing, Ethos applies only to AMP for Endpoints.

Spero Engine

Spero is a machine learning–based technology that proactively identifies threats that were previously unknown. It uses active heuristics to gather execution attributes, and because the underlying algorithms come up with generic models, it can identify malicious software based on its general appearance rather than based on specific patterns or signatures.

Indicators of Compromise

If you look up "indicator of compromise" on Wikipedia (http://en.wikipedia.org/wiki/ Indicator_of_compromise), this is what you see: "an artifact observed on a network or in an operating system that with high confidence indicates a computer intrusion."

There may be artifacts left on a system after an intrusion or a breach, and they can be expressed in a language that describes the threat information, known as indicators of compromise (IOCs). The sets of information describe how and where to detect the signs of the intrusion or breach. IOCs can be host-based and/or network-based artifacts, but the scan actions are carried out on the host only.

IOCs are very high-confidence indicators, and they may describe numerous specific items, including FileItem, RegistryItem, EventLogItem, ProcessItem, and ServiceItem. You can lean the IOC language in more detail at http://www.openioc.org.

Figure 5-3 shows an example of an IOC.

```xml
<?xml version="1.0" encoding="us-ascii"?>
<ioc xmlns:xsi="http://www.w3.org/2001/XMLSchema-instance" xmlns:xsd="http://www.w3.org/2001/XMLSchema" id="af2e8c80-13db-4a57-9
9ac-460ccd192333" last-modified="2012-06-04T21:33:52" xmlns="http://schemas.mandiant.com/2010/ioc">
  <short_description>Flamer,Skywiper</short_description>
  <description>IOCs to detect the presence of the Flamer framework</description>
  <authored_by>Jaime Blasco, Alienvault</authored_by>
  <authored_date>2012-06-04T15:15:17</authored_date>
  <links />
  <definition>
    <Indicator operator="OR" id="9aa42d5a-3bc6-446e-b19c-1b2a4b909b5a">
      <Indicator operator="AND" id="2e1b945c-2587-412c-9b9d-51a28d23f652">
        <IndicatorItem id="8be295c7-879c-4499-b1ee-ca03873decf8" condition="contains">
          <Context document="RegistryItem" search="RegistryItem/Path" type="mir" />
          <Content type="string">HKEY_LOCAL_MACHINE\SOFTWARE\Microsoft\Windows NT\CurrentVersion\Drivers32</Content>
        </IndicatorItem>
        <IndicatorItem id="4becb7bf-5f45-4c9b-8c7b-130a7e8cbe26" condition="contains">
          <Context document="RegistryItem" search="RegistryItem/Text" type="mir" />
          <Content type="string">wavesup3.drv</Content>
        </IndicatorItem>
        <Indicator operator="OR" id="1f4f8b85-b307-487a-897c-197492cb51f4">
          <IndicatorItem id="3d9496b4-10fa-4b65-b72b-8f289c914c91" condition="is">
            <Context document="RegistryItem" search="RegistryItem/ValueName" type="mir" />
            <Content type="string">wave9</Content>
          </IndicatorItem>
          <IndicatorItem id="c729ed47-513d-436d-b164-919ff4cd2d3d" condition="is">
            <Context document="RegistryItem" search="RegistryItem/ValueName" type="mir" />
            <Content type="string">wave8</Content>
          </IndicatorItem>
        </Indicator>
      </Indicator>
      <Indicator operator="AND" id="14868529-c95f-4576-af9c-23f9d2923107">
        <IndicatorItem id="5225f2f2-8293-42c5-92a7-fbb5afb1cda8" condition="contains">
          <Context document="RegistryItem" search="RegistryItem/Path" type="mir" />
          <Content type="string">\Control\Lsa\Authentication Packages</Content>
        </IndicatorItem>
        <IndicatorItem id="48c2cd98-5324-4780-a06c-0e6b7ecd780b" condition="contains">
          <Context document="RegistryItem" search="RegistryItem/Text" type="mir" />
          <Content type="string">mssecmgr.ocx</Content>
        </IndicatorItem>
      </Indicator>
      <Indicator operator="OR" id="c702bea5-317a-4232-855a-090cd61c8e5e">
        <IndicatorItem id="209070e1-50d7-489d-af11-e0f2b3df23d5" condition="contains">
          <Context document="ProcessItem" search="ProcessItem/HandleList/Handle/Name" type="mir" />
          <Content type="string">TH_POOL_SHD_PQOISNG</Content>
        </IndicatorItem>
        <IndicatorItem id="f64f68ac-5d94-49e2-b59d-d614db8dc122" condition="contains">
          <Context document="ProcessItem" search="ProcessItem/HandleList/Handle/Name" type="mir" />
          <Content type="string">microsoft shared_msaudio_wpgfilter.dat</Content>
        </IndicatorItem>
```

Figure 5-3 *Example of an Indicator of Compromise*

Device Flow Correlation

Device flow correlation provides a kernel-level view into network I/O. It allows for blocking or alerting on network activity, traced back to the initiating process itself. It enables internal and external networks to be monitored, leverages IP reputation data, and offers URL/domain logging. The flow points are extra telemetry data and are not file disposition specific.

Cisco provides intelligence on many malicious destinations, including generic command and control (CnC) servers, phishing hosts, zero-access CnC servers, and more.

Advanced Analytics

Advanced analytics consists of a set of multifaceted engines that provide big data context beyond a single host and beyond a single file. Advanced analytics highlights files executed in an environment, from least common to most. This can aid in identifying previously undetected threats that may have only been seen by a small number of users.

Dynamic Analysis with Threat Grid

Cisco AMP Threat Grid is not a single tool. It is a full solution for dynamic malware analysis and threat intelligence. It performs high-speed, automated analysis with adjustable runtimes while not exposing any tags or other indicators that malware could use to detect that it is being observed.

Threat Grid provides video playbacks, a glovebox for malware interaction and operational troubleshooting, a process graph for visual representation of process lineage, and a threat score with behavior indicators.

It searches and correlates all data elements of a single sample against billions of sample artifacts collected and analyzed over years, leveraging global and historic context. This enables an analyst to better understand the relevancy of a questionable sample as it pertains to the analyst's own environment.

Threat Grid was architected from the ground up as a cloud solution with an API designed to integrate with existing IT security solutions and to create custom threat intelligence feeds. It can automatically receive submissions from other solutions and pull the results into your environment.

Many think that Threat Grid is a sandboxing solution. It is much more than just that, however; sandboxing is a piece of the solution, and Threat Grid's sandboxing functions are performed in a way that evades detection by malware. Threat Grid uses an outside-in approach, with no presence in the virtual machine. The sandboxing's dynamic analysis includes an external kernel monitor, dynamic disk analysis that illuminates any modifications to the physical disk (such as the master boot record), monitoring user interaction, video capture and playback, process information, artifacts, and network traffic.

Threat Grid supports the following samples and object types:

- Executable files (.EXE) and libraries (.DLL)

- Java archives (.JAR)

- Portable document format (.PDF)

- Office documents (.RTF, .DOC, .DOCX, .XLS, .XLSX, .PPT, .PPTX)

- ZIP containers (.ZIP)

- Quarantine containers

- URLs

- HTML documents

- Flash

Note   At this writing, Threat Grid is a key part of the Cisco AMP cloud, but it is not yet available as part of the private cloud (local/onsite) offering.

The Retrospective Framework

Retrospection means taking a look at what has already transpired; it involves tracking system behavior regardless of disposition, focusing on uncovering malicious activity. Retrospection could be viewed as the "incident response mode," using continuous analysis to reactively act on a file that was assigned a clean disposition once but was later found to have a bad disposition.

The retrospective framework is designed to show the trajectory of a malicious file, with a goal of 30 days of telemetry data, as illustrated in Figure 5-4. Even files that are originally given a clean verdict are tracked, and if a clean file is later found to be malicious, all connectors that have seen the file are notified to quarantine the file retrospectively.

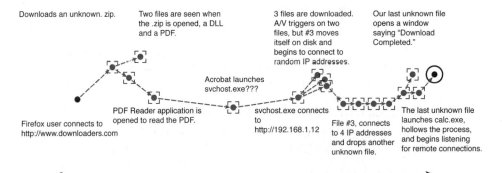

Figure 5-4   *Trajectory Illustrated*

The Cloud

As you will see throughout this book, the AMP cloud is the centralized location for all management and reporting. Figure 5-5 shows an example of an AMP cloud dashboard. The dashboard shows indicators of compromise and allows you to drill into them.

From the dashboard, you can provision endpoints, download agents, run reports, and more.

Figure 5-5   *Example of an AMP Cloud Dashboard*

Private Cloud

The AMP cloud is available in a private version. Administrators can run their own private cloud with many of the features from the public cloud, but not all. With the private offering, you may choose to host all components within your own data center or perhaps in another cloud environment, like Cisco's InterCloud or Amazon Web Services (AWS).

The option to host the AMP cloud in your own data center is often selected by organizations that reside outside the United States and have very strict controls on where data may reside. In addition, some organizations, such as government agencies, have requirements for data storage being on premises.

The private cloud product is shipped as a virtual machine that you can run in your own VMware environment. The private cloud may be operated in two ways: in cloud proxy mode and in air gap mode.

Note   At this writing, the private cloud is available only for AMP for Endpoints and AMP for Networks. In addition, support of Threat Grid with the private cloud is planned but not yet available.

Cloud Proxy Mode

Cloud proxy mode operates the private cloud within the confines of your own data center or other cloud infrastructure. The AMP for Networks and AMP for Endpoints connectors all communicate to the private cloud. However, the private cloud maintains a connection to the public cloud for certain communications:

- **File disposition checks:** File disposition is still determined by the public cloud. The file hashes are passed on to the public cloud over an SSL session using TCP port 443 or TCP port 32137. The public cloud is known as the *upstream server,* and the FQDN that you connect to is cloud-pc.amp.sourcefire.com.

- **Product updates:** The AMP private cloud can be configured for automatic or manual updates, leveraging a yum repository named packages.amp.sourcefire.com that uses an SSL session over TCP port 443.

- **Support:** Cisco TAC is able to remotely access the device for diagnostic purposes and customer assistance. The remote access uses SSH over TCP port 443.

Figure 5-6 illustrates the cloud proxy mode.

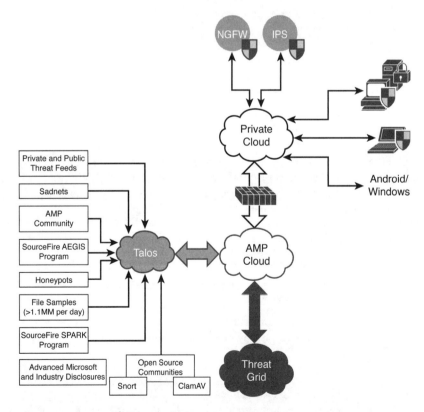

Figure 5-6 *Private Cloud Proxy Mode*

Air Gap Mode

As its name indicates, air gap mode creates a private cloud instance that is completely isolated and has no external access to the public cloud. Updates must be completed manually, and remote support is challenging. However, this mode provides the highest levels of confidentiality. Figure 5-7 illustrates air gap mode.

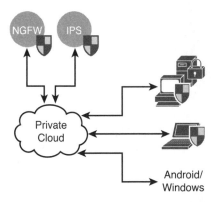

Figure 5-7   *Private Cloud Air Gap Mode*

Installing the Cisco AMP Private Cloud

The AMP private cloud is available as an Open Virtualization Archive (.ova) format file, for import into a VMware virtual environment. At this writing, the only supported virtual environment for the private cloud is VMware ESX 5 or newer. Unofficially, however, the virtual appliance works on VMware Fusion and VMware Workstation, though this is unsupported.

Installing the private cloud in air gap mode requires more resources than the cloud proxy mode installation. These are the minimum requirements:

■ **Cloud proxy mode:** 32 GB RAM, 8 CPUs, 238 GB minimum free disk space

■ **Air gap mode:** 128 GB RAM, 8 CPUs, 1 TB minimum free disk space

After you deploy the OVA template, you connect to the console of the VM in order to configure the private cloud, as shown in Figure 5-8. You need to configure the network so the private cloud configuration can be completed through its web interface.

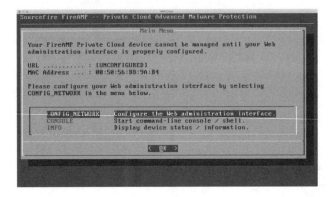

Figure 5-8 *DHCP or Static IP*

DHCP is required if you will be installing in demo mode, while a static IP address and external DNS servers are required for a production install. You need to click **No** and provide valid IP stack information, as shown in Figures 5-9 and 5-10.

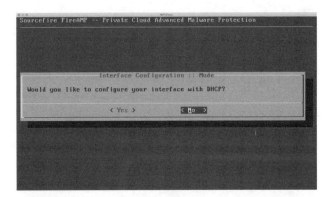

Figure 5-9 *DHCP or Static IP*

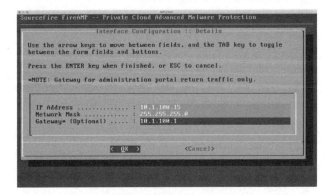

Figure 5-10 *Static IP Interface Configuration*

You then click **Yes** to apply the changes to the interface, as shown in Figure 5-11. The main menu returns, with a randomized password that you use to administer the private cloud through the web interface, as shown in Figure 5-12.

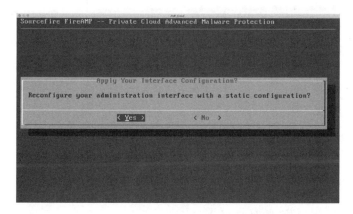

Figure 5-11 *Applying Your Interface Configuration*

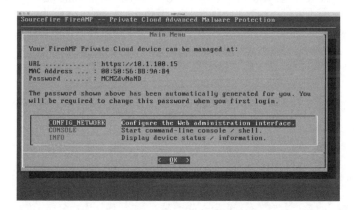

Figure 5-12 *AMP Private Cloud Device Management*

Connect to your private cloud with a web browser using HTTPS, as shown in Figure 5-13, and log in with a random password such as the one displayed in Figure 5-12.

Figure 5-13 *Logging into the AMP Private Cloud Web Interface*

Once you have successfully logged in, you are prompted to change the one-time password that the system generated, as shown in Figure 5-14, and then you have to accept the license agreement, shown in Figure 5-15. If you step away from the browser for an extended period of time, it times out, and you need to log in with the newly set password of your choosing instead of the one-time system-generated password.

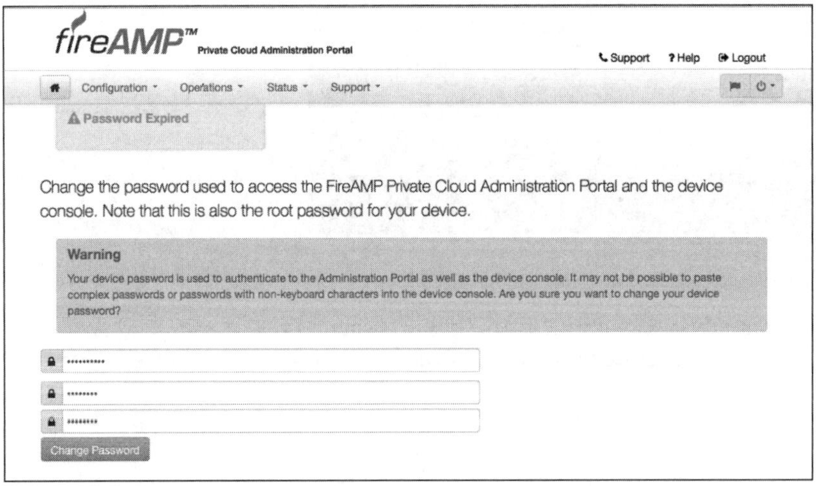

Figure 5-14 *Changing the Password*

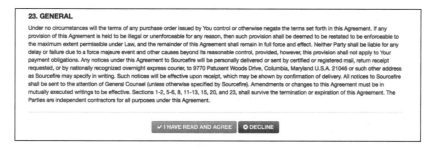

23. GENERAL

Under no circumstances will the terms of any purchase order issued by You control or otherwise negate the terms set forth in this Agreement. If any provision of this Agreement is held to be illegal or unenforceable for any reason, then such provision shall be deemed to be restated to be enforceable to the maximum extent permissible under Law, and the remainder of this Agreement shall remain in full force and effect. Neither Party shall be liable for any delay or failure due to a force majeure event and other causes beyond its reasonable control, provided, however, this provision shall not apply to Your payment obligations. Any notices under this Agreement to Sourcefire will be personally delivered or sent by certified or registered mail, return receipt requested, or by nationally recognized overnight express courier, to 9770 Patuxent Woods Drive, Columbia, Maryland U.S.A. 21046 or such other address as Sourcefire may specify in writing. Such notices will be effective upon receipt, which may be shown by confirmation of delivery. All notices to Sourcefire shall be sent to the attention of General Counsel (unless otherwise specified by Sourcefire). Amendments or changes to this Agreement must be in mutually executed writings to be effective. Sections 1-2, 5-6, 8, 11-13, 15, 20, and 23, shall survive the termination or expiration of this Agreement. The Parties are independent contractors for all purposes under this Agreement.

Figure 5-15 *Accepting the License Agreement*

At this point, you can restore a previously backed up private cloud or proceed with a clean installation. To install a new private cloud, you click **Start** for a clean installation, as shown in Figure 5-16.

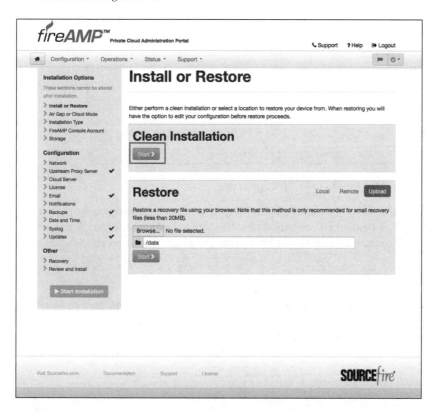

Figure 5-16 *Choosing a Clean Installation or to Restore from Backup*

You are now prompted to choose between air gap and cloud proxy mode, as shown in Figure 5-17. Cloud proxy mode requires an Internet connection to send disposition queries to the public cloud and to receive content updates as well as software updates, as described earlier in this chapter.

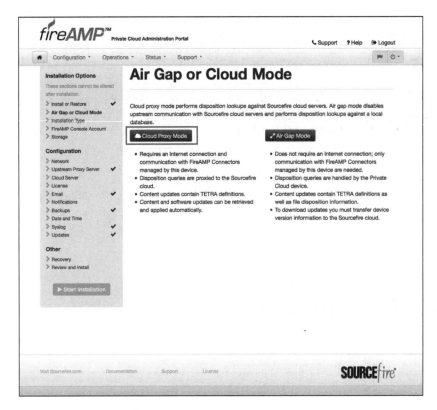

Figure 5-17   *Cloud Proxy Mode or Air Gap Mode*

Next, you choose the installation type. In this case, you can choose demo mode, which requires DHCP to be used rather than a static IP address. Demo mode also skips some of the installation requirements, so it can be installed on a laptop or other smaller VM host.

In order to see all the installation options, you click **Next** under Production, as shown in Figure 5-18.

For a production installation, a license file is required. Click **Browse** to locate the license file, enter the passphrase to decrypt the key, and then click **Upload**, as shown in Figure 5-19. The license is then installed.

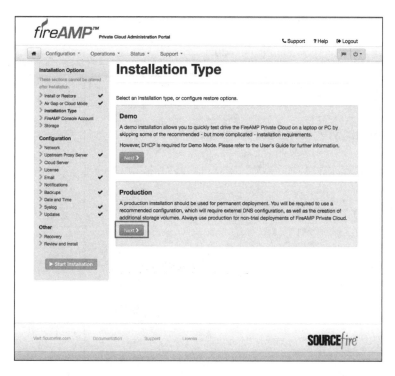

Figure 5-18   *Choosing the Demo or Production Installation Type*

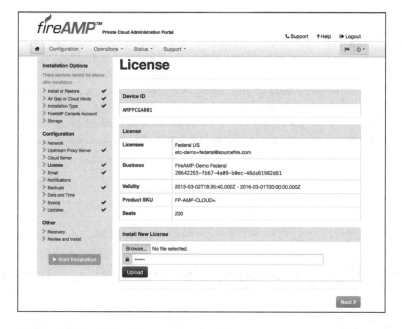

Figure 5-19   *Uploading the License File*

Next, you are asked to create a console account, which you use to initially log into the cloud, create additional accounts, and set up groups. Create your console account and password and click **Next**, as shown in Figure 5-20.

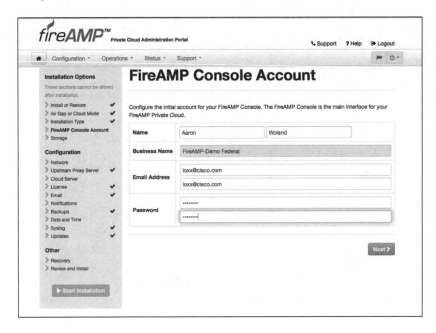

Figure 5-20   *Creating the Console Account*

After creating the console account, you see a summary screen for your storage capabilities. There are two main tabs: Automatic Configuration and Manual Configuration. The automatic configuration adjusts partition sizes based on the number of connectors that you configure the cloud for and the number of days of history that you wish to retain. Figure 5-21 shows the automatic configuration screen. With this mode, you simply state the number of connectors to plan for and the number of days to store the data. The connectors are the endpoints or network AMP devices that will be using this private cloud. Warnings appear for any misconfigurations where not enough storage is available.

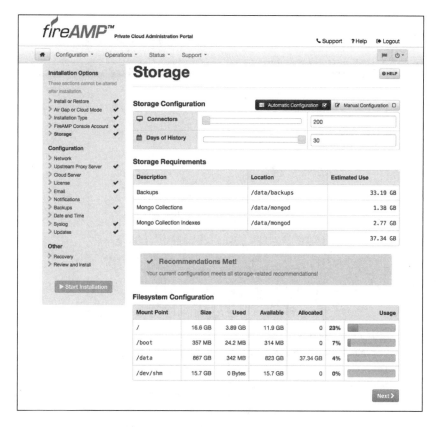

Figure 5-21 *Automatic Configuration of Storage*

As shown in Figure 5-22, the manual configuration gives you more control, and you can determine how much space to allocate for each of the collections (archives, default, documents, executables, events, and DFC). Again, warnings appear for any misconfigurations where not enough storage is available.

Note If you manually misconfigure the file system and the database grows too large for the disk partition, you will need to do a full backup, reinstallation, and restoration in order to change the partition sizes. Therefore, it is recommended that you use the automatic option.

Figure 5-22   *Manual Configuration of Storage*

The next screen is the Network Configuration page. The top half of the screen is fairly self-explanatory. Here you see the administrative portal being hosted on the interface (eth0) and the IP address that you configured at the command line. What is new here is that the second interface (eth1) needs to be configured. The eth1 interface is known as the *production interface* and is used to connect to the Internet for updates, communication with the public cloud, and communication with all the connectors (endpoints and network AMP systems).

Figure 5-23 shows the VMware configuration, where you can see two network adapters. Both NICs can be on the same network segment, as shown in Figure 5-23. They do not have to be in the same VLAN, but they can be. Figure 5-24 shows the top half of the network configuration page, with both eth0 and eth1 configurations displayed.

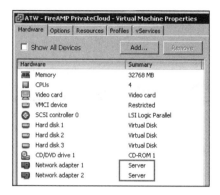

Figure 5-23 *VMware Configuration Showing Two NICs*

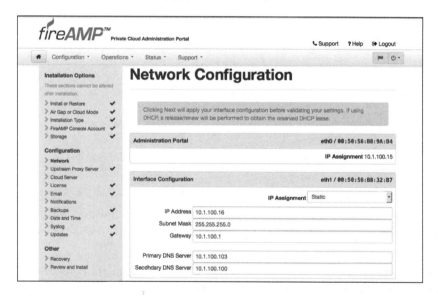

Figure 5-24 *Top Portion of the Network Configuration Page*

With the eth1 configuration complete, you come to a rather confusing part of the setup. You need to enter two required fully qualified domain names (FQDNs) and one optional one. What confuses people with this portion of the setup is that the FireAMP Console FQDN, the Cloud Server FQDN, and the Defense Center FQDN are all referring to exactly the same host—the host that you are currently configuring. That's right: You need to have two or three entries in DNS that all point to the IP address configured for the eth1 interface, as shown for the DNS server displayed in Figure 5-25.

atw-ampcloud	Host (A)	10.1.100.15
cloud	Host (A)	10.1.100.16
console	Host (A)	10.1.100.16
amp-dc	Host (A)	10.1.100.16

Figure 5-25 *DNS A Records for the FQDNs*

You need to enter these FQDNs into the corresponding fields of the configuration screen, as shown in Figure 5-26. When you are sure that the names exist correctly in both the DNS server and the configuration screen, click **Next (Applies Configuration)** to move on.

Note   The endpoints and the private cloud need the ability to resolve these DNS names. If the endpoints cannot resolve these names, they will fail to register to the cloud.

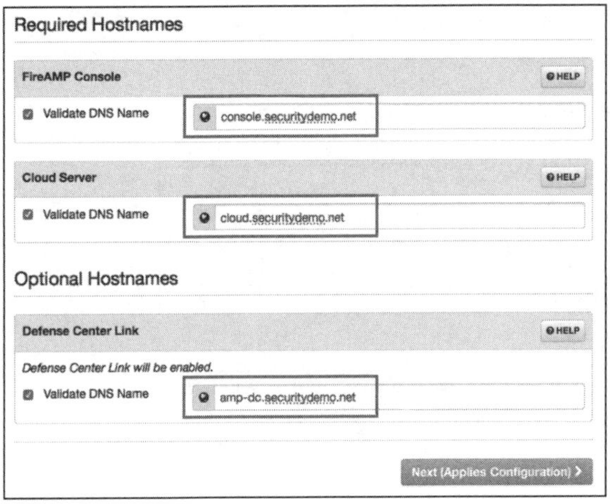

Figure 5-26   *Lower Portion of the Network Configuration Page*

When the network configuration is complete, the next step is to select which upstream cloud should be used, along with the port and security settings related to that cloud connection, as shown in Figure 5-27.

The upstream server selection can be either the North American cloud, the European cloud, or a custom cloud name, as shown in Figure 5-28.

Note   The custom server is not used in the majority of deployments because it is designed for multitiered private cloud deployments, which are rare.

There are no geographical requirements for the upstream public cloud infrastructure. The cloud server selection that you make should be based on latency: Choose the one with the lowest latency. The next drop-down is the protocol selection: either SSL (TCP port 443) or TCP (port 32137). Cisco best practice is to use TCP port 32137 because the communication is already encrypted and the SSL port adds additional overhead and uses more bandwidth. Figure 5-29 shows the drop-down choices.

Figure 5-27   *Cloud Server Configuration*

Figure 5-28   *Upstream Cloud Server Selection Choices*

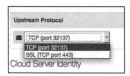

Figure 5-29   *Protocol Selection*

The cloud server identity section shown in Figure 5-27 and Figure 5-29 lists this AMP cloud server's unique identity and the certificates that represent this cloud server's identity for any downstream private clouds.

Click **Next** to move on from the cloud server configuration and set up a recipient or recipients of administrative email notifications, as shown in Figure 5-30. The emails may contain notices of low disk space, backup success or failure, failed sanity checks, and more items of this nature.

Figure 5-30 *Setting Notifications*

Date and time configuration is next. Network Time Protocol (NTP) plays a critical role in all network security solutions, ensuring time accuracy and synchronization. It ensures that log entries will always be accurate and provide valid, useful reports. All events are stored in UTC time, so selecting a time zone is not necessary. The time zone will be adjusted upon display to the console UI, so the admin is not stuck working in UTC. Figure 5-31 shows the date and time configuration screen.

Figure 5-31 *Setting Date and Time*

Note NTP updates occur through the public interface (eth1), allowing you to choose an NTP source on the public Internet, if that is preferred.

The next screen is for a recovery file. A recovery file is like a backup, and it contains all the cloud configuration and the server keys shown in Figure 5-27. You should store the recovery file in a very safe location because if you lose the recovery key, you will never be able to restore your configuration. In addition, every one of your FireAMP connectors will need to be reinstalled. In other words, without the original key, you have to reinstall the private cloud infrastructure with all new keys.

To complete this step, simply download the backup file through your browser by clicking the blue **Download** button (see Figure 5-32) and save the pre-install-backup.tgz file to your local disk. Then upload it right back to the server by clicking the **Browse** button on the same page. You can click **Next** and proceed with the installation after the file is validated.

Figure 5-32 *Setting Up Recovery*

Finally, you see the Review and Install screen, as shown in Figure 5-33. This is your last chance to review all the configuration options before you install. When you are certain you have selected all the correct options, click **Start Installation**, and the installation proceeds, with a status screen like the one shown in Figure 5-34.

Figure 5-33   *Review and Install*

Figure 5-34   *Installing the Device*

As the screen warns, you should leave your browser on the page and not try to refresh it manually. As the installation finishes, it sends an email notification like the one shown in Figure 5-35.

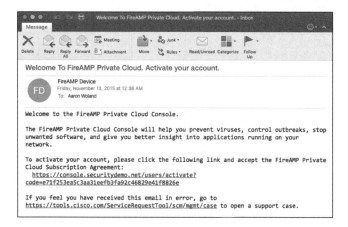

Figure 5-35 *Email Notification*

When the installation is complete, the **Reboot** button becomes active (see Figure 5-36). Click **Reboot** when the process finishes to reboot the appliance, and the server reboots and displays the message shown in Figure 5-37.

Figure 5-36 *Successful Installation*

Figure 5-37   *Rebooting*

After the appliance reboots, the web interface for the administrative interface (eth0) that you were using to configure the appliance displays key metrics like those shown in Figure 5-38.

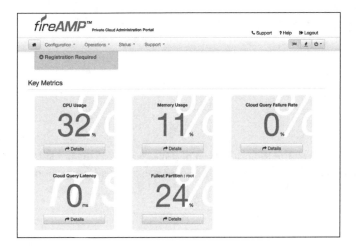

Figure 5-38   *Key Metrics*

Now you can connect to the web interface for the eth1 interface by connecting to the console FQDN that you configured, as shown in Figure 5-39. You log in using the console account you created during the setup process.

Figure 5-39   *Login Screen*

The subscription agreement is displayed next. Scroll to the bottom and select the check box, as shown in Figure 5-40, and click **Continue**.

Figure 5-40 *Subscription Agreement*

After logging in, you are presented with a setup wizard to configure your first policies for Windows or Mac AMP connectors. The endpoint policies are examined in more detail in Chapter 8, "Cisco AMP for Endpoints."

Summary

In this chapter you have learned all about the role of the AMP cloud for performing file disposition checks. You have learned about the intelligence that feeds the AMP cloud and the AMP view of security as including a prevention framework and a retrospection framework. You have learned about public and private clouds and seen how to complete an installation of a private cloud instance.

Chapter 6

Cisco AMP for Networks

This chapter dives into the Advanced Malware Protection (AMP) for Networks connector. The following topics are covered in this chapter:

■ How AMP for Networks fits in the AMP architecture

■ The functions of AMP for Networks

■ The components and configuration of malware and file policies

■ The types of files and what actions are available for them

Introduction to Advanced Malware Protection (AMP) for Networks

The network is the best place to see across an organization, uncover, and discover. It provides unprecedented visibility to activity at a macro-analytical level. However, to remediate malware, you need to be on the host. This is why AMP has the following connectors: AMP for Networks, AMP for Endpoints, and AMP for Content Security Appliances.

What Is That Manager Called, Anyway?

While the AMP connectors are installed differently and act in different places in networks, they all speak to the AMP clouds. In addition, AMP for Networks and AMP for Endpoints connectors share a common management platform that has gone by a few different names since Cisco acquired SourceFire. Thanks to the acquisition and the branding strategy from Cisco, you might see the management center being referred to as SourceFire Defense Center (SFDC), Cisco FireSIGHT Management Center (FMC), or even Cisco Firepower Management Center (FMC). At this writing, the latest and hopefully final name for the management system is Cisco Firepower Management Center (FMC).

Form Factors

You can install AMP for Networks on any Cisco FirePOWER security appliance right alongside the firewall and IPS; however, there are dedicated AMP appliances as well. When it comes down to it, though, AMP appliances and FirePOWER appliances are actually the same. They can all run all the same services. Are you thoroughly confused? Stated a different way, Cisco AMP for Networks is the AMP service that runs on an appliance that is examining traffic flowing through a network. It can be installed in a standalone form or as a service on a FirePOWER IPS or even a Cisco ASA with FirePOWER Services.

At this writing, the AMP appliance lineup included the AMP7150, AMP8050, AMP8150, AMP8350, AMP8360, AMP8370, and AMP8390. These appliances range from 500 Mbps to 20 Gbps of throughput.

What Does AMP for Networks Do?

AMP for Networks and all the AMP connectors are designed to find malicious files and provide retrospective analysis, illustrate trajectory, and point out how far malicious files may have spread.

The AMP for Networks connector examines, records, tracks, and sends files to the cloud. It creates an SHA-256 hash of the file and compares it to the local file cache. If the hash is not in the local cache, it queries the Defense Center (DC). The DC has its own cache of all the hashes that it has seen before, and if it hasn't previously seen this hash, the DC queries the cloud. Unlike with AMP for Endpoints, when a file is new, it can be analyzed locally and doesn't have to be sent to the cloud for all analysis, and it also examines and stops the file in flight, as it is traversing the appliance.

Figure 6-1 illustrates the many AMP for Networks connectors sending the file hash to the DC, which in turn sends it to the cloud if the hash is new. The connectors could be running on dedicated AMP appliances, as a service on a SourceFire next-generation IPS (NGIPS), on an ASA with FirePOWER Services, or even on the newer next-generation firewall (NGFW) known as Firepower Threat Defense (FTD).

It's very important to note that only the SHA-256 hash is sent unless you configure the policy to send files for further analysis in Threat Grid.

AMP can also provide retrospective analysis. The AMP for Networks appliance keeps data from what occurred in the past. When a file's disposition is changed, AMP provides a historical analysis of what happened, tracing an incident/infection. With the help of AMP for Endpoints, retrospection can reach out to that host and remediate the bad file, even though that file was permitted in the past.

This capability of retrospection is useful when a file is considered normal and then is later reconsidered to be malicious.

AMP for Networks deals with malicious files, and it also allows an organization to implement file control—even if malware is present.

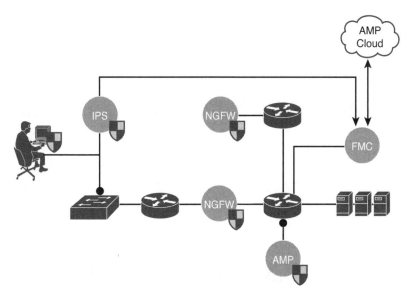

Figure 6-1 *AMP Connectors Talking to the DC and Then the Cloud*

In order for the AMP policies to be used, you must have at least one SourceFire device with an active malware license. Figure 6-2 shows an example of the license screen located at **System > Licenses**. Notice that there are two devices listed, an ASA5515-X with FirePOWER Services and a virtual SourceFire NGIPS (NGIPSv), both of which have malware licenses.

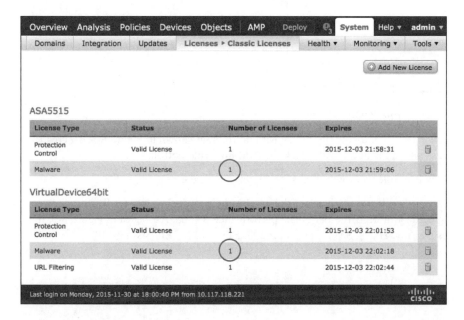

Figure 6-2 *Malware Licenses*

Where Are the AMP Policies?

When you look at the Firepower Management Center (FMC), you don't see the AMP policies named the same way they're named in other tools. They are configured under **Policies > Access Control > Malware & File**, as shown in Figure 6-3.

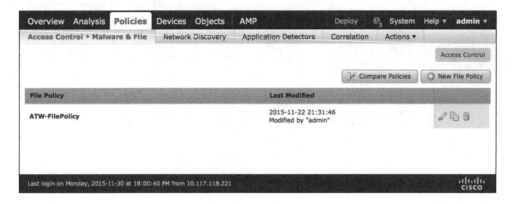

Figure 6-3   *Malware & File Policies Page*

Create a new file policy by clicking **New File Policy** in the upper-right corner and providing a name in the New File Policy dialog box, as shown in Figure 6-4. Remember to provide a detailed description that will help you understand the purpose of the policy. Click **Save** to create the policy and move into the configuration.

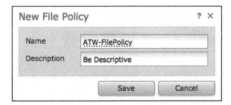

Figure 6-4   *New File Policy Dialog*

You now have a brand-new file policy with no rules, as shown in Figure 6-5. To create your first rule in the new policy, click the **Add File Rule** button.

The View File Rule window appears, as shown in Figure 6-6.

To create a file rule, you first select the application protocol to inspect for files. The more specific your rule, the better the performance will be. As shown in Figure 6-7, the choices are Any, HTTP, SMTP, IMAP, POP3, FTP, and NetBIOS-ssn (SMB).

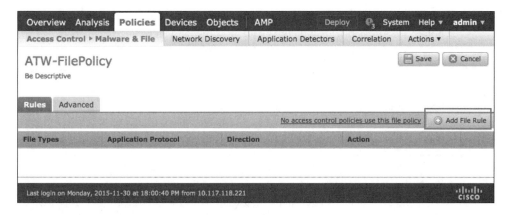

Figure 6-5 *New File Policy Without Rules*

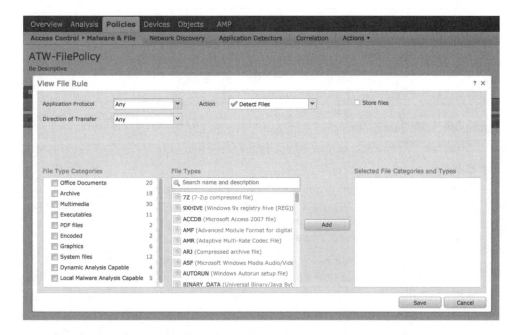

Figure 6-6 *View File Rule Window*

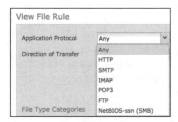

Figure 6-7 *Application Protocols*

You must also specify the direction of the file transfer through the network appliance. The choices are Any, Upload, and Download, as shown in Figure 6-8.

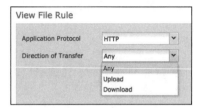

Figure 6-8   *Direction of Transfer*

The action you choose next determines what to do with files. As shown in Figure 6-9, the actions are Detect Files, Block Files, Malware Cloud Lookup, and Block Malware.

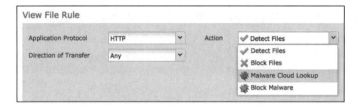

Figure 6-9   *File Rule Actions*

File Rules

The first traditional file rule action is the Detect Files rule action. Detecting files logs the detection of the specific files but does not interfere with the file's traversal through the network. Think of it as a "monitor mode" or an audit style rule. You can store the files that meet the rule for further evaluation.

The next traditional file rule action is the Block Files rule action, which resets the file transfer connection. Just like the detection rule action, this blocking action has an option to store the files.

Malware Cloud Lookup is the first of AMP rule actions, and it requires a valid malware license. This rule action is like a monitor mode or an audit rule for AMP, where the AMP connector obtains and logs the disposition of the file but does not stop the transmission of the files. As with the other rules, you have the ability to store the triggering files, only this time the options are to store file types: Malware, Unknown, Clean, and/or Custom.

Block Malware is the second AMP rule action, and it naturally requires a valid malware license. This rule action works the same way as Malware Cloud Lookup, except it adds an option to reset the connection by sending a TCP reset.

With both malware lookup options you have four choices:

- **Spero Analysis for EXEs:** Spero Analysis is machine learning that leverages heuristics to determine zero-day malware.

- **Dynamic Analysis:** This sends the files themselves to be analyzed by Threat Grid.

- **Capacity Handling:** When you use dynamic analysis and the cloud is not reachable, the files can be stored locally.

- **Local Malware Analysis:** This examines the file using locally installed antivirus software (at this writing, ClamAV, an open source product owned by Cisco SourceFire).

File Disposition Types

As mentioned earlier in the chapter, there are four file dispositions: Malware, Unknown, Clean, and Custom. One other disposition is Unavailable. The list that follows describes these file dispositions in detail:

- **Malware:** This disposition indicates that the AMP cloud categorized the file as malware or local malware analysis identified malware during the file scan, using the local antivirus software. Another possibility for this file disposition is that the file's threat score exceeded the malware threshold defined in the file policy.

- **Clean:** This disposition indicates that the AMP cloud categorized the file as clean. It is also possible to manually add a file to the clean list, which shows the file with the Clean disposition.

- **Unknown:** This disposition indicates that the system queried the AMP cloud, but the AMP cloud has not categorized the file.

- **Custom:** This disposition indicates that a user added the file to the custom detection list, possibly for data loss prevention (DLP) purposes or a static location of the file instead of a dynamic one.

- **Unavailable:** This disposition might mean the AMP for Networks system could not query the AMP cloud.

Determining What Files to Match

The file rule must understand what file types to examine. To make it easier, the system organizes file types into categories. You can use these categories to help locate certain file types more easily. When you have the file types you want in the middle column (aptly named File Types) of the View File Rule dialog, click the **Add** button to select them for matching in the rule.

You do not have to add the individual file types; you can select the entire category. Simply select the category on the left, click **All types in selected Categories** in the middle, and then click **Add**. The chosen categories and file types are maintained in the right column. Click **Save** to save the final file rule.

Figure 6-10 shows the file rule with file types and categories mixed together in the right column.

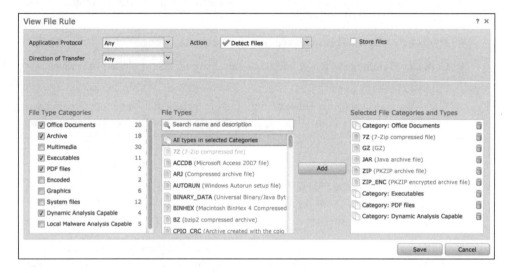

Figure 6-10 *What File Types to Match*

What About Those "Zippy" Type Files?

Zip and other archive files contain other files within them. The contents of an archive file are examined, and the disposition of an archive file is assigned based on the files inside it. If any of the files are determined to be malware, the archive file is assigned the Malware disposition. If any of the files are unknown, the archive file is marked as Unknown.

All the files within the archive must be found to be clean in order for the archive to be assigned the Clean disposition.

Advanced File Policies

A file policy is made up of one or more file rules. In addition to the rules, you can set some global settings for all the file rules within a file policy. As shown in Figure 6-11, the advanced options are broken into two different categories:

■ **General:**

■ **First Time File Analysis:** If this option is disabled, all files detected for the first time are marked as Unknown. When this option is enabled, the files are analyzed based on the options selected in the file rule.

■ **Enable Custom Detection List:** If this option is enabled and a file is on the custom detection list, that file is blocked.

- **Enable Clean List:** If this option is enabled and a file is on the clean list, that file is allowed.

- **Mark files as malware based on dynamic analysis threat score:** In this drop-down list you select a threshold score. Files are considered malware when their score is equal to or worse than the threshold value.

■ **Archive File Inspection:**

- **Inspect Archives:** With this option disabled, AMP bypasses inspecting archive files, even when they are selected in the file rule. If you disable the inspection of archive files, AMP creates a hash of the archive file itself and performs the lookup for that SHA, which is not very useful.

- **Block Encrypted Archives:** Because you cannot decrypt these archives and examine the files within the archive, you can simply choose to treat all encrypted archives as possibly malicious and therefore block them.

- **Block Uninspectable Archives:** This option allows you to block archive files with contents that the system is unable to inspect for reasons other than encryption; this could be due to file corruption or an archive within an archive exceeding the specified maximum archive depth.

- **Max Archive Depth:** This option determines how many levels of archive stacking the system should decompress and examine. Think of it as a Russian nesting doll: Files can be in a zip that is within a tar.gz file, which is in a 7zip compressed archive.

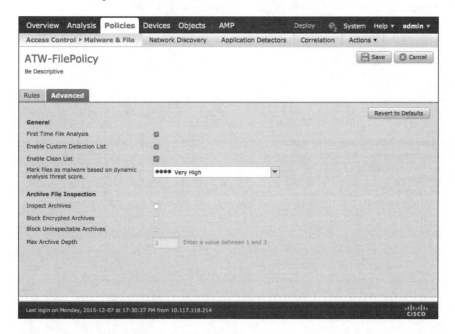

Figure 6-11 *File Policy Advanced Settings*

When you're ready to push the policies out to the AMP for Networks–capable systems, click **Deploy**, as shown in Figure 6-12. As shown in Figure 6-13, you now see a list of capable devices that can use this file policy. Select the devices to receive the new policy and then click **Deploy**.

Figure 6-12   *Deploying the Policies*

Figure 6-13   *Selecting the Appliances to Push Policy To*

Summary

There are different types of AMP connectors on an endpoint and throughout a network. AMP for Networks connectors exist on FirePOWER appliances, ASA with FirePOWER Services, and the newer Firepower Threat Defense (FTD) appliances.

AMP for Networks policies are configured in the Firepower Management Center (FMC) with the Malware & File policies and then deployed to AMP-capable appliances. The file policies determine which types of files to examine, how to examine them, which protocols to examine for the files, and what to do with them.

Chapter 7

Cisco AMP for Content Security

This chapter dives into the Advanced Malware Protection (AMP) for Content Security connector. This chapter covers the following topics:

- How AMP for Content Security fits in the AMP architecture

- The components and configuration of file reputation and file analysis services

- The reporting for file reputation and file analysis services

Introduction to AMP for Content Security

The Cisco Advanced Malware Protection (AMP) architecture uses connectors that examine files on the endpoint or in transit to and from the network. AMP for Content Security appliances play a key role in the perimeter security of a network, examining key traffic flows that represent common attack vectors; they are therefore a perfect location for detecting and blocking malware.

Figure 7-1 illustrates a network with many different AMP connectors existing on endpoints, next-generation intrusion prevention systems (NGIPS), AMP appliances, and Email Security Appliances (ESAs) and Web Security Appliances (WSAs).

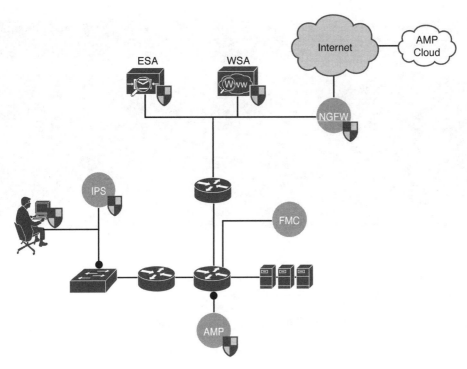

Figure 7-1   *Network with AMP Connectors*

Content Security Connectors

AMP connectors are implemented in different ways. The AMP for Networks connectors that you learned about in Chapter 6, "Cisco AMP for Networks," are managed by the Firepower Management Center (FMC) and configured through file policies.

AMP for Content Security appliances rely on a concept called *reputation scoring*, which involves reputations of websites, email senders, and files. Therefore, it shouldn't come as a surprise that the capabilities on AMP for Content Security appliances are referred to as file reputation filtering and file analysis.

Figure 7-2 illustrates the file evaluation used by AMP for Content Security. If the Web-Based Reputation Score (WBRS) is configured to scan, the appliance simultaneously scans the file for malware and sends an SHA-256 of the file to the AMP cloud. In addition, if it is a Microsoft executable file, it sends the Spero fingerprint of the PE header. Spero is a machine learning–based technology that proactively identifies threats that were previously unknown. If the file's reputation and scan results are both determined to be clean, the file is released and delivered to the end user.

If the file is deemed to be malicious, either through file reputation or based on a local scan result, the configured action is taken. If the file reputation is unknown and it matches the criteria for file upload, the appliance uploads it to Threat Grid in the cloud for analysis.

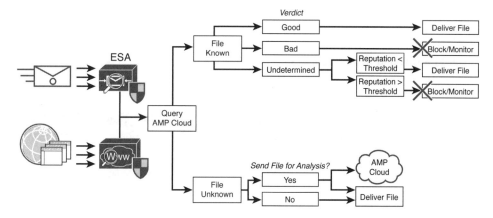

Figure 7-2 *Content AMP Flows*

Configuring Cisco AMP for Content Security

Before you can configure AMP for Content Security, you must first have the correct licensing (known as "feature keys") on your appliances. The feature keys enable the service on the appliance and allow you to configure the settings for the AMP services.

Configuring the Web Security Appliance (WSA) for AMP

Two features in the WSA correspond to AMP: file reputation and file analysis. Figure 7-3 shows the feature keys for a WSA and points out the file reputation and file analysis feature keys.

CISCO Cisco S300V
Web Security Virtual Appliance

| Reporting | Web Security Manager | Security Services | Network | System Administration |

Feature Keys

Success — No new feature keys are available.

Feature Keys for Serial Number: 4238486ABA7AD3C24880-709F91C24100

Description	Status	Time Remaining	Expiration Date
Cisco L4 Traffic Monitor	Active	367 days	Sun Dec 18 18:59:59 2016
Cisco HTTPS Proxy	Active	367 days	Sun Dec 18 18:59:59 2016
File Reputation	Active	367 days	Sun Dec 18 18:59:59 2016
Cisco Web Usage Controls	Active	367 days	Sun Dec 18 18:59:59 2016
Sophos	Active	367 days	Sun Dec 18 18:59:59 2016
File Analysis	Active	367 days	Sun Dec 18 18:59:59 2016
Webroot	Active	367 days	Sun Dec 18 18:59:59 2016
Cisco Web Proxy & DVS Engine	Active	367 days	Mon Dec 19 17:05:23 2016
Cisco AnyConnect Secure Mobility	Dormant	367 days	Sun Dec 18 18:59:59 2016
Cisco Web Reputation Filters	Active	367 days	Sun Dec 18 18:59:59 2016

Figure 7-3 *AMP Feature Keys*

The WSA must have access to the AMP cloud. Remember that the naming of each Cisco product may vary (for example, the AMP cloud is sometimes called File Reputation and Analysis Services). You configure the AMP cloud settings under **Security Services > Anti-Malware and Reputation**, as shown in Figure 7-4.

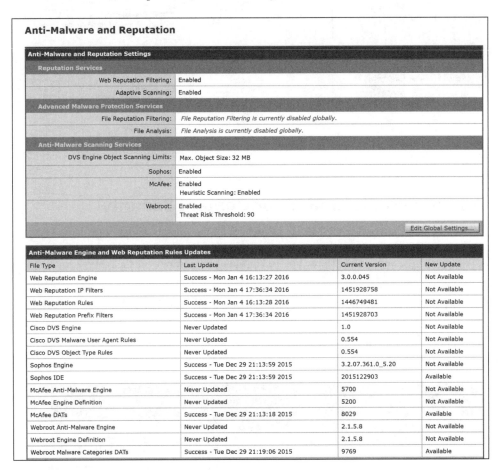

Figure 7-4   *Anti-Malware and Reputation Screen*

To configure the AMP services, click **Edit Global Settings**. Figure 7-5 shows the resulting Edit Anti-Malware and Reputation Settings screen. To enable AMP, simply select the check box next to **Enable File Reputation Filtering**.

Clicking Submit takes you to the license agreement page, where you must click **Accept**, as shown in Figure 7-6.

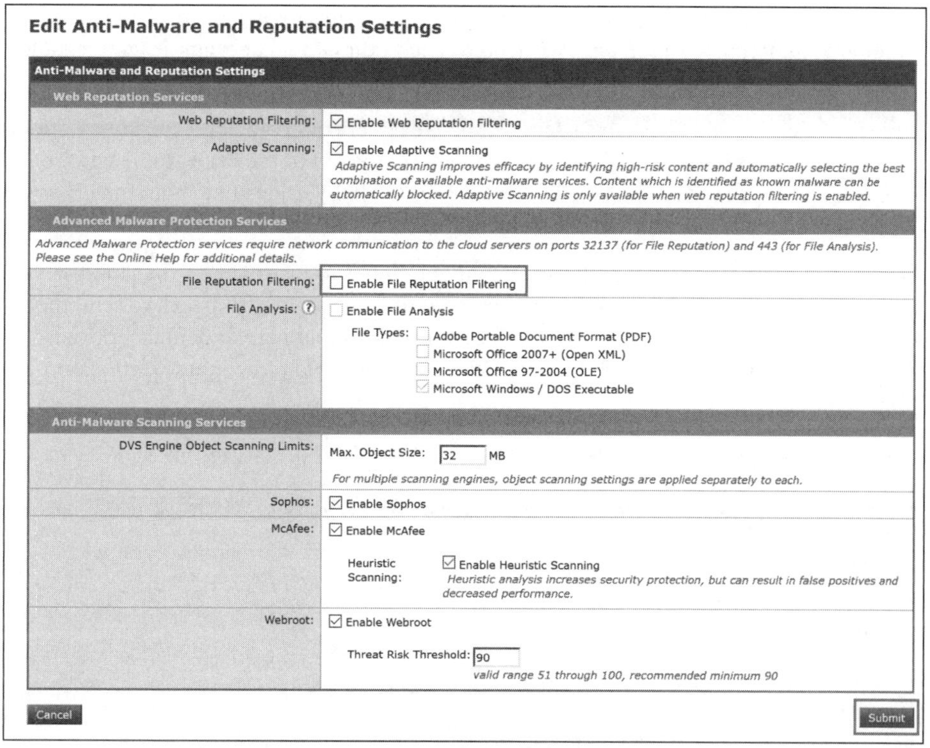

Edit Anti-Malware and Reputation Settings

Anti-Malware and Reputation Settings

Web Reputation Services

Web Reputation Filtering: ☑ Enable Web Reputation Filtering

Adaptive Scanning: ☑ Enable Adaptive Scanning

Adaptive Scanning improves efficacy by identifying high-risk content and automatically selecting the best combination of available anti-malware services. Content which is identified as known malware can be automatically blocked. Adaptive Scanning is only available when web reputation filtering is enabled.

Advanced Malware Protection Services

Advanced Malware Protection services require network communication to the cloud servers on ports 32137 (for File Reputation) and 443 (for File Analysis). Please see the Online Help for additional details.

File Reputation Filtering: ☐ Enable File Reputation Filtering

File Analysis: ⓘ ☐ Enable File Analysis

File Types: ☐ Adobe Portable Document Format (PDF)
☐ Microsoft Office 2007+ (Open XML)
☐ Microsoft Office 97-2004 (OLE)
☑ Microsoft Windows / DOS Executable

Anti-Malware Scanning Services

DVS Engine Object Scanning Limits: Max. Object Size: `32` MB

For multiple scanning engines, object scanning settings are applied separately to each.

Sophos: ☑ Enable Sophos

McAfee: ☑ Enable McAfee

Heuristic Scanning: ☑ Enable Heuristic Scanning
Heuristic analysis increases security protection, but can result in false positives and decreased performance.

Webroot: ☑ Enable Webroot

Threat Risk Threshold: `90`
valid range 51 through 100, recommended minimum 90

Cancel   Submit

Figure 7-5 *Edit Anti-Malware and Reputation Settings Screen*

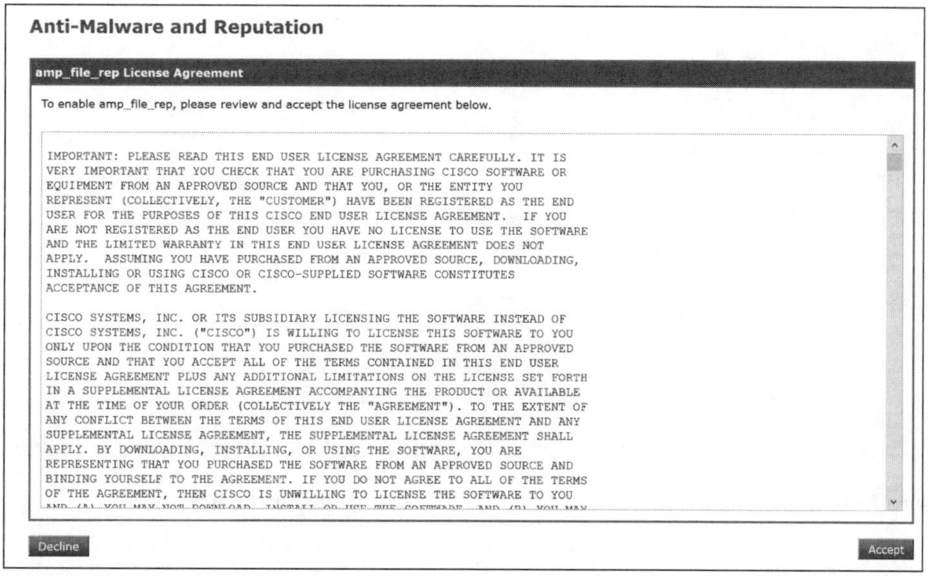

Anti-Malware and Reputation

amp_file_rep License Agreement

To enable amp_file_rep, please review and accept the license agreement below.

IMPORTANT: PLEASE READ THIS END USER LICENSE AGREEMENT CAREFULLY. IT IS
VERY IMPORTANT THAT YOU CHECK THAT YOU ARE PURCHASING CISCO SOFTWARE OR
EQUIPMENT FROM AN APPROVED SOURCE AND THAT YOU, OR THE ENTITY YOU
REPRESENT (COLLECTIVELY, THE "CUSTOMER") HAVE BEEN REGISTERED AS THE END
USER FOR THE PURPOSES OF THIS CISCO END USER LICENSE AGREEMENT. IF YOU
ARE NOT REGISTERED AS THE END USER YOU HAVE NO LICENSE TO USE THE SOFTWARE
AND THE LIMITED WARRANTY IN THIS END USER LICENSE AGREEMENT DOES NOT
APPLY. ASSUMING YOU HAVE PURCHASED FROM AN APPROVED SOURCE, DOWNLOADING,
INSTALLING OR USING CISCO OR CISCO-SUPPLIED SOFTWARE CONSTITUTES
ACCEPTANCE OF THIS AGREEMENT.

CISCO SYSTEMS, INC. OR ITS SUBSIDIARY LICENSING THE SOFTWARE INSTEAD OF
CISCO SYSTEMS, INC. ("CISCO") IS WILLING TO LICENSE THIS SOFTWARE TO YOU
ONLY UPON THE CONDITION THAT YOU PURCHASED THE SOFTWARE FROM AN APPROVED
SOURCE AND THAT YOU ACCEPT ALL OF THE TERMS CONTAINED IN THIS END USER
LICENSE AGREEMENT PLUS ANY ADDITIONAL LIMITATIONS ON THE LICENSE SET FORTH
IN A SUPPLEMENTAL LICENSE AGREEMENT ACCOMPANYING THE PRODUCT OR AVAILABLE
AT THE TIME OF YOUR ORDER (COLLECTIVELY THE "AGREEMENT"). TO THE EXTENT OF
ANY CONFLICT BETWEEN THE TERMS OF THIS END USER LICENSE AGREEMENT AND ANY
SUPPLEMENTAL LICENSE AGREEMENT, THE SUPPLEMENTAL LICENSE AGREEMENT SHALL
APPLY. BY DOWNLOADING, INSTALLING, OR USING THE SOFTWARE, YOU ARE
REPRESENTING THAT YOU PURCHASED THE SOFTWARE FROM AN APPROVED SOURCE AND
BINDING YOURSELF TO THE AGREEMENT. IF YOU DO NOT AGREE TO ALL OF THE TERMS
OF THE AGREEMENT, THEN CISCO IS UNWILLING TO LICENSE THE SOFTWARE TO YOU

Decline   Accept

Figure 7-6 *Accepting the License Agreement*

After you accept to the license agreement, the GUI redirects you back to the main Anti-Malware and Reputation screen. You need to click **Edit Global Settings** again to enable the file analysis service.

When you enable the file analysis service, the GUI asks you to agree to the license for that service, and after you click **Accept**, you are redirected to the main Anti-Malware and Reputation screen again. You must click **Edit Global Settings** one more time if you want to change the file types that will be analyzed.

There is also an area for more advanced configuration, such as changing the cloud server to use for file reputation and setting the cloud (public or private) to which to send the file for analysis. You also configure the reputation threshold here; it defaults to whatever threshold is being conveyed by the cloud. Normally, you leave these settings at their defaults.

Figure 7-7 shows the final file reputation and file analysis settings for the WSA.

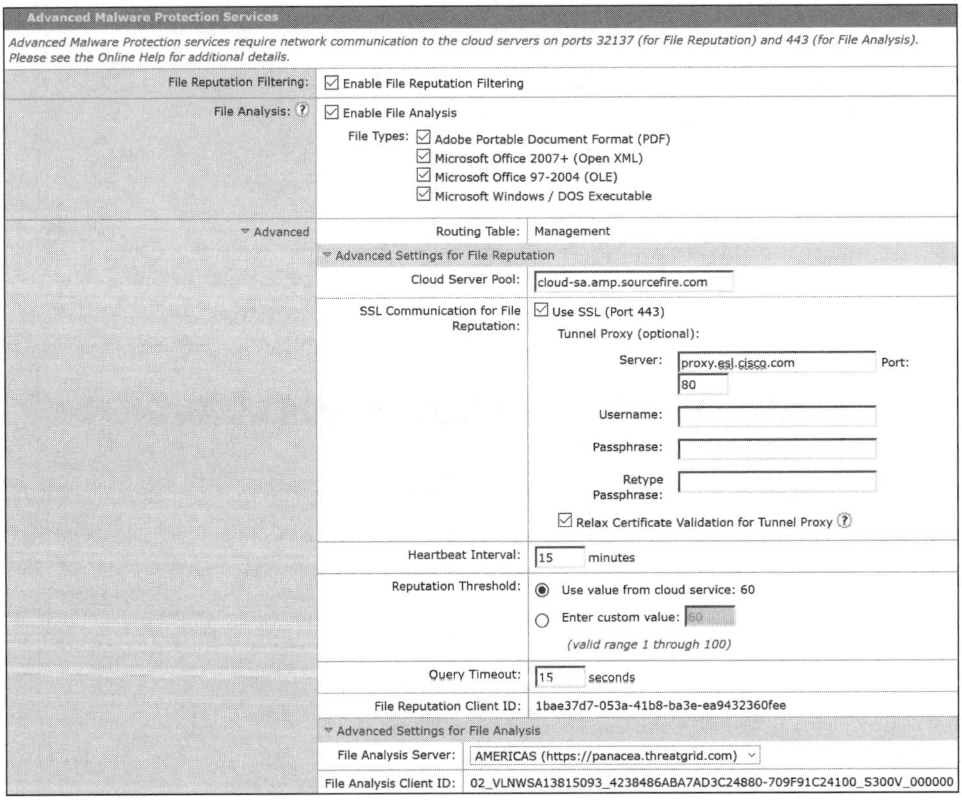

Figure 7-7 *Final File Reputation and File Analysis Settings for the WSA*

Configuring the Email Security Appliance (ESA) for AMP

Just like the WSA, the ESA has two feature keys: file reputation and file analysis. Figure 7-8 shows the feature keys for a Cisco ESA and points out the file reputation and file analysis feature keys, as well as the menu item for configuring AMP.

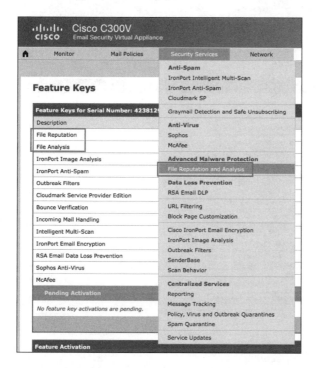

Figure 7-8   *ESA Feature Keys and Menu*

The ESA must have the capability to reach the AMP cloud. As you saw in Figure 7-8, you configure the AMP cloud settings under **Security Services > File Reputation and Analysis**. Initially, the service is disabled, as shown in Figure 7-9.

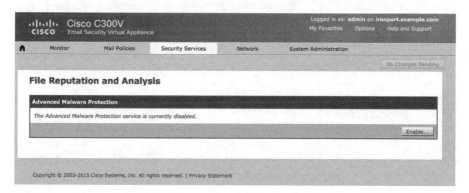

Figure 7-9   *Security Services > File Reputation and Analysis*

Configuring file reputation and analysis requires clicking the **Enable** button shown in Figure 7-9. The GUI then prompts you to accept the license agreement, as shown in Figure 7-10.

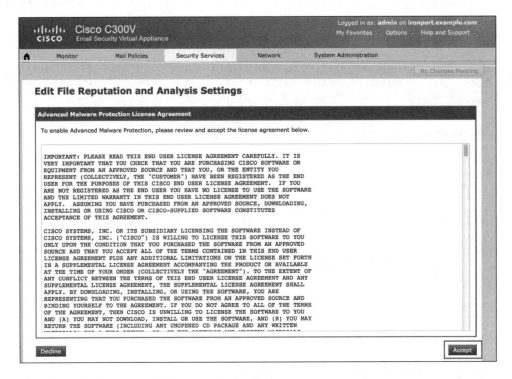

Figure 7-10 *Accepting the License Agreement*

After you accept the license agreement, the AMP service is enabled for both file reputation and file analysis, as shown in Figure 7-11.

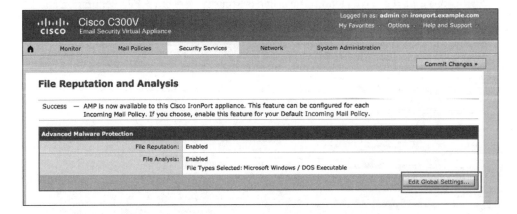

Figure 7-11 *AMP Services Enabled*

To configure the enabled services, click **Edit Global Settings,** and all the settings for AMP are displayed, as shown in Figure 7-12.

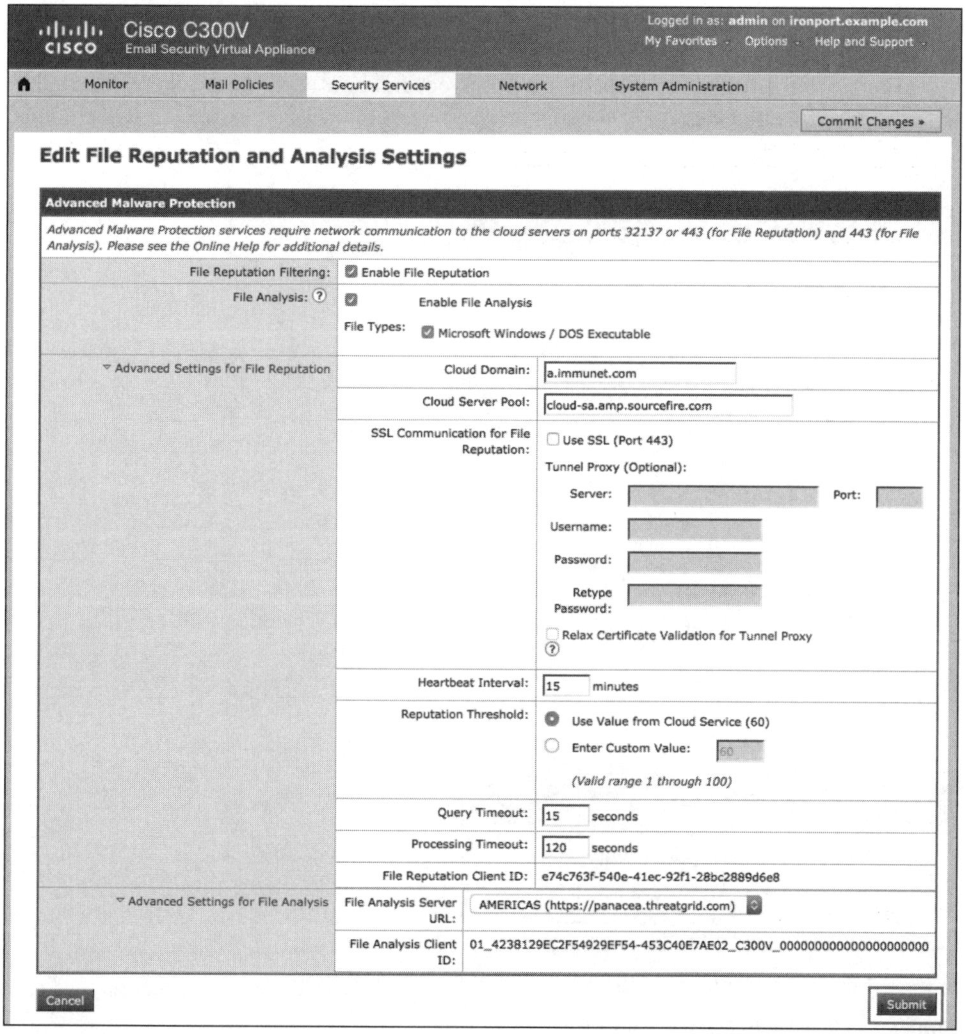

Figure 7-12   *AMP Settings*

There is also an area for more advanced configuration, such as changing the cloud server to use for file reputation and setting the cloud (public or private) to which to send the file for analysis. If AMP must go through an upstream proxy (another proxy server between the ESA and the AMP cloud), you configure this here as well. You also configure the reputation threshold here; it defaults to whatever threshold is being conveyed by the cloud. Normally, you would leave these settings at their defaults.

As with all other configuration changes with AMP for Content Security appliances, you must click **Commit Changes** for the configuration to take effect.

AMP Reports

A number of reports show AMP-related activity. Figure 7-13 shows an example of an AMP report from ESA. Summaries are in the charts at the top, while the files identified as threats are listed at the bottom. You can see in the report the file hashes that were matched, the actual name of the threat observed, and how many threats were detected, monitored, or blocked.

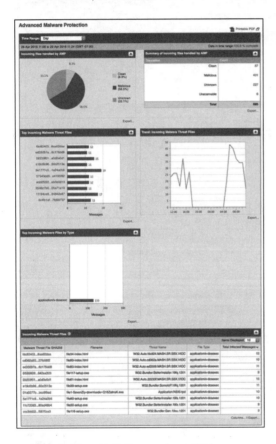

Figure 7-13   *AMP Report from ESA*

Figure 7-14 shows an example of an AMP report from WSA. This report is called the File Analysis report, and it allows you to search for a specific file hash at the top, shows the latest analysis in the middle, and shows any pending files at the bottom.

To determine whether a file was successfully sent to the cloud, you can use the File Analysis report or the **tail** CLI command. If you use **tail**, you can choose option 2 for **amp_logs**, as shown in Figure 7-15.

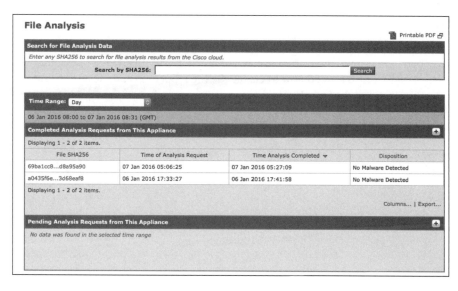

Figure 7-14 *AMP Report from WSA*

Figure 7-15 *tail amp_logs*

Summary

This chapter examines how AMP for Content Security fits into the overall AMP architecture. You have learned the feature names and how to verify that feature keys are installed. You have also learned how to enable the file reputation and file analysis services on the WSA and the ESA. In addition, you have seen a few of the reports that are available in AMP for Content Security.

Chapter 8

Cisco AMP for Endpoints

In this chapter, you will learn the following:

- Introduction to Cisco AMP for Endpoints

- Custom detections

- Application control

- AMP for Windows

- AMP for Mac

- AMP for Linux

- AMP for Android

- Installing all flavors of AMP for Endpoints

- Using the AMP cloud console

This chapter provides an overview of Cisco Advanced Malware Protection (AMP) for Endpoints. This chapter looks at where AMP for Endpoints fits into the AMP architecture. You'll also learn about the types of AMP for Endpoints connectors, how to create policies for them, and how to install them. The chapter describes how to use the AMP cloud console, and you will even get a look at AMP detecting and remediating malware.

After Cisco acquired SourceFire, the solution previously known as FireAMP was renamed AMP for Endpoints. Throughout the console interface and even within the connectors, you will see a confusing mix of terminology, and in a number of place, you will still see the term FireAMP. The figures in this chapter even show some instances of this. Cisco is updating its products all the time, though, so expect that the user interface will be updated at some point.

Introduction to AMP for Endpoints

Throughout this book, you have been learning about the various Cisco next-generation security products and technologies. You have learned that security technologies and processes should not just focus on detection but should also provide the capability to mitigate the impact of an attack. Organizations must maintain visibility and control across the extended network during the full attack continuum:

■ Before an attack takes place

■ During an active attack

■ After an attacker starts to damage systems or steal information

In Chapter 5, "Introduction to and Architecture of Cisco AMP," you learned all about the components that make up the AMP architecture and the AMP cloud. You learned that the AMP solution enables malware detection, blocking, continuous analysis, and retrospective views with the following features:

■ **File reputation:** AMP allows you to analyze files inline and block or apply policies.

■ **File sandboxing:** AMP allows you to analyze unknown files to understand true file behavior.

■ **File retrospection:** AMP allows you to continue to analyze files for changing threat levels.

Remember that the architecture of AMP can be broken down into three main components: the AMP cloud, AMP client connectors, and intelligence sources. This chapter focuses on the AMP for Endpoints client connector.

Figure 8-1 illustrates the cloud architecture, showing how AMP receives intelligence from many sources and a variety of client connectors.

AMP for Endpoints provides more than just endpoint-level visibility into files. It also provides cloud-based detection of malware, in which the cloud constantly updates itself. This enables very rapid detection of known malware because the cloud resources are used instead of endpoint resources. This architecture has a number of benefits. With the majority of the processing power being performed in the cloud, the endpoint software remains very lightweight. The cloud is able to provide a historical view of malware activity, segmented into two activity types:

■ **File trajectory:** What endpoints have seen the files

■ **Device trajectory:** Actions the files performed on given endpoints

With the data storage and processing in the cloud, the AMP solution is able to provide powerful and detailed reporting, as well as provide very robust management.

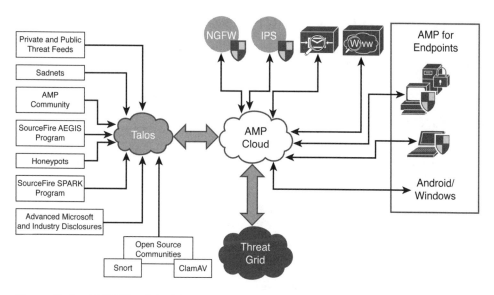

Figure 8-1 *AMP Cloud Architecture*

The AMP for Endpoints agent is also able to take action. For example, it can block malicious network connections based on custom IP blacklists or intelligent dynamic lists of malicious IP addresses.

What Is AMP for Endpoints?

AMP for Endpoints is the connector that resides on—you guessed it—endpoints. It resides on Windows, Mac, Linux, and Android endpoints. Unlike traditional endpoint protection software that uses a local database of signatures to match a known bad piece of software or a bad file, AMP for Endpoints remains lightweight, sending a hash to the cloud and allowing the cloud to make intelligent decisions and return the verdicts Clean, Malware, and Unknown.

Figure 8-2 illustrates the AMP for Endpoints architecture.

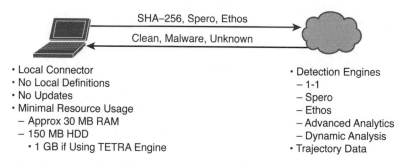

• Local Connector
• No Local Definitions
• No Updates
• Minimal Resource Usage
  – Approx 30 MB RAM
  – 150 MB HDD
    • 1 GB if Using TETRA Engine

• Detection Engines
  – 1-1
  – Spero
  – Ethos
  – Advanced Analytics
  – Dynamic Analysis
• Trajectory Data

Figure 8-2 *AMP for Endpoints Architecture*

Connections to the AMP Cloud

AMP for Endpoints connectors must be able to reach the AMP cloud. That means the agents may have to be able to go through firewalls and proxy servers to reach the Internet.

Firewalls, Destinations, and Ports, Oh My!

If traversing a firewall and/or web proxy to reach the Internet, those products must allow connectivity from the AMP connector to the following servers over HTTPS (TCP 443):

- **Event Server:** Enterprise-event.amp.sourcefire.com (for US), enterprise-event.eu.amp.sourcefire.com (for Europe)

- **Management Server:** Enterprise-mgmt.amp.sourcefire.com (for US), enterprise-mgmt.eu.amp.sourcefire.com (for Europe)

- **Policy Server:** policy.amp.sourcefire.com.s3.amazonaws.com (for US), policy.eu.amp.sourcefire.com.s3.amazonaws.com (for Europe)

- **Error Reporting:** crash.immunet.com (for US), crash.eu.amp.sourcefire.com (for Europe)

- **Endpoint IOC Downloads:** https://endpoint-ioc-prod-us.s3.amazonaws.com (for US), https://endpoint-ioc-prod-eu.s3.amazonaws.com (for Europe)

To allow a connector to communicate with Cisco cloud servers for file and network disposition lookups, a firewall must allow the clients to connect to the following server over TCP 443 by default or TCP 32137:

- **Cloud Host:** cloud-ec.amp.sourcefire.com (for US), cloud-ec.eu.amp.sourcefire.com (for Europe)

In order to upload files for analysis, clients must be able to access the following server over TCP 80:

- **Submission Server:** submit.amp.sourcefire.com (for US), submit.eu.amp.sourcefire.com (for Europe)

If you have TETRA enabled on any of your AMP Connectors, you must allow access to the following server over TCP 80 for signature updates:

- **Update Server:** update.immunet.com (for both US and Europe)

Outbreak Control

With a solution as powerful and extensive as AMP for Endpoints, it is difficult to determine where to start describing how to configure and use the system; however, it makes logical sense to begin with Outbreak Control because the objects you create within Outbreak Control are key aspects of endpoint policies.

Outbreak Control allows you to create lists that customize AMP for Endpoints to your organization's needs. You can view the main lists from the AMP cloud console by clicking the **Outbreak Control** menu, which offers options in the following categories: Custom Detections, Application Control, Network, and Endpoint IOC (indicators of compromise), as shown in Figure 8-3.

Figure 8-3 *Outbreak Control Menu*

Custom Detections

You can think of custom detections as a blacklist. You use them to identify files that you want to detect and quarantine. When a custom detection is defined, not only do endpoints quarantine matching files when they see them, but any AMP for Endpoints agents that have seen the file before the custom detection was created can also quarantine the file through retrospection, also known as cloud recall.

Simple custom detection allows you to add file signatures for files, while the advanced custom detections are more like traditional antivirus signatures.

Simple Custom Detections

Creating a simple custom detection is similar to adding new entries to a blacklist. You define one or more files that you are trying to quarantine by building a list of SHA-256 hashes. If you already have the SHA-256 hash of a file, you can paste that hash directly into the UI, or you can upload files directly and allow the cloud to create the SHA-256 hash for you.

To create a simple custom detection, navigate to **Outbreak Control > Custom Detections > Simple**, and the list of all existing simple custom detections appears, as shown in Figure 8-4. To add a new one, you must type it in the Name box and click **Save**, as shown in Figure 8-4. The detection is then added to the list, as shown in Figure 8-5, and automatically edited—with the contents displayed on the right side.

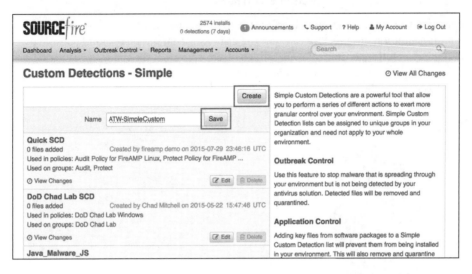

Figure 8-4   *Custom Detections—Simple*

Figure 8-5   *Detection Added and Contents on the Right Side*

If you already have the SHA-256 hash of a file, simply paste it in, add a note, and click Save; otherwise, you can upload a file, add a note, and click Upload, as shown in Figure 8-5. Once the file is uploaded, the hash is created and shown on the bottom-right side, as shown in Figure 8-6. You must click **Save**, or the hash will not be stored as part of your simple custom detection.

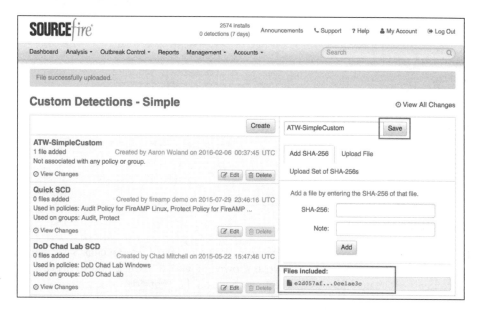

Figure 8-6 *Saving a Simple Custom Detection*

Advanced Custom Detections

Simple custom detections just look for the SHA-256 hash of a file. Advanced custom detections offer many more signature types to the detection, based on ClamAV signatures, including the following:

- File body-based signatures

- MD5 signatures

- MD5, PE section–based signatures

- An extended signature format (with wildcards, regular expressions, and offsets)

- Logical signatures

- Icon signatures

To create an advanced custom detection, navigate to **Outbreak Control > Custom Detections > Advanced**, and the list of all existing advanced custom detections appears, as shown in Figure 8-7.

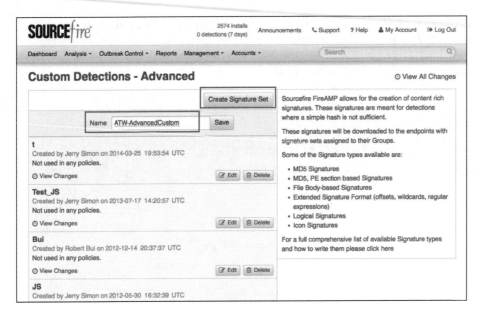

Figure 8-7   *Custom Detections—Advanced*

To add a new custom detection, you must type it in the **Name** box and click **Save**, as shown in Figure 8-7, to add it to the list, as shown in Figure 8-8. Click **Edit** to display the contents of the new advanced detection object on the right side.

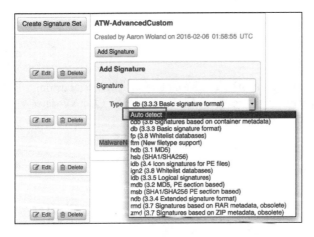

Figure 8-8   *Adding an Advanced Custom Detection*

As shown in Figure 8-8, the ClamAV signature types can be auto-detected, or you can manually select them from the drop-down list. In Figure 8-9, the ClamAV signature string 5d47b318b55c130ef30702026605ed6b:35411:Exploit.PDF-28520 was pasted in with a type Auto Detect, and the **Create** button was clicked. You can see there that the UI correctly converted it to hdb: Exploit.PDF-28520.UNOFFICIAL.

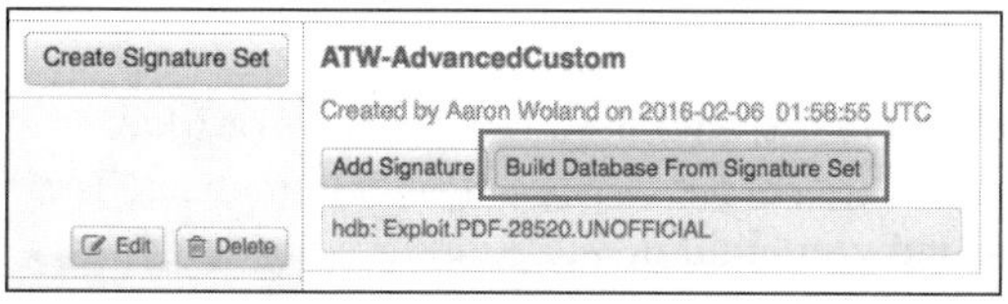

Figure 8-9 *Adding a Signature*

Next, you click the **Build Database From Signature Set**, and a success message is displayed, showing the successful creation of the advanced custom detection signature set, as shown in Figure 8-10.

Figure 8-10 *Successfully Built Advanced Detection*

A View Changes link is visible with every custom detection, both simple and advanced. The AMP cloud maintains an audit log for each of the detection lists, and you can view it by clicking that link. Figure 8-11 shows an example of the audit log.

Figure 8-11 *Audit Log for an Advanced Custom Detection*

Android Custom Detections

Android detections are defined separately from the ones used by Windows or Mac. These detections provide granular control over Android devices in an environment. The detections look for specific applications, and you build them by either uploading the app's .apk file or selecting that file from the AMP console's inventory list.

You can choose to use Android custom detections for two main functions: outbreak control and application control.

When using an Android custom detection for outbreak control, you are using the detection to stop malware that is spreading through mobile devices in the organization. When a malicious app is detected, the user of the device is notified and prompted to uninstall it.

You don't have to use these detections just for malware, but you can also use them to stop applications that you don't want installed on devices in your organization. This is what SourceFire refers to as *application control*. Simply add apps to an Android custom detection list that you don't want installed, and APM notifies the user of the unwanted application and prompts the user to uninstall it, just as if it were a malicious app.

To create an Android custom detection, navigate to **Outbreak Control > Custom Detections > Android** to display the list of all existing Android custom detections, if any exist. Click **Create** to add a new one, and give it a name, as shown in Figure 8-12. Then click **Save**.

Once the new Android detection is created, you click **Edit** to add the Android apps that you wish to detect as either malware or unwanted.

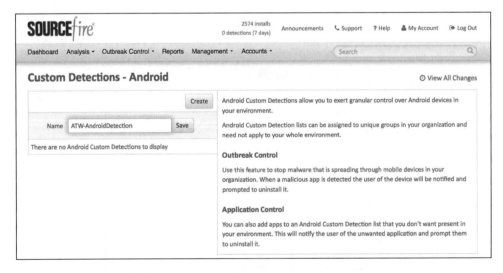

Figure 8-12   *Custom Detections—Android*

IP Blacklists and Whitelists

You can use outbreak control IP lists in conjunction with device flow correlation (DFC) detections. DFC allows you to flag or even block suspicious network activity. You can use policies to specify the behavior of AMP for Endpoints when a suspicious connection is detected and also to specify whether the connector should use addresses in the Cisco intelligence feed, the custom IP lists you create yourself, or a combination of both.

You use an IP whitelist to define IPv4 addresses that should not be blocked or flagged by DFC. AMP bypasses or ignores the intelligence feeds as they relate to the IPv4 addresses in the whitelist.

You use IP blacklists to create DFC detections. Traffic that matches entries in the blacklist are flagged or blocked, as the DFC rule dictates.

To create an IP list, navigate to Outbreak Control > Network > IP Blacklists & Whitelists, as shown in Figure 8-13.

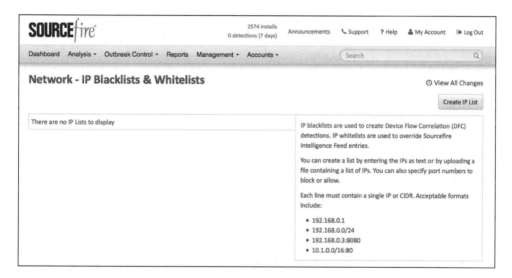

Figure 8-13   *Network—IP Blacklists & Whitelists*

Here you click **Create IP List** to start a new IP list, and you're brought to the **New IP List** configuration screen, where you can either create an IP list by typing the IPv4 addresses in classless interdomain routing (CIDR) notation or by uploading a file that contains a list of IPs. You can also specify port numbers to block or allow. After the list is created, you can edit it only by downloading the resulting file and uploading it back to the AMP console. Figure 8-14 shows the New IP List screen, with a mixture of entries entered as text.

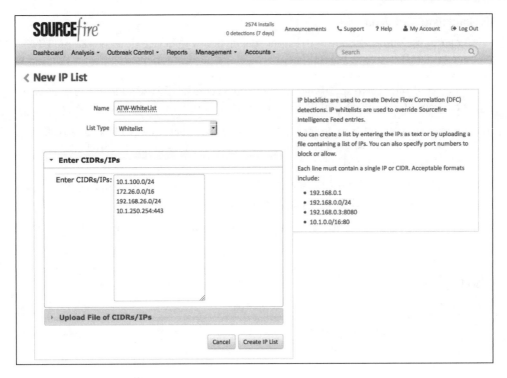

Figure 8-14   *New IP List Screen*

You name the list, choose whether it is a whitelist or a blacklist, and enter a series of IPv4 addresses, one line at a time. Each line must contain a single IP or CIDR. Acceptable formats include the following:

- **10.1.100.0/24**: A standard network range designated by network-/mask-length CIDR notation

- **192.168.26.26**: A single IPv4 address

- **10.1.250.254:443**: A single IPv4 address with a port specified (UDP and TCP)

- **10.250.1.1/16:8443**: A CIDR-notated network range with a port specified (UDP and TCP)

You click **Create IP List** to create the text file in the cloud console, and your new IP list is shown on the screen. If you click **Edit**, you can change the name of the IP list. To update the contents of the list, you must click **Download** and then delete the list. Then you create a new list with the same name and upload the modified file. An IP list can contain up to 100,000 lines or be a maximum of 2 MB in size.

As for custom detections, the AMP console maintains an audit trail for IP lists that you can view by clicking **View Changes**.

Application Control

Like files, applications can be detected, blocked, and whitelisted. As with the other files, AMP does not look for the name of the application but the SHA-256 hash.

To create a new application control list for blocking an application, navigate to **Outbreak Control > Application Control > Blocking**. One thing you must credit the SourceFire AMP team with is that it sure understands the concept of consistency in GUIs. This GUI works just like so many other areas of the interface. If any existing blocking lists exist, they are displayed here, as shown in Figure 8-15. As you would expect, to create a new list, you click **Create**. You must name the list and click **Save** before you can add any applications to the blocking list.

Figure 8-15   *Outbreak Control > Application Control > Blocking*

Once the list has been created and saved, click **Edit** to add any applications. If you already have the SHA-256 hash, add it. Otherwise, you can upload one application at a time and have the AMP cloud console calculate the hash for you, as long as the file is not larger than the 20MB limit. You can also upload an existing list. Figure 8-16 shows a blocking list with an existing application hash shown at the bottom of the right-hand column, while another file is being uploaded for hash calculation.

Application whitelists work the same way. Navigate to **Outbreak Control > Application Control > Whitelisting** to see a list of any existing whitelists. Click **Create** to add a new one, provide it a name, and click Save, as shown in Figure 8-17.

Figure 8-16 *Adding Application Hashes to the Blocking List*

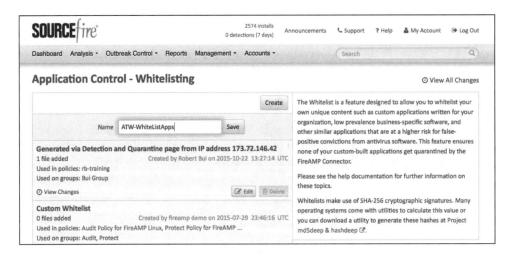

Figure 8-17 *Outbreak Control > Application Control > Whitelisting*

Once the list has been created and saved, click **Edit** to add any applications. If you already have the SHA-256 hash, add it. Otherwise, you can upload one application at a time and have the AMP cloud console calculate the hash for you, as long as the file is not larger than the 20 MB limit. You can also upload an existing list. Figure 8-18 shows a whitelist with an existing application in the list (SafeGuardPDFViewer.exe).

Don't forget to click **Save** after adding the hash to the list.

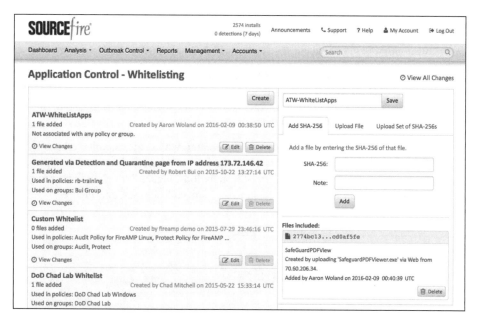

Figure 8-18 *Adding Application Hashes to a Whitelist*

Exclusion Sets

There is one more object that you should try to create before you build your policies, and that is an exclusion set. An exclusion set is a list of directories, file extensions, or even threat names that you do not want the AMP agent to scan and definitely not to convict as malware.

You can use an exclusion set to resolve conflicts with other security products or mitigate performance issues by excluding directories that contain large files that are frequently written to, like databases. If you are running an antivirus product on computers with the AMP for Endpoints connector, you should exclude the location where that product is installed.

It's important to remember that any files stored in a location that has been added to an exclusion set will not be subjected to application blocking, simple custom detections, or advanced custom detections.

These are the available exclusion types:

- **Threat:** This type excludes specific detections by threat name.

- **Extension:** This type excludes files with a specific extension.

- **Wildcard:** This type excludes files or paths using wildcards for filenames, extensions, or paths.

- **Path:** This type excludes files in a given path.

For Windows, path exclusions may use constant special ID lists (CSIDL), which are Microsoft given names for common file paths. For more on CSIDL, see https://msdn .microsoft.com/en-us/library/windows/desktop/bb762494%28v=vs.85%29.aspx.

To create a new exclusion set, navigate to **Management > Exclusions**. Here you see a list of any existing exclusions and can create new ones. Click **Create Exclusion Set**, provide a name, and click **Save**. The contents of the exclusion set are automatically listed on the right side.

As shown in Figure 8-19, new exclusion sets are created with some default exclusions. Many of these exclusions are specific to the default installation paths of antivirus products and designed to cover a large variety of installations. Figure 8-19 shows an example of a Windows exclusion set. Figure 8-20 shows a Mac exclusion set, and Figure 8-21 shows a Linux exclusion set.

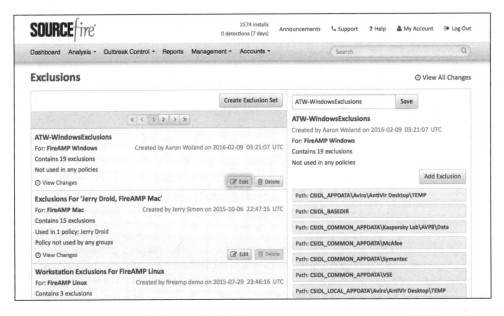

Figure 8-19 *Creating a Windows Exclusion Set*

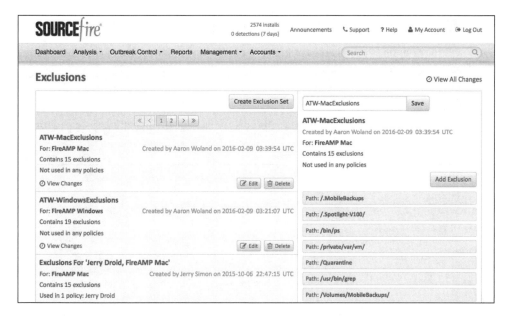

Figure 8-20   *Creating a Mac Exclusion Set*

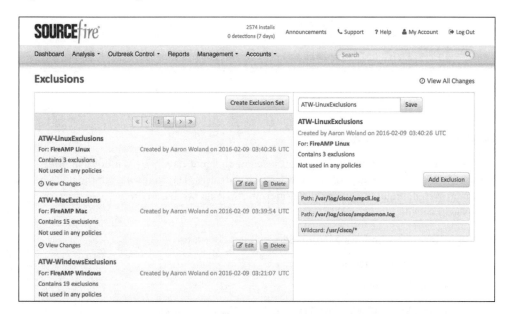

Figure 8-21   *Creating a Linux Exclusion Set*

The Many Faces of AMP for Endpoints

AMP for Endpoints is available for multiple platforms: Windows, Android, Mac, and Linux. You can see the available connectors from the cloud console by navigating to **Management > Download Connector.** Here you see the types of endpoints, as shown in Figure 8-22.

The following sections go through the options for each of the operating systems shown in Figure 8-22.

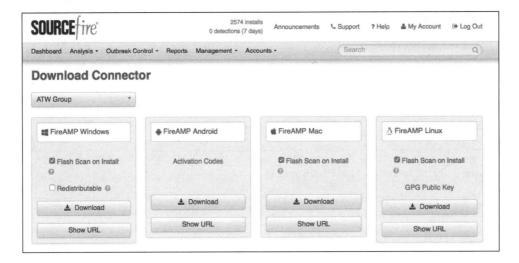

Figure 8-22   *AMP Connector Types*

AMP for Windows

The Windows AMP connector supports many different flavors of Windows in both 32-bit and 64-bit variants of those Windows platforms. The following are the minimum system requirements for the Windows AMP agents, based on the operating system version:

- **Microsoft Windows XP with Service Pack 3 or later:**

  - 500 MHz or faster processor

  - 256 MB RAM

  - 150 MB available hard disk space for cloud-only mode

  - 1 GB available hard disk space for TETRA

- **Microsoft Windows Vista with Service Pack 2 or later:**
    - 1 GHz or faster processor
    - 512 MB RAM
    - 150 MB available hard disk space for cloud-only mode
    - 1 GB available hard disk space for TETRA
- **Microsoft Windows 7:**
    - 1 GHz or faster processor
    - 1 GB RAM
    - 150 MB available hard disk space for cloud-only mode
    - 1 GB available hard disk space for TETRA
- **Microsoft Windows 8 and 8.1 (requires AMP Connector 3.1.4 or later):**
    - 1 GHz or faster processor
    - 512 MB RAM
    - 150 MB available hard disk space for cloud-only mode
    - 1 GB available hard disk space for TETRA
- **Microsoft Windows 10 (requires AMP Connector 4.3.0 or later):**
    - 1 GHz or faster processor
    - 1 GB RAM (32-bit) or 2 GB RAM (64-bit)
    - 150 MB available hard disk space for cloud-only mode
    - 1 GB available hard disk space for TETRA
- **Microsoft Windows Server 2003:**
    - 1 GHz or faster processor
    - 512 MB RAM
    - 150 MB available hard disk space for cloud-only mode
    - 1 GB available hard disk space for TETRA
- **Microsoft Windows Server 2008:**
    - 2 GHz or faster processor
    - 2 GB RAM
    - 150 MB available hard disk space for cloud-only mode
    - 1 GB available hard disk space for TETRA

■ **Microsoft Windows Server 2012 (requires AMP Connector 3.1.9 or later):**

   ■ 2 GHz or faster processor

   ■ 2 GB RAM

   ■ 150 MB available hard disk space for cloud-only mode

   ■ 1 GB available hard disk space for TETRA

Windows Policies

There are many policy options for Windows. From the AMP cloud console, navigate to **Management > Policies > Windows**, where you can see existing AMP policies for Windows as well as create new ones (see Figure 8-23).

Figure 8-23 *AMP Windows Policies*

Click **Create Policy** and then select **FireAMP Windows** from the drop-down as shown in Figure 8-24, and click **Create Policy**.

Figure 8-24 *Selecting the Connector OS*

In the New Policy Window, select the custom detections, app blocking, whitelists, and exclusions created earlier, as shown in Figure 8-25. When they are all selected, click **Create Policy** to save the policy.

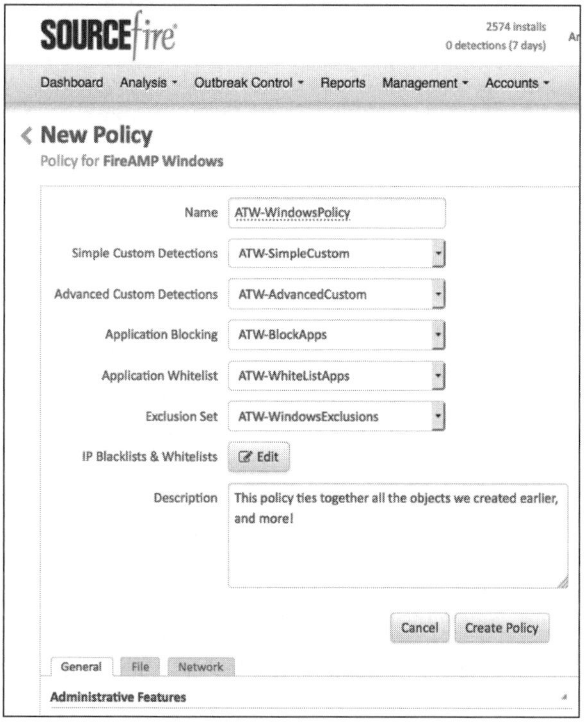

Figure 8-25 *Creating a Windows Policy*

Click **Edit** for the newly created Windows policy and scroll to the bottom. This is where a lot of the AMP agent configuration and customization takes place. There are three tabs for AMP connector configurations: General, File, and Network.

General Tab

The General tab for a Windows policy has the basic settings for the AMP for Endpoints connector, such as proxy settings and update schedules. There are five component areas within the General tab: Administrative Features, Connector Identity Persistence, Client User Interface, Proxy Settings, and Product Updates. Each of these areas is explained in the sections that follow. One very nice UI feature here is that a blue informational icon appears whenever a default setting is changed, as shown in Figure 8-26.

Figure 8-26   *The Windows Policy General Tab*

Administrative Features

As you can see in Figure 8-26, there are nine configurable settings in the Administrative Features section of the General tab:

- **Send User Name in Events:** This relates to the username that has launched the process. This setting is useful for tracking down who was on a system that may be seeing malware.

- **Send Filename and Path Info:** This setting enables the AMP agent to send the filename and path information to the AMP cloud so that they are visible in the Events tab, device trajectory, and file trajectory. Unchecking this option stops this information from being sent.

- **Heartbeat Interval:** This option sets how often the AMP agent should call home to the AMP cloud. During the call home connection, the agent checks whether there are any policy updates, any updates or scans to perform, or any files to restore via cloud recall or by the administrator.

- **Confirm Cloud Recall:** Cloud recall (also known as retrospection) can find every connector that has seen a specific file and attempt to quarantine it when the connector calls home on its heartbeat interval. This check box adds a required action for a system admin to confirm before recalling any files.

- **Connector Log Level and Tray Log Level:** This option allows you to change the default log level to debug, when directed by Cisco Technical Assistance Center (TAC).

- **Connector Protection:** Selecting this check box requires a password for stopping the AMP service or the uninstalling the AMP agent.

- **Connector Protection Password:** This option sets the password for the connection protection.

- **Automated Crash Dump Uploads:** When this option is enabled, the connector automatically sends crash dumps to Cisco for analysis in the event of connector crashes.

Connector Identity Persistence

Connector Identity Persistence is an odd section to show in the interface. It is actually not available unless enabled by TAC. Identity persistence is used in virtual environments when systems are cloned or reimaged. This setting maintains a consistent event log by binding a connector to a MAC address or hostname so that a new event log is not created every time a new virtual session is started or a computer is reimaged. You can choose to apply this setting with granularity across different policies or across your entire organization. There are five configuration options for identity persistence, as shown in Figure 8-27:

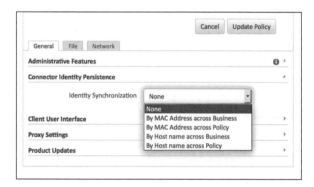

Figure 8-27 *Connector Identity Persistence*

- **None:** Connector logs are not synchronized with new connector installs under any circumstance. This is the default setting unless changed by support.

- **By MAC Address across Business:** New connectors look for the most recent connector that has the same MAC address to synchronize with across all policies in the business that have Identity Synchronization set to a value other than None.

- **By MAC Address across Policy:** New connectors look for the most recent connector that has the same MAC address to synchronize with within the same policy.

- **By Hostname across Business:** New connectors look for the most recent connector that has the same hostname to synchronize with across all policies in the business that have Identity Synchronization set to a value other than None.

- **By Host name across Policy:** New connectors look for the most recent connector that has the same hostname to synchronize with within the same policy.

Client User Interface

The Client User Interface section allows you to configure what the end user sees on the Windows system. Many organizations prefer to show the agent icon in the system tray, so it is obvious that the agent is running, but they often choose to hide all notifications so that users are not bothered by the connector. There are six different options, as shown in Figure 8-28:

- **Start Client User Interface:** Simply put, this option hides the user interface or shows it. The agent is running either way. This setting offers you the option of keeping it out of the system tray. When you change this option, it takes effect at the next agent restart.

- **Cloud Notifications:** This option controls whether you see those fun balloon pop-ups from the agent icon in the Windows system tray. When this option is selected, a pop-up appears when the agent is successfully connected to the cloud, and it displays the number of users and detections registered to the cloud.

- **Verbose Notifications:** When this option is enabled, the end user is completely harassed by a series of text boxes that pop up from the Windows system tray icon, telling about nearly every file that traverses the AMP connector. *Leave this option unselected* unless you are in the process of active troubleshooting or you just want to punish your end users.

Figure 8-28   *Client User Interface*

- **Hide Cataloging Notifications:** This option relates to endpoint IOC scans and hides the user notification about cataloging. Note that when you select this option, you hide a disk-intensive process of cataloging artifacts from the system to be used in comparisons with IOCs.

- **Hide File Notifications:** Selecting this option keeps malicious file notifications from being displayed when a file is convicted or quarantined by the AMP agent.

- **Hide Network Notifications:** Selecting this option causes messages to not display when a malicious network connection is detected or blocked by AMP.

It is highly recommended that you keep any interactivity with the end user to an absolute minimum. End users often get frustrated and annoyed when burdened by notifications that they don't understand or don't care to understand.

Proxy Settings

In today's world of mobile workstations, configuring a hard-coded proxy server may not always be the best-practices configuration. However, with the wonderful cloud-based technologies available, such as the Cisco Cloud Web Security solution (blatant plug), you may wish to configure the AMP agent to always use that cloud proxy solution. Proxy servers and some of the complications they bring are covered in more detail later in this chapter, but in the meantime, let's take a look at the Proxy Settings section in the General tab, as displayed in Figure 8-29.

Figure 8-29 *Proxy Settings*

By populating the Proxy Settings sections of the General tab, you can configure a hard-coded proxy server for the agents that receive this policy. As you can see in Figure 8-29, basic and NT LAN Manager (NTLM) authentications are both supported, as are straight HTTP proxy and Secure Sockets (SOCKS) proxy. If you use NTLM, be sure to use the *DOMAIN\USER* notation for the account.

Product Updates

The policy that is applied to the AMP connector determines whether and when to update to a newer version. You select the version from the Product Version drop-down, choose a time window for the updates to occur, and tell the agent how often to check for updates. Figure 8-30 shows the Product Updates settings.

Figure 8-30 *Product Updates*

A reboot is required for the running AMP agent to reflect an upgrade. The Product Updates section lets you specify whether to not reboot the system, to ask the user if it's okay to proceed with a reboot, or to simply reboot the system, as shown in Figure 8-30.

File Tab

You use the File tab to configure the settings and behavior of file scanning in the AMP for Endpoints agent. For example, you can specify which engines to use, set up scheduled scans, and specify cache settings. There are six component areas of the File tab: Modes, Cache Settings, Engines, Ethos, Cloud Policy, and Scheduled Scans. Figure 8-31 shows the File tab with the Modes component area expanded.

Figure 8-31 *File Tab*

Modes

The Modes section of the File tab allows you to specify how the AMP connector should behave during file moves or copies as well as how it should behave when a file is executed. These are the available options in the Modes section:

- **Monitor File Copies and Moves:** This option is either selected or not. It determines whether AMP should care about files when they are moved or copied within or off the system.

- **File Conviction Mode:** This option is set to either Audit or Quarantine. In other words, is this a monitor-only deployment, or should the AMP agent take action?

- **Monitor Process Execution:** This option is set to either on or off. This setting determines whether AMP should care about executable files when they are run.

- **On Execute Mode:** This option is set to either Passive or Active. In other words, should the file lookup happen before the executable is allowed to run, or should they occur in parallel? When the endpoint has another antivirus product installed, it is best to leave this set to Passive to avoid performance issues.

- **Maximum Scan File Size:** Any file larger than this setting will not be scanned by AMP.

- **Maximum Archive Scan File Size:** Any archive file (ZIP, TAR, etc.) larger than this setting will not be scanned by AMP.

Cache Settings

As you know, the AMP connector focuses on the disposition that the AMP cloud assigns to the SHA-256 hash of a file. The hash and the disposition are stored in a local cache for better performance and to reduce redundant lookups of the same hash value. The settings in the Cache Settings section of the File tab determine how long the hashes should remain in the cache. As Figure 8-32 shows, there are four different cache settings, all of which are configured as the number of seconds before checking those file hashes again:

- **Malicious Cache TTL:** This setting specifies how long to hold on to the disposition of a file hash when it has been deemed malicious. The default is 1 hour.

- **Clean Cache TTL:** This setting specifies how long to hold on to the information when a file has been assigned a clean disposition. The default is 7 days.

- **Unknown Cache TTL:** This setting specifies how long to store the disposition of files that receive an Unknown disposition. The default is 1 hour.

- **Application Blocking TTL:** This setting specifies how long an outbreak control blocking list is cached. The default is 1 hour.

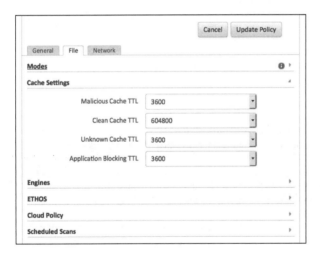

Figure 8-32   *Cache Settings Section*

Engines

As shown in Figure 8-33, the Engines section is used to configure the use of one or all of the three engines:

- **Offline Engine (TETRA):** This setting is configured to be disabled (default) or TETRA, which is a full client-side antivirus solution. Do not enable the use of TETRA if there is an existing antivirus product in place. The default AMP setting is to leave TETRA disabled, as it changes the nature of the AMP connector from being a very lightweight agent to being a "thicker" software client that consumes more disk space for signature storage and more bandwidth for signature updates. When you enable TETRA, another configuration subsection is displayed, allowing you to choose what file scanning options you wish to enable, as shown in Figure 8-34.

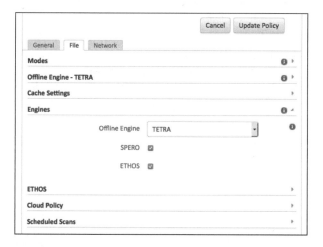

Figure 8-33 *Engines Settings Section*

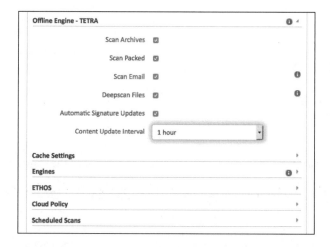

Figure 8-34 *Optional TETRA Settings*

- **Spero:** Spero is a machine learning–based technology that proactively identifies threats that were previously unknown. It uses active heuristics to gather execution attributes, and because the underlying algorithms come up with generic models, they can identify malicious software based on its general appearance rather than basing identity on specific patterns or signatures.

- **Ethos:** Ethos is a "fuzzy fingerprinting" engine that uses static or passive heuristics. Disabling Ethos in this section hides the Ethos menu from the File tab altogether.

Ethos

As just mentioned, Ethos is a "fuzzy fingerprinting" engine that uses static or passive heuristics. Think of it as Cisco's file-grouping engine. It groups families of files together, and when variants of a malware are detected, it marks the Ethos hash as malicious and instantly detects entire families of malware.

Ethos can be a bit resource intensive, and therefore it is enabled only for file move and copy by default, as shown in Figure 8-35. When scanning on copy or move, AMP allows the copy or move action to finish and then queues another thread to calculate the Ethos for a file. That same passive performance luxury is not available for the On Execute or On Scan settings.

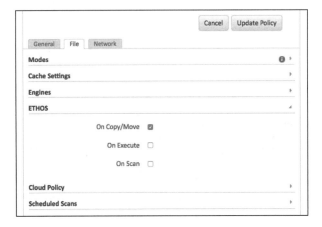

Figure 8-35   *Ethos Settings Section*

Cloud Policy

The Cloud Policy settings refer to the Ethos and Spero engines. Because both Ethos and Spero are classified as generic engines, you can tune how false-positive-prone an Ethos or Spero hash is. The Cloud Policy section provides up to three configurable thresholds, as shown in Figure 8-36.

Figure 8-36 *Cloud Policy Settings Section*

- **Detection Threshold per Ethos Hash:** When this option is selected, a single Ethos hash can convict a single SHA of unknown disposition a maximum number of times. The default is 10, meaning that Ethos will not convict any SHA-256 seen 10 times in 24 hours by the entire community. If you encounter a situation where the detection threshold has been reached but feel that the detection is not a false positive and want to keep convicting the particular SHA, you should add it to an advanced custom detection list.

- **Detection Threshold per Spero Hash:** This is exactly like the Detection Threshold per Ethos Hash option, except it refers to Spero.

- **Step-Up Enabled:** When this option is selected, additional Spero groupings can be turned on if the network is considered "massively infected." These Spero groupings, or trees, are more false positive prone but do a better job of detecting malware. The definition of "massively infected" is based on the Step-Up threshold setting.

- **Step-Up Threshold:** This option's setting determines whether a connector is "massively infected." The default is 5, meaning that if 5 SHA one-to-one detections are found in 30 seconds, the system is considered "massively infected," and additional Spero trees are enabled for the next 30 seconds.

Scheduled Scans

Scheduled scans are typically deemed unnecessary with AMP for Endpoints. This is because files are being scanned as they are moved, copied, or executed. So to keep the processing low and the performance higher, no scans are scheduled by default. This does not, however, preclude you from configuring some scheduled scans per policy, as shown in Figure 8-37.

Figure 8-37   *Scheduled Scans Settings Section*

Multiple scans can be configured to occur daily, weekly, and/or monthly. Scans can be flash, full, or custom scans, and they can be configured to occur at specific times. A flash scan examines the processes running in memory, along with the files and registry settings associated with those running processes. A full scan examines the processes running in memory, their associated registry settings, and all the files on the entire disk. A custom scan is configured to look at files in a specific path. Figure 8-38 shows an example of the configuration window that pops up when you add a scheduled scan.

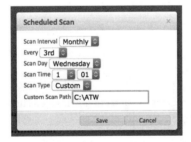

Figure 8-38   *Adding a Scheduled Scan*

Network Tab

You use the Network tab to configure device flow correlation (DFC) and, in fact, DFC is the only configuration section in the Network tab. As described earlier in this chapter, DFC allows you to flag or even block suspicious network activity.

As you can see in Figure 8-39, you can enable or disable DFC from the Network tab. In addition, you specify here whether the detection action should be **Audit** or **Blocking**. In other words, you specify whether this policy should dictate a monitor-only mode or actually take action on the file. If you select Blocking, you can choose to terminate the parent process of the network connection and quarantine the malicious file. Finally, you can set Data Source to SourceFire, Custom, or both.

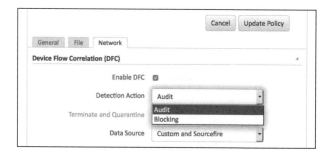

Figure 8-39   *Network Tab*

Known Incompatible Software

At this writing, AMP for Windows has interaction incompatibility with the following security software:

- Check Point's ZoneAlarm
- Carbon Black
- Res Software's AppGuard

AMP for Mac

Unlike AMP for Windows, AMP for Mac is supported only on 64-bit versions of the popular Mac OS. The following are the minimum system requirements for the Mac AMP agents, based on the operating system version:

- **Apple OS X 10.7:**
  - 2 GB RAM
  - 65 MB available hard disk space
- **Apple OS X 10.8:**
  - 2 GB RAM
  - 65 MB available hard disk space
- **Apple OS X 10.9:**
  - 2 GB RAM
  - 65 MB available hard disk space
- **Apple OS X 10.10 (requires AMP Mac Connector 1.0.6 or later):**
  - 2 GB RAM
  - 65 MB available hard disk space

■ **Apple OS X 10.11 (requires AMP Mac Connector 1.0.7 or later):**

  ■ 2 GB RAM

  ■ 65 MB available hard disk space

MAC Policies

There are many policy options for Macs. From the AMP cloud console, navigate to **Management > Policies > Mac** to see existing AMP policies for Mac and create new ones, as shown in Figure 8-40.

Click **Create Policy** and then select **FireAMP Mac** from the drop-down, as shown in Figure 8-40, and click **Create Policy**.

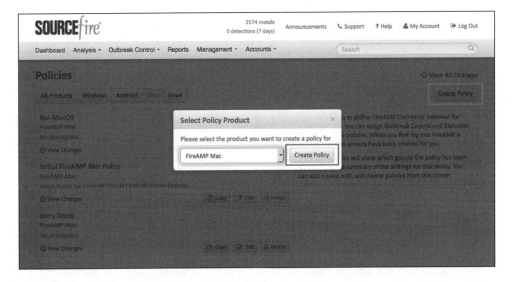

Figure 8-40 *Creating a Mac Policy*

In the New Policy Window that appears, provide a name and select the custom detections, app blocking, whitelists, and exclusions created earlier, as shown in Figure 8-41. When they are all selected, click **Create Policy** to save the policy.

Click **Edit** for the newly created Mac policy and scroll to the bottom. This is where a lot of the AMP agent configuration and customization takes place. Just as with a Windows policy, the AMP connector configurations are presented in three tabs for Mac: General, File, and Network.

Figure 8-41 *Creating a Mac Policy*

General Tab

The General tab for a Mac policy provides the basic options for the AMP for Endpoints connector, such as proxy settings and update schedules. As shown in Figure 8-42, there are four component areas in the General tab: Administrative Features, Client User Interface, Proxy Settings, and Product Updates. These areas are explained in the following sections.

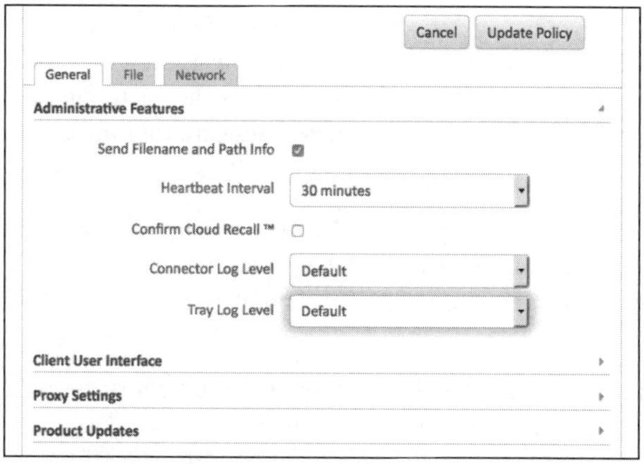

Figure 8-42 *Mac Policy General Tab*

Administrative Features

As you can see in Figure 8-42, there are five configurable settings in the Administrative Features section of the General tab:

- **Send Filename and Path Info:** This option enables the AMP agent to send the filename and path information to the AMP cloud so that they are visible in the Events tab, device trajectory, and file trajectory. Unchecking this option stops this information from being sent.

- **Heartbeat Interval:** This option sets how often the AMP agent should call home to the AMP cloud. During the call home connection, the agent checks whether there are any policy updates, any updates or scans to perform, or any files to restore via cloud recall or by the administrator.

- **Confirm Cloud Recall:** Cloud recall (also known as retrospection) can find every connector that has seen a specific file and attempt to quarantine it when the connector calls home on its heartbeat interval. This check box adds a required action for a system admin to confirm before recalling any files.

- **Connector Log Level:** This option allows you to change the default log level to debug, when directed by Cisco TAC.

- **Tray Log Level:** This option allows you to change the default log level to debug, when directed by Cisco TAC.

Note This section has no options for sending the username, connector protection options, or crash dumps. Those are Windows-specific options.

Client User Interface

The Client User Interface section of the General tab allows you to configure what the end user sees on a Mac system. Many organizations prefer to show the agent icon in the menu bar, so it is obvious that the agent is running, but they often choose to hide all notifications so that the users are not bothered by the agent. There are four different options, as shown in Figure 8-43:

- **Start Client User Interface:** Simply put, this option hides the user interface or shows it. The agent is running either way. This setting offers you the option of keeping it out of the menu bar. When you change this option, it takes effect at the next connector restart.

- **Cloud Notifications:** This option controls whether you see those fun notification pop-outs that come from the upper-left side of the screen on a Mac (the Notification Center). When this option is selected, a pop-out appears when the agent is successfully connected to the cloud, and it displays the number of users and detections registered to the cloud. Your end users will normally not thank you for these messages, which don't make any sense to them.

- **Hide File Notifications:** Selecting this option hides malicious file notifications from being displayed when a file is convicted or quarantined by the AMP agent.

- **Hide Network Notifications:** Selecting this option hides messages when a malicious network connection is detected or blocked by AMP.

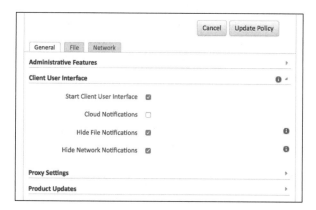

Figure 8-43 *Client User Interface Section*

It is highly recommended that you keep any interactivity with the end user to an absolute minimum. End users often get frustrated and annoyed when burdened by notifications that they don't understand or don't care to understand.

Proxy Settings

The options in the Proxy Settings section for Mac are exactly the same as for the Windows connector. To do our part to save the planet and use less paper, please see the "Proxy Settings" section for Windows, earlier in this chapter.

Product Updates

The options in the Product Updates section for Mac are exactly the same as for the Windows connector. Please see the "Product Updates" section for Windows, earlier in this chapter.

File Tab

You use the File tab to configure the settings and behavior of file scanning in the AMP for Endpoints agent, such as which engines to use, setting up scheduled scans, and cache settings. There are five component areas of the file tab: Modes, Offline Engine—ClamAV, Cache Settings, Engines, and Scheduled Scans.

Modes

The options in the Modes section for Mac are exactly the same as for the Windows connector. Please see the "Modes" section for Windows, earlier in this chapter.

Offline Engine—ClamAV

This section is available only when ClamAV has been selected for the Offline Engine option in the Engines portion of the File tab.

The Windows connector uses TETRA for offline scanning. The Mac connector uses ClamAV, which is an open source full antivirus product, owned by Cisco SourceFire. Just like TETRA, ClamAV is signature based and takes up more disk space and processor power on the Macs.

As shown in Figure 8-44, the only configurable option for ClamAV is Content Update Interval. By default, it checks for new or updated AV signatures to be downloaded every 24 hours. Just as on Windows, compatibility with other antivirus software solutions can be an issue, so never enable Offline Engine—ClamAV if another antivirus product is installed on the computer.

Figure 8-44 *Offline Engine—ClamAV*

Cache Settings

The options in the Cache Settings section for Mac are exactly the same as for the Windows connector. Please see the "Cache Settings" section for Windows, earlier in this chapter.

Engines

As stated in the "Offline Engine—ClamAV" section, the Engines section of the File tab is where you enable or disable ClamAV in the Mac connector policy.

Scheduled Scans

The options in the Scheduled Scans section for Mac are exactly the same as for the Windows connector. Please see the "Scheduled Scans" section for Windows, earlier in this chapter.

Network Tab

Just as with the AMP for Windows connector, you use the Network tab to configure DFC. As described earlier in this chapter, DFC allows you to flag or even block suspicious network activity.

As you can see in Figure 8-45, the options here are even fewer for Mac than they are for Windows. DFC can be enabled or disabled, and Detection Action may be set to Audit or Blocking.

Figure 8-45 *Network Tab*

AMP for Linux

AMP for Linux gets a bit interesting. First of all, there are more flavors of Linux than you can count, and Cisco certainly cannot be expected to support and test every one. At this writing, only the CentOS and Red Hat Linux variants are supported, and only the 64-bit versions of those Linux flavors are supported. The system requirements are as follows:

- **CentOS 6.4/6.5/6.6:**

    - 1 GB RAM

    - 400 MB available hard disk space

- **Red Hat Enterprise Linux 6.5/6.6:**

    - 1 GB RAM

    - 400 MB available hard disk space

Note   AMP for Linux may not install properly on custom kernels.

Linux Policies

Just as with the Windows and Mac operating systems, there are many policy options for Linux. From the AMP cloud console, navigate to **Management > Policies > Linux**, where you can see existing AMP policies for Linux and create new ones.

Click **Create Policy** and then select **FireAMP Linux** from the drop-down and click **Create Policy**.

In the New Policy window that appears, provide a name and select the custom detections, app blocking, whitelists, and exclusions created earlier, as shown in Figure 8-46. When they are all selected, click **Create Policy** to save the policy.

Figure 8-46　*Creating a Linux Policy*

Click **Edit** for the newly created Linux policy and scroll to the bottom to find the three tabs General, File, and Network.

General Tab

Just as for Windows and Mac, the General tab for a Linux policy has the basic settings for the AMP for Endpoints connector, such as proxy settings and update schedules.

There are only four component areas in the General tab: Administrative Features, Client User Interface, Proxy Settings, and Product Updates. Only the items that are different from the Windows and Mac policy options are discussed here. You can look to earlier sections for descriptions of any other options.

Administrative Features

The only difference in configuration of administrative features on Linux as compared to Mac is the lack of a system tray log for which to set the level. Only the connector log exists, and therefore only connector log settings can be changed from Default to Debug.

Client User Interface

The Client User Interface section provides two options: Hide File Notifications and Hide Network Notifications. As always, silence seems to be golden for the AMP connector, so hiding notifications may be wise for your environment.

File Tab

The File tab for Linux is exactly the same as it is for the Mac connector. ClamAV is the antivirus product for Linux that is built into the AMP connector, and it can be enabled and configured for periodic updates, just as the Mac connector can.

Network Tab

Just as with the Mac and Windows connectors, the Network tab for Linux is used to enable or disable DFC. However, Linux does not have a blocking mode for DFC; it is only capable doing audits.

AMP for Android

The AMP for Android connector requires Android 2.1 or higher running on ARM and Intel Atom processors with 4 MB of free space on the device.

Unlike with Windows and Mac, there are not many policy options for Android. From the AMP cloud console, navigate to **Management > Policies > Android**, where you can see existing AMP policies for Android and create new ones.

Click **Create Policy** and then select **FireAMP Android** from the drop-down and click **Create Policy.**

In the New Policy window that appears, provide a name and select the custom detection created earlier, as shown in Figure 8-47. There is only one option to configure at the bottom of the policy, Heartbeat Interval, as shown in Figure 8-47.

Figure 8-47   *Creating an Android Policy*

Installing AMP for Endpoints

You have created policies for the different endpoints. The next step is to assign those policies to groups so you can begin to deploy the AMP connectors to the many endpoints in your organization.

Groups, Groups, and More Groups

Before you move on to installing AMP for Endpoints onto hosts, we should really discuss an important organization component: groups. The AMP administrative console uses groups to organize and manage computers according to function, location, or other criteria that you determine. Policies get assigned to groups and can inherit from parent groups for greater control.

For example, you might create a group for each department of line of business; however, there could be additional controls required, based on the country of origin in which the computer normally resides.

Navigate to **Management > Groups**, where you see a list of all the top-level groups in your organization. You can create, edit, or delete the groups from this screen. If a group has child groups within it, this is indicated as shown in Figure 8-48.

To create a new group, click the **Create Group** button shown in Figure 8-48. To create a new group, you provide a group name, description, and parent group (if any) and you can assign existing known computers to it, as shown in the upper right of Figure 8-49. At the bottom of the screen, you can make this new group a parent by assigning other existing groups to it as children.

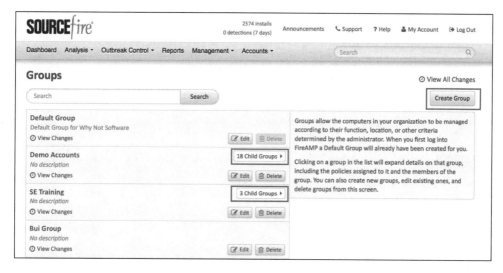

Figure 8-48 *Top-Level Groups*

In addition, as you can see in Figure 8-49, you can assign existing policies to the group. This is where you select the policies you just created in this chapter.

Click **Save** to save the new group.

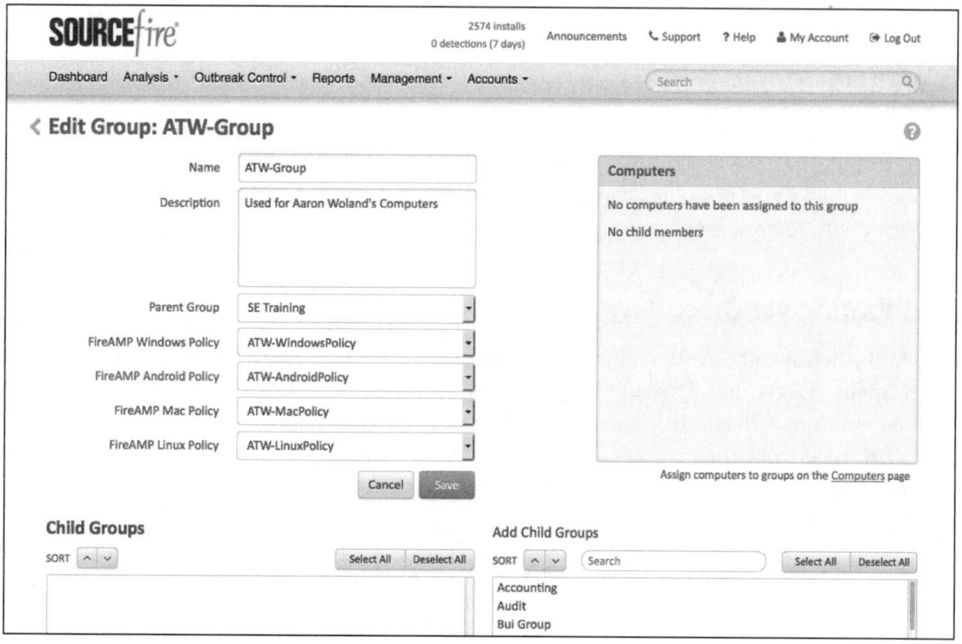

Figure 8-49 *Creating a New Group*

Download Connector

Earlier in the chapter you saw the Download Connector screen, located at **Management > Download Connector** (see Figure 8-50). Here you can download installation packages for each type of AMP for Endpoints connector, or you can copy the URL from where those connectors can be download. Before downloading a connector, select the appropriate group so the correct policies will be assigned and the installed computers will appear in the correct group.

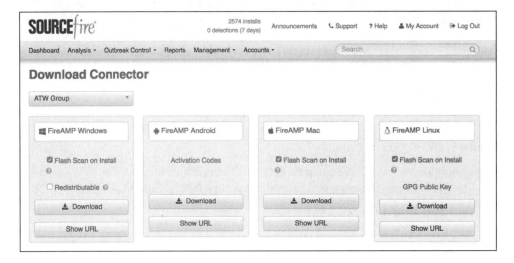

Figure 8-50 *Download Connector Screen*

The installer may be placed on a network share, distributed via management software, or distributed via the Cisco AnyConnect Secure Mobility Client. The download URL can be emailed to users so they can download and install it themselves; this can be convenient with remote users.

Distributing via Cisco AnyConnect

At this writing, the AMP connector is not part of the Cisco AnyConnect Secure Mobility Client, but you can use the AMP Enabler add-on to AnyConnect to aid in the distribution of the AMP connector to clients who use AnyConnect for remote access VPN, secure network access, posture assessments with Cisco's Identity Services Engine, and more. Figure 8-51 shows the AnyConnect Secure Mobility Client with the AMP Enabler tile.

Figure 8-51 *AnyConnect Security Mobility Client*

Installing AMP for Windows

On the Download Connector screen shown in Figure 8-50, Windows is the first operating system. As you can see in Figure 8-52, there are a few options to select when choosing to download the AMP installer for Windows.

Figure 8-52 *Downloading AMP for Windows*

There is an option to have the connector perform a flash scan during the install process. The flash scan checks processes currently running in memory and should be performed on each install.

The second check box is an option to enable a redistributable file. This option is not enabled by default, and when you click **Download** with this disabled (the default), you download a very small (around 500 KB) bootstrapper file to install the AMP connector. This type of installer is also referred to as a "stub installer."

A stub installer determines whether a computer is running a 32- or 64-bit operating system and connects to the cloud to download and install the appropriate version of the

AMP connector. The connector is configured with your policies, based on the group assignment.

If you select the Redistributable option and then click **Download**, you download a much larger executable (around 30 MB) that contains the full installation, both 32- and 64-bit versions.

You can place the executable file on a network share or push it to all the computers in a group via a tool like Microsoft System Center Configuration Manager (SCCM) or Active Directory Group Policies in order to install the AMP connector on multiple computers. The bootstrapper and redistributable installer also both contain a policy.xml file, which contains your assigned policies and is used as a configuration file for the install. Administrative rights are required for installing the connector interactively.

Figure 8-53 shows the UI displaying the URL to send to the end users. Figure 8-54 shows an end user connecting to the installer stub through the download URL entered into their browser. The stub installer is downloaded, and when it's executed, the Windows security subsystem asks for permission to run the installer, as shown in Figure 8-55. You click **Yes** to continue with the installation and download the full agent with the policies, as shown in Figure 8-56.

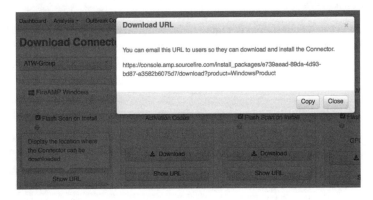

Figure 8-53 *The Download URL*

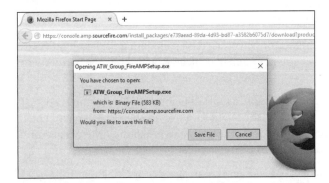

Figure 8-54 *Downloading the Stub Installer*

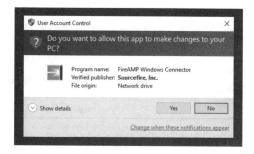

Figure 8-55 *Windows Security Prompt*

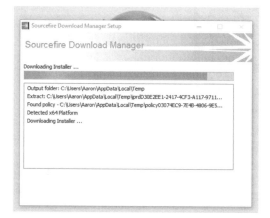

Figure 8-56 *Installing the Agent on Windows*

When the agent is installed on a Windows endpoint and the user interface is configured to be visible, the AMP icon is in the system tray; clicking that system tray icon brings up the summary window. Both the system tray icon and the summary window are shown in Figure 8-57.

Figure 8-57 *System Tray Icon and Summary Window*

As shown in Figure 8-57, the summary window includes the current status of the connection to the AMP cloud, the last date the system was scanned, and the assigned policy. If you click **Settings**, you see the settings that are configured in the policy, as shown in Figure 8-58.

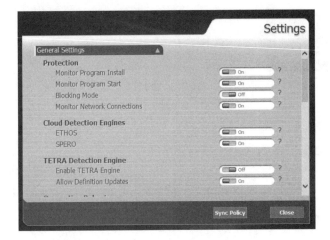

Figure 8-58   *Local GUI Displaying Settings*

Installing AMP for Mac

The process of installing AMP for Mac is very similar to the installation process for Windows. First, you select the group, but instead of downloading a Windows executable file, you download a PKG file to install the AMP connector. Or you can copy the URL, just as with Windows. Also as with Windows, a Mac user must have admin privileges to install the connector. Figure 8-59 shows the downloading of the PKG file.

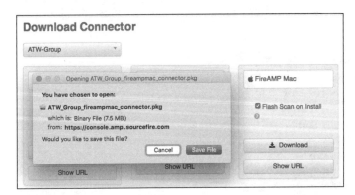

Figure 8-59   *Downloading the Mac PKG File*

The PKG file is only about 7 MB, as there is no "redistributable" equivalent. When the end user runs the PKG file, the step-by-step installation begins, as shown in Figure 8-60.

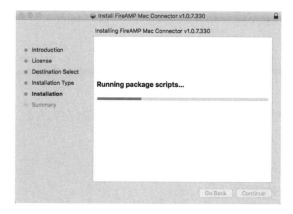

Figure 8-60   *Mac Installation GUI*

When the agent is installed, if the user interface is configured to be visible, there is an AMP icon in the menu bar. Clicking the menu bar icon allows you to trigger an on-demand scan, sync the policy to the cloud, or get into the settings, as shown in Figure 8-61.

Figure 8-61   *Menu Bar Icon and Menu*

You can click **Settings** to bring up the main AMP for Mac GUI. As you can see in Figure 8-62, this GUI has four sections: Events, Policy, Scan, and About. This is quite different from the Windows agent: You cannot see or change the policy in the Mac GUI.

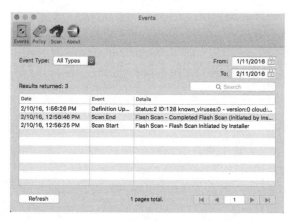

Figure 8-62   *The Events Section of the AMP for Mac GUI*

The Events tab in the GUI lists all the logged activities for quarantines, detection, update, and scans.

Figure 8-63 shows the Policy section of the GUI, which provides some visibility into the configuration, but not any settings to change.

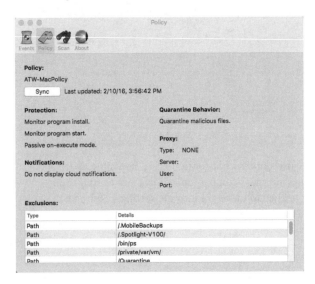

Figure 8-63   *Policy Section*

Figure 8-64 shows the Scan section of the GUI, which allows you to initiate a flash, full, or custom scan. It also shows any scans scheduled from the centralized policy.

Figure 8-65 shows the About section of the GUI, which lists the AMP connector version.

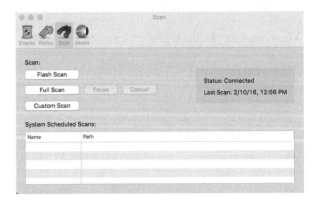

Figure 8-64   *Scan Section*

Figure 8-65 *About Section*

Installing AMP for Linux

Downloading the Linux connector provides you with an RPM (Red Hat Package Manager, aka RPM Package Manager) file to be installed. The installer is about 16MB and also contains the policy.xml file, which is used as a configuration file for your settings. There is also a link to download the GPG key, which is required for connector updates via the central policy. Figure 8-66 shows the screen where the GPG key can be copied or downloaded.

Figure 8-66 *GPG Public Key*

You can install the RPM via **rpm** or the **yum** toolset. To install via RPM, you use the **rpm -i** command and option. For yum, use **sudo yum localinstall [***install-file***] -y**. Figure 8-67 shows an example of using the **rpm** command.

Figure 8-67 *Installing the Connector via **rpm***

If you plan on pushing connector updates via policy, you need to import the GPG key into your RPM DB. Here's how you do this:

Step 1.   Verify the GPG key by clicking the GPG Public Key link on the Download Connector page, as shown in Figure 8-66. Compare the key from that link to the one at /opt/cisco/amp/etc/rpm-gpg/RPM-GPG-Key-cisco-amp. Figure 8-68 shows the contents of that public key file, for comparison.

Figure 8-68 *cat RPM-GPG-KEY-cisco-amp*

Step 2.   Run the following command from a terminal to import the key: **[sudo] rpm --import /opt/cisco/amp/etc/rpm-gpg/RPM-GPG-KEY-cisco-amp**

Step 3.   Verify that the key was installed by running the following command from a terminal: **rpm -q gpg-pubkey --qf '%{name}-%{version}-%{release} --> %{summary}\n'**

Step 4.   Look for a GPG key from SourceFire in the output.

The Linux connector has a command-line interface (CLI), as shown in Figure 8-69.

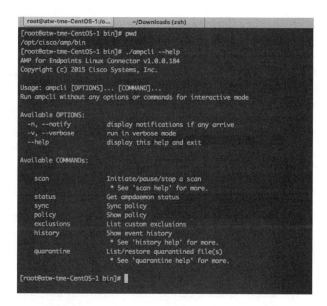

Figure 8-69 *Linux AMP CLI*

Installing AMP for Android

AMP for Android comes in the form of an app. An end user can obtain the app if you send a link to the app, send the app directly, or allow the user to download the app from the Google Play Store.

Android Activation Codes

Before you can successfully install the app on an Android endpoint, an activation code is required. Activation codes are generated in the console GUI and do not have expiration dates by default.

In the Download Connector screen, click **Activation Codes** in the FireAMP Android box, as shown in Figure 8-70.

Figure 8-70 *Download Connector for Android*

In the Android Activation Codes screen, click **Create** to generate a new code, and you get a small form to fill out, including the new code value. The Activation Limit setting is how many connectors may be activated using this license code. You can choose an expiration date for the use of the code to prevent any new activations with the code from that date forward. An expiration date does not disable the connectors that were previously activated by the code. Finally, you select the group that will use the activation code. Only a single activation code can be applied to a group at a time, so make sure you have assigned a high enough activation limit for the number of devices in the group you are applying the code to. Don't worry, though: You can later return to the screen and edit the code to extend the activation limit. You can also delete the old code and create a new code for the same group. Again, deleting a code does not deactivate the connectors that were previously activated; it simply prevents any new users from activating their app with that code.

Click **Create** at the bottom of the screen to create the new activation code and ensure that you notate the code for use in the next steps. Figure 8-71 shows the connector code being generated.

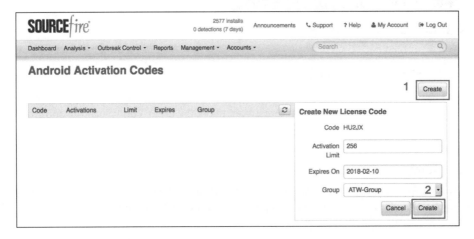

Figure 8-71 *Generating the AMP Connector Code*

Deploying the AMP for Android Connector

AMP for Android comes in the form of an app. An end user can obtain the app if you send a link to the app, send the app directly, or allow the user to download the app from the Google Play Store. Using the Google Play Store is often considered the easiest method, since it is trusted to all Android devices by default and doesn't require changing security settings on the device to allow apps to be installed from other sources.

Figure 8-72 shows the app in the Google Play Store. Click **Install** to download and install it. When the installation is complete, open the app. You are prompted to accept the license agreement, as shown in Figure 8-73.

Figure 8-72 *Downloading the AMP Connector App*

Figure 8-73 *License Agreement*

Next, you are asked to enter the activation code and provide an identifying name for the Android device, as shown in Figure 8-74. If the code is active and valid, you see a success message and then the main AMP app window, as shown in Figure 8-75.

Figure 8-74 *Entering the License Code*

Figure 8-75 *AMP Main App Window*

Clicking Settings in the Android AMP connector is a bit different from clicking Settings in the other connectors, as the only option displayed is to change the device name, as shown in Figure 8-76.

Figure 8-76   *Settings*

Proxy Complications

AMP for Endpoints needs to reach the AMP cloud through an Internet connection, and that connection may require traversing a proxy server. Sometimes there are complications with this process.

Proxy Server Autodetection

AMP for Endpoints can use multiple mechanisms to support anonymous proxy servers. A specific proxy server or path to a proxy auto-config (PAC) file can be defined in Policies, or the connector can discover the endpoint proxy settings from the Windows registry.

The FireAMP connector can be set to discover endpoint proxy settings automatically. When the connector detects proxy setting information, it attempts to connect to the FireAMP management server to confirm that the proxy server settings are correct. The connector first uses the proxy settings specified in the policy. If the connector is unable to establish a connection to the FireAMP management server, it attempts to retrieve proxy settings from the Windows registry on the endpoint. The connector attempts to retrieve the settings only from systemwide settings and not from per-user settings.

If the connector is unable to retrieve proxy settings from the Windows registry, it attempts to locate the PAC file. This can be specified in policy settings or determined using Web Proxy Auto-Discovery (WPAD). If the PAC file location is specified in policy, it has to begin with http or https. Note that the PAC files supported are only ECMAScript based and must have a .pac file extension. If the PAC file is hosted on a web server, the proper MIME type, application/x-javascript-config, must be specified. Because all connector communications are already encrypted, https proxy is not supported. For version 3.0.6 of the connector, a SOCKS proxy setting cannot be specified using a PAC file.

The connector attempts to rediscover proxy settings after a certain number of cloud lookups fail. This ensures that when laptops are outside the enterprise network, the connector is able to connect when network proxy settings are changed.

Incompatible Proxy Security Configurations

Some proxy and web security configurations are incompatible with AMP:

- **Websense NTLM credential caching:** The currently supported workaround for AMP is either to disable NTLM credential caching in Websense or to allow the AMP connector to bypass proxy authentication exception.

- **HTTPS content inspection:** HTTPS content inspection breaks the AMP endpoint agent's communication with the cloud due to certificate pinning and strong authentications. The currently supported workaround is either to disable HTTPS content inspection or to set up exclusions for the AMP connector.

- **Kerberos/GSSAPI authentication:** The AMP connector does not work with these authentication methods. The currently supported workaround is either to use basic or NTLM authentication or to set up an authentication exception.

Using the Cloud Console

When endpoints are running and reporting to the cloud, you see a populated dashboard and can look for malware, threats, and indicators of compromise.

Figure 8-77 shows the AMP dashboard, indicating that one of the computers with an AMP connector loaded has indicators of compromise, five counts of malware detected on it, and even a list of the malware threats.

If you click **Threat Detected** link in the Indications of Compromise section on the dashboard (see Figure 8-77), you are taken to the Events tab, but the filters are prepopulated, as shown in Figure 8-78.

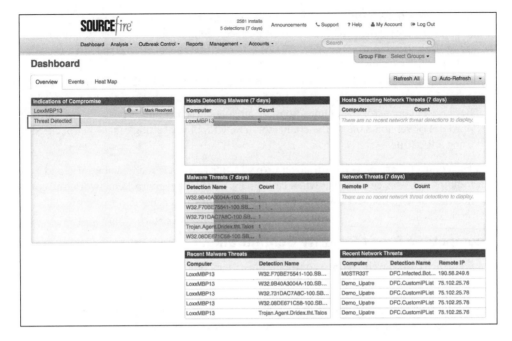

Figure 8-77   *Dashboard*

Immediately, you can see that all the malware has the status Quarantine: Success. This means AMP was able to isolate and block the malware. If you drill into one of the pieces of malware detected, you can get more information about the filename, the path, the parent, and more. You can also look into the file trajectory and computer trajectory (see Figure 8-78) to attempt to see where else the file has been and where else the infected computer has been.

If you navigate to **Analysis > Events**, you get an unfiltered view of all events. If you scroll down, you can see vulnerable applications being reported. As you can see in Figure 8-79, the Windows client that AMP was installed on had a vulnerable version of Java on it, and the vulnerability CVEs are listed.

Upon recognizing systems with vulnerable applications, you can contact the desktop team to have the system updated. Or you can have an indicator of compromise trigger a correlation action in the Firepower Management Center (FMC) that uses a remediation with Cisco Identity Services Engine (ISE) to quarantine the endpoint on the network. This type of solution is known as rapid threat defense with Firepower Management Center and ISE.

File   Computer
Trajectory   Trajectory

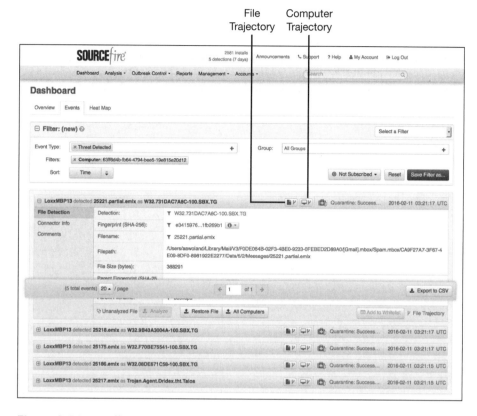

Figure 8-78 *Drilling into the Events*

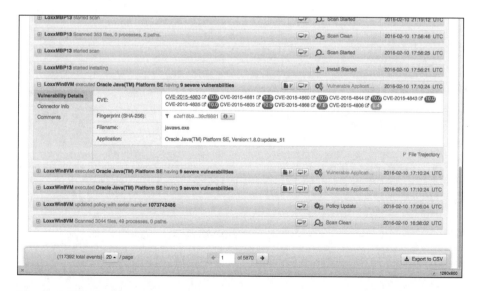

Figure 8-79 *Bad Java*

Summary

This chapter provides more than an overview of Cisco's AMP for Endpoints. It reviews the overall AMP architecture and where AMP for Endpoints fits into that architecture. You have learned about the types of AMP for Endpoints connectors, created policies for each of them, and gone through their installations. You have used the AMP cloud console to see whether AMP has detected and remediated malware and detected and reported on threats, and you have seen how to follow file and computer trajectories.

Chapter 9

AMP Threat Grid: Malware Analysis and Threat Intelligence

This chapter covers the following topics:

- Cisco AMP Threat Grid cloud

- On-premises Cisco AMP Threat Grid appliance

This chapter introduces the cloud and on-premises Cisco AMP Threat Grid deployment options. These two types of deployments present different options, including the Cisco AMP, Email Security Appliance (ESA), and Web Security Appliance (WSA).

Threat Grid is a deep threat analysis solution that leverages many identification techniques, including sandboxing. It can be architected as a cloud or on-premises solution. It does deep analysis of file samples that are submitted to the AMP Threat Grid cloud or appliance. Cisco AMP Threat Grid analyzes files based on behavioral indicators and malware knowledge information and provides accurate and context-rich malware analytics. The analysis results can be used for updating file disposition in the cloud that is used by other cloud deployments.

Cisco AMP Threat Grid

Cisco AMP Threat Grid is a cloud and on-premises malware analysis solution that was first introduced in FirePOWER v6.0.

Note Cisco customers can deploy an on-premises Cisco Threat Grid appliance if they do not wish to send any file information to the Cisco cloud or if they are worried about bandwidth utilization.

With either an on-premises or cloud installation, security engineers can use Cisco AMP Threat Grid to quickly correlate a single malware sample or hundreds of observed activities and characteristics against millions of samples in order to study malware behavior in a historical context. This helps them defend against targeted attacks and threats from advanced malware. Cisco AMP Threat Grid also can generate detailed reports, including important behavioral indicators and threat scores that allow security analysts to quickly prioritize and recover from advanced attacks.

Cisco AMP Threat Grid is not a single tool. It is a malware analysis and threat intelligence solution. It crowdsources malware from a closed community and analyzes all samples, using highly secure proprietary techniques including static and dynamic analysis. It performs automated analysis with adjustable runtimes while not exposing any indicators that malware could use to detect that it is being observed and analyzed. That way, Cisco AMP Threat Grid can still operate and analyze malware that changes behavior to avoid analysis in sandbox environments.

Many think that the Cisco AMP Threat Grid offering is just a sandboxing solution, but it is much more than just that. Sandboxing is a piece of the solution, and its sandbox functions are performed in a way that evades detection by malware. AMP Threat Grid uses an outside-in approach and has no presence in the virtual machine. The sandboxing's dynamic analysis includes an external kernel monitor, dynamic disk analysis that illuminates any modifications to the physical disk (such as the master boot record [MBR]), monitoring of user interaction, video capture and playback, and monitoring of process information, artifacts, and network traffic. The following are some of the object types Cisco AMP Threat Grid supports:

- Executable files (.EXE) and libraries (.DLL)

- Java archives (.JAR)

- Portable document format (.PDF)

- Office documents (.RTF, .DOC, .DOCX, .XLS, .XLSX, .PPT, .PPTX)

- ZIP containers (.ZIP)

- Quarantine containers

- URLs

- HTML documents

- Flash

Among its outputs, Cisco AMP Threat Grid provides video playback, the Glovebox feature for malware interaction and troubleshooting, a process graph for visual representation of process lineage, and a threat score with behavior indicators of malware. The Glovebox feature helps analysts dissect and interact with the malware in real time by recording all activity for future playback and reporting. It correlates sample malware data elements against billions of sample artifacts historically collected and analyzed in order to match well-known malicious behaviors. The threat score provided for analyzed malware is based on severity and confidence. In addition, the more than 450 behavioral indicators, sourced from around the globe, can show an analyst if a piece of malware is malicious, suspicious, or benign—and why—which eliminates guesswork and helps an analyst make better decisions more quickly.

Cisco AMP Threat Grid is integrated with Cisco security technologies that span from the network edge to the endpoint, including Cisco AMP for Networks, Cisco ASA with FirePOWER Services, Cisco Firepower Threat Defense, Cisco Email Security Appliance, Cisco Web Security Appliance, and Cisco AMP for Endpoints. In combination, these tools give organizations more visibility than ever before. Information across many platforms can be correlated and synthesized so organizations can make faster, better decisions to more quickly eliminate threats and reduce the harm caused by malware.

Cisco AMP Threat Grid also provides highly accurate, easy-to-integrate security content feeds that help organizations generate context-rich threat intelligence that is both actionable and specific. The feeds are available in a number of standardized formats:

- JavaScript Object Notation (JSON)

- Cyber Observable Expression (CybOX)

- Structured Threat Information Expression (STIX)

- Comma-separated values (CSV)

- Snort rules

Customized feed formats are also available for particular security products. Using the powerful application programming interface (API), you can import threat information into your security technologies, including security information and event management (SIEM) solutions, graphical visualization tools, and more to automate detection and response to even the most sophisticated threats. Cisco AMP Threat Grid's threat intelligence allows administrators to look into markets and industries of interest. An analyst can understand the relevancy of the executable sample as it pertains to the environment and look at specific threat information for specific types of data and take proactive, preventive action.

Among the security personnel who can benefit from Cisco AMP Threat Grid are incident response and security operation team members and information security executives. Incident response teams use Cisco AMP Threat Grid to analyze malware submissions; search for malicious files, registry keys, and URLs; and run malicious code in Glovebox. Security operation teams generate threat scores, prioritize malware cleanup and remediation, and submit suspicious code for analysis. Threat Grid empowers a security team to act faster on malware, offers a more complete security solution by integrating with existing technologies, and accelerates detection of advanced attacks.

The rest of this chapter presents specifics of the cloud and appliance deployment options for Cisco AMP Threat Grid and briefly presents details on how to configure them.

Cisco AMP Threat Grid Cloud Solution

The Cisco AMP cloud includes multiple analytics engines constantly correlating data. Threat Grid is one of them. The analysis results generated by AMP engines are used to update the AMP signatures. Other machine-learning engines are used to refine signatures and reevaluate detections of indicators that have already been caught. AMP does not serve as a static signature repository. Decision making and intelligent operations take place in real time, evolving constantly based on the data that is received.

As mentioned previously, AMP Threat Grid's cloud solution allows users to submit malware samples to the cloud for analysis and receive detailed reports that identify important malware behavioral indicators and assign threat scores. Security teams can then rapidly prioritize and recover from advanced attacks. Figure 9-1 shows the Firepower Management Center (FMC) with the AMP cloud located in U.S. and EU data centers. An AMP private cloud option is also available for organizations that do not want malware information shared in the cloud.

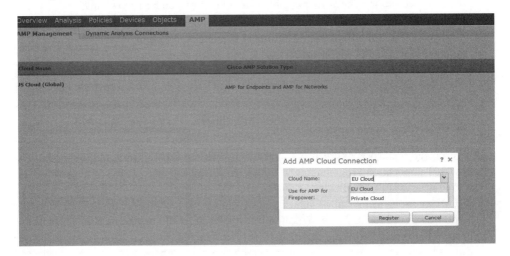

Figure 9-1   *AMP Cloud Location*

Cisco AMP Threat Grid can be accessed via a portal page. Files can be submitted for analysis using the browser. All the results can be easily retrieved from the web page. Malware samples can also be compared with other samples and searched for. In addition, with Cisco AMP Threat Grid cloud, you can define the malware runtime from 5 to 30 minutes.

Threat Grid exposes an API that integrates with existing security solutions and can create custom threat intelligence feeds. It can automatically receive submissions from other products and pull the results in the environment. Cisco AMP Threat Grid's analysis, threat intelligence correlation, and feeds retrieval can be automated and integrated with existing security solutions using the API. Security tools can also access and integrate with it by using the Threat Grid API.

Administrators can navigate to **AMP > Dynamic Analysis Connections** in FMC (see Figure 9-2) to configure cloud HTTPS connections that the Cisco ASA with FirePOWER Services or Cisco Firepower Threat Defense will be using to get attribute and dynamic analysis updates to verify whether malware samples are malicious. Cisco ESA and WSA also integrate with Cisco Threat Grid cloud, leveraging a similar outbound HTTPS connection configured in the File Reputation Filtering and File Analysis page.

Figure 9-2 *AMP Dynamic Analysis Connections*

Cisco AMP Threat Grid On-Premises Appliance

Even though the Cisco AMP Threat Grid cloud-based solution can serve many organizations well, others might require no outbound connections to the cloud transferring information externally. Organizations with such compliance and policy restrictions can submit malware samples to the AMP Threat Grid on-premises appliance for local analysis and ensure policy enforcement and compliance. The appliance also has the capability to manually update its knowledge base while complying with corporate or regulatory policies to keep all information within logical boundaries and not transfer it externally.

The Cisco AMP Threat Grid appliances (TG5000 and TG5500) are hosted in a Cisco UCS C220 hardware server. They can analyze 1500 and 5000 samples per day, respectively.

Similarly to the cloud, with the Cisco AMP Threat Grid appliance, malware samples are analyzed using static and dynamic analysis techniques, and the results are correlated against millions of analyzed malware artifacts; however, in the case of the on-premises appliance, information is not sent out of an organization's logical boundaries. Security teams can quickly correlate a single malware sample's activity and characteristics against other samples to analyze its behaviors in historical and global contexts to defend against targeted attacks or general threats from advanced malware.

As shown in Figure 9-2, in FMC administrators can navigate to **AMP > Dynamic Analysis Connections** to create new connections to the Cisco AMP Threat Grid appliance rather than using the public cloud to analyze files traversing an ASA with FirePOWER Services or Cisco Firepower Threat Defense (FTD). These connections allow the firewall to connect the Threat Grid appliance to get files analyzed and find their posture. The Cisco ESA and Cisco WSA offer similar integration with Threat Grid. If the system is configured to connect to an on-premises appliance, it can use the default public cloud connection for public report retrieval. If the appliance cannot generate a dynamic analysis report about a file, it queries the Cisco AMP cloud. In an on-premises appliance deployment, public cloud reports returned to the system by the cloud are scrubbed and returned with limited data.

The initial configuration of a device (Cisco ASA with FirePOWER Services, Cisco FTD, Cisco ESA, or Cisco WSA) consists of configuring Secure Sockets Layer (SSL) certificates so the appliance can communicate, registering the device in the appliance, creating a user, and configuring the device to connect to the appliance, as demonstrated in Figure 9-3. In the Cisco ESA and Cisco WSA, Cisco AMP Threat Grid dynamic file analysis is enabled in the File Reputation Filtering and File Analysis page.

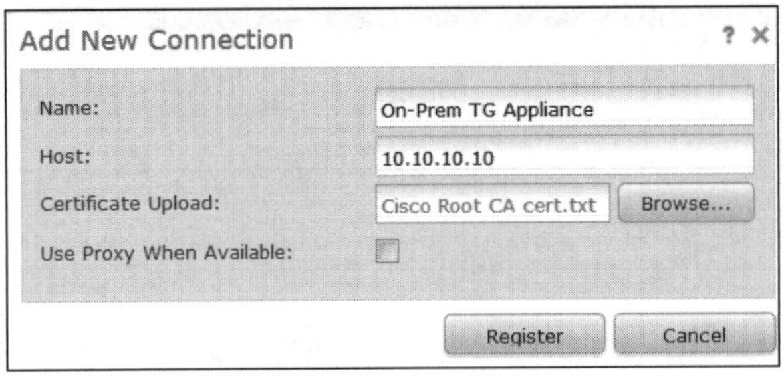

Figure 9-3   *Adding a New Connection to a Cisco AMP Threat Grid Appliance*

The appliance itself has an administrator interface, a clean interface that connects to the trusted inside network, and a dirty interface for the untrusted network. Access to the appliance is from the administrator interface, using the graphical user interface in a browser. The web interface allows for file submission for analysis, report generation about malware activities and network traffic, result retrieval, sample searches, and comparison.

To analyze malware, an administrator has the opportunity to run and interact with it in Glovebox for 5 to 30 minutes to observe its behaviors. Malware analysis, threat intelligence correlation, and feeds retrieval are other features the web interface offers. These can also be automated and integrated with existing security solutions using the API. A powerful representational state transfer (REST) API allows organizations to integrate the appliance with existing security infrastructure, such as gateways, proxies, and SIEM platforms. The API can also be used to automatically consume submissions from third-party endpoint agents, deep-packet-inspection platforms, and investigation tools. Numerous partner solution integrations showcase that functionality. Finally, the user interface offers customizable workflows that are designed for security operations center (SOC) malware analysts and forensic investigators to perform their day-to-day operations.

Default Users

The default Cisco AMP Threat Grid portal administrator username is **admin**, and the password is **changeme**.

The default Cisco AMP Threat Grid OpAdmin administrator's password is "threatgrid," which is the same as the Threat Grid portal user password, and it is maintained in the OpAdmin interface.

As previously mentioned, the Cisco AMP Threat Grid appliance is a Cisco UCS server. It also comes with the Cisco Integrated Management Controller (CIMC) for low-level server administration. The default username for the CIMC is **admin**, and the default password is **password.**

> **Tip**   It is highly recommended that you change the device password and that you use strong passwords to increase the security posture of the device and to reduce its attack surface.

Once the user accounts are set up, the administrators or other users can log in and begin submitting malware samples for analysis.

Network Segment Configuration

As mentioned previously, the Cisco AMP Threat Grid appliance has three required networks:

- **Administrative (admin) network:** This network must be configured in order to configure the appliance.

- **Clean network:** This network is used for inbound trusted traffic (requests) to the appliance, including traffic from other integrated systems (for example, Cisco ESA, Cisco WSA).

- **Dirty network:** This network is used for outbound traffic, including malware traffic.

> **Tip**   A best practice is to configure a dedicated external IP address for the appliance that is different from your corporate IP address in order to protect your internal network.

Summary

This chapter provides an overview of the Cisco AMP Threat Grid solution, which offers an efficient and granular file analysis and context-rich and accurate malware analytics. This chapter also explains how Cisco AMP Threat Grid can be used in conjunction with Cisco AMP to offer a complete malware protection and analysis solution that operates throughout the attack continuum—before, during, and after a malware compromise— and helps organizations understand what malware is attempting to do, the threats it poses, and how to defend against it. The cloud-based AMP Threat Grid solution offers flexibility of deployment and off-the-shelf analytics from the Cisco AMP cloud. On-premises AMP Threat Grid deployments, on the other hand, serve organizations that want to use Cisco AMP Threat Grid's granular analysis without transferring information to the cloud.

Chapter 10

Introduction to and Deployment of Cisco Next-Generation IPS

The chapter covers the following topics:

- NGIPS basics

- Deployment design considerations

- The NGIPS deployment lifecycle

Attackers have constantly improved their methodologies of exploiting gaps in security by concealing their malicious activities and potential intrusions in spite of the security controls used in an infrastructure. Detection challenges are introduced by complicit users, misaligned policies, sophisticated attackers, naïve users, complex geopolitical relations, dynamic threats, and more. Next-generation intrusion prevention systems (NGIPS) has become a very important component of security architectures, providing protection against traditional and sophisticated types of attacks.

This chapter introduces NGIPS and compares it with legacy intrusion prevention systems (IPS). It presents a number of design concepts, principles, and challenges for NGIPS deployment. The chapter also explores some basic deployment scenarios and explains the basic design considerations security architects need to address when deploying NGIPS. The chapter concludes with coverage of the NGIPS deployment lifecycle followed in most NGIPS deployments.

NGIPS Basics

The following sections introduce the basic concepts of NGIPS and how it compares to legacy IPS. The following sections also present Cisco NGIPS products and their capabilities as well as peek at some basic deployment modes and scenarios. After reading these sections, you will be familiar with NGIPS and Cisco NGIPS and ready to move into NGIPS deployment design concepts.

Legacy IPS Versus NGIPS

Legacy IPS were traditionally used in network infrastructures to protect against known security threats. Often, two concepts were used: IPS and intrusion detection systems (IDS). IDS mostly detect and generate alerts for various attacks or intrusion attempts, whereas IPS can also prevent and mitigate attacks. The remainder of this section focuses on IPS, but you should note that there are no significant differences between the methodologies used in IPS and IDS for attack detection.

Legacy IPS depend mostly on matching signature-based patterns to identify and potentially prevent malicious activity. These are some of their basic characteristics of legacy IPS:

- They are sometimes deployed behind a firewall when providing IPS functionality (inline). Often, an IPS is also placed in the network without a firewall in front of it.

- They often look for attempts to exploit a vulnerability and not for the existence of a vulnerability.

- Legacy IPS often generate large amounts of event data that are difficult to correlate.

- They focus on individual indicators/events without focusing on contextual information to take action.

- Legacy IPS require manual tuning for better efficacy.

Thus, legacy IPS suffer from certain shortcomings, including the following:

- They often need to be operated in conjunction with other products or tools (firewalls, analytics, and correlation tools).

- They are sometimes not very effective and may be ignored.

- Their operation costs and the operating resources they need are high.

- They can leave infrastructures imperfectly covered against attackers.

NGIPS supplement legacy IPS functionality with more capabilities, such as the following:

- **Application awareness and control:** NGIPS provide visibility into Layer 7 applications and can protect against Layer 7 threats.

- **Content awareness of the information traversing the infrastructure:** For example, knowledge about files transferred between two hosts can be used to identify viruses transferred and the trajectory of a virus infection in a system.

- **Contextual awareness:** This helps better understand alerts and automatically deduce comprehensive information about the events taking place, which makes the NGIPS less complex and means it requires less tuning.

■ **Host and user awareness:** The infrastructure offers more conclusive information about the events taking place.

■ **Automated tuning and recommendations:** This allows an administrator to follow recommendations and tune signatures specifically to his environment.

■ **Impact and vulnerability assessment of the events taking place:** The impact of a security event identified by the system can be evaluated based on the information available for the environment. For example, a Windows system that is identified to secure a vulnerability cannot be severely impacted by an attempt to exploit the vulnerability against it.

Thus, it is clear that in the threat landscape of both today and in the future, NGIPS functionality has an important role in protecting and providing coverage against known attacks and new types of exploits.

Cisco NGIPS Capabilities

Modern networks constantly evolve, as do miscreants and their attack methods. People and machines that could misbehave reside inside and outside a network infrastructure. Devices are communicating in many different forms. The interconnected infrastructure with attackers that could be located anywhere is called the *any-to-any* challenge. Almost all modern environments face this challenge. Cisco is a leader in NGIPS, offering Cisco Firepower NGIPS products that can provide protection against constantly evolving attack surfaces in these environments.

Modern security tools need to integrate directly into the network fabric in order to maximize performance and efficiency. Responses need to be comprehensive and simple. Protection must be continuous. Network controls should not be implemented disparately and individually. To abide by these modern security requirements, Cisco follows a new security model that looks at the actions needed before, during, and after attacks that apply to mobile devices, virtual machines, endpoints, or more (see Figure 10-1). The Cisco Firepower NGIPS functionality operates mostly in the during phase of the attack continuum, but all phases are covered by the integrated capabilities of the Cisco Firepower product portfolio.

The following are some of the key differentiators of the Cisco NGIPS portfolio from other vendors:

■ Trusted security engine and security intelligence provided by Cisco

■ Security automation and behavioral and retrospective analysis

■ Network and context awareness and visibility

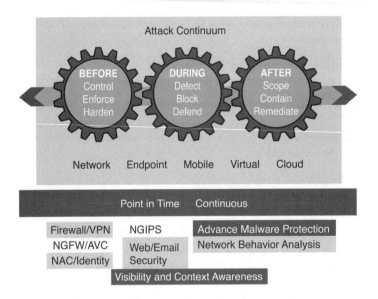

Figure 10-1   *The Attack Continuum and Where Security Functions Fall*

The Cisco Firepower NGIPS engine is based on well-defined open source Snort. Snort, originally created by SourceFire, is an open source IPS tool that is widely used in the industry. The Cisco Snort IPS rules in Snort are developed by the Cisco TALOS team and are open for inspection. They are built based on collective security intelligence by Cisco TALOS and a variety of other sources. The rule set offers broad product and threat coverage. In addition, third-party rules can be integrated and customized in the Cisco NGIPS.

The Cisco NGIPS products include the following:

- **Cisco ASA5500-X with FirePOWER Services:** Multiple ASA5500-X products for different performance requirement can run FirePOWER Services to leverage Cisco NGIPS capabilities in software (5506-X, 5512-X) or hardware modules (ASA5585-X).

- **Cisco Firepower next-generation firewall (NGFW) appliances (4100, 9300 series):** Threat-centric security appliances are available for service providers that run Firepower Threat Defense (FTD). FTD includes Application Visibility and Control (AVC), optional Firepower NGIPS, Cisco Advanced Malware Protection (AMP), and URL filtering.

- **Cisco Firepower appliances (7000, 8000 series):** Standalone NGIPS appliances are available for different performance requirements.

- **vNGIPS:** Firepower Virtual NGIPS is available for virtual environments.

The following are some of the most important capabilities of Cisco NGIPS:

- **Threat containment and remediation:** Cisco Firepower NGIPS provides protection against known and new threats. Its features include file analysis, packet- and flow-based inspection, and vulnerability assessment.

- **Application visibility:** Cisco Firepower NGIPS offers deep inspection and control of application-specific information for better efficacy.

- **Identity management:** NGIPS policies can be enforced by using contextual user information.

- **Security automation:** Cisco Firepower NGIPS includes automated event impact assessment and policy tuning.

- **Logging and traceability management:** This can be used in retrospective analysis.

- **High availability and stacking:** Cisco Firepower NGIPS provides redundancy and performance by leveraging multiple devices.

- **Network behavioral analysis:** Key behavioral indicators and threat scores help analysts prioritize and recover from attacks.

- **Access control and segmentation:** Access policies can be applied to separate traffic profiles in the network.

- **Real-time contextual awareness:** NGIPS discovers and provides information about applications, users, devices, operating systems, vulnerabilities, services, processes, files, and threat data related to IT environments.

To leverage its capabilities, NGIPS needs a robust and comprehensive management platform. For NGIPS management, Cisco offers the following:

- Cisco Firepower Management Center (FMC) (appliance or virtual) for multiple devices

- Cisco ASDM (which, at this writing, can be used only in some ASA with FirePOWER Services models)

As shown in Figure 10-2, there are two connectivity flows between the FMC and the NGIPS that offer device policy configuration from FMC to the NGIPS and information collection from the NGIPS to FMC for further intelligent analysis and reporting.

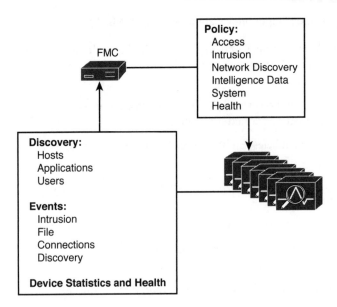

Figure 10-2   *FMC Connection Flow with NGIPS Devices*

The following are some of the features provided in the Cisco FMC:

- Policy management

- Display of event and contextual information, using various formations

- Health and performance monitoring

- Notifications and alerts filtering

- Correlation, vulnerabilities, indications of compromise, and remediation features for real-time threat response

- Custom reporting

- High availability

By combining top-notch platforms, research, and management, Cisco offers a complete NGIPS tool set that allows a security architect to build secure and simple-to-operate architectures.

NGIPS Modes

As in legacy IPS, NGIPS can operate in two different modes: inline and monitoring. *Inline mode* is the most common mode for a device used for prevention. Inline NGIPS can be placed between two assets that communicate or at a point that aggregates traffic from various sources—between a switch and a firewall or between a router and a switch—to block and mitigate threats. Two of the interfaces of the NGIPS are used in an inline pair for traffic to enter and exit the device after being inspected. Based on the configured policies, traffic can be dropped, allowed, or reset.

The caveat with inline NGIPS (Figure 10-3) is that in the event of a software failure or a loss of power, all traffic is dropped. The *fail-open* capability can be used for such situations to allow traffic to hardware bypass the device and avoid traffic loss. *Fail-open* should not be used when the security policy doesn't allow for traffic to go unaccounted for or uninspected.

Figure 10-3 *NGIPS in Inline Mode*

Inline mode offers two more modes of operation: routed and switched. In routed mode (see Figure 10-4), the device operates at Layer 3, as a router would. In switched mode (see Figure 10-5), the NGIPS is in transparent mode and doesn't show in the path as a Layer 3 hop. It uses two interfaces in a VLAN pair and bridges them together.

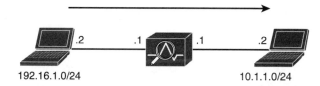

Figure 10-4 *NGIPS in Router Inline Mode*

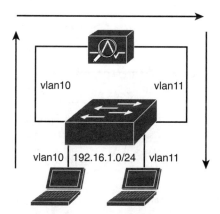

Figure 10-5 *NGIPS in Switched Inline Mode*

Monitoring (passive) mode is the mode where the NGIPS does usually not prevent attacks. The device uses one interface to silently inspect traffic and identify malicious activity without interrupting traffic flow (see Figure 10-6). It is usually connected to a switch's span port, a mirrored port, or a network tap interface. Even though in monitoring mode the device doesn't block traffic, there is an option to reset malicious connections, but that should not be considered as a mitigation mechanism as it can't guarantee attack prevention.

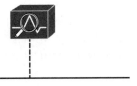

Figure 10-6 *NGIPS in Monitoring (Passive) Mode*

All Cisco NGIPS products (ASA FirePOWER Services modules, Firepower Threat Defense, NGIPS appliances, and vNGIPS) can operate in the modes described. Specifically for the ASA FirePOWER Services module, the modes and how they can be configured are presented in Chapter 2, "Introduction to and Design of Cisco ASA with FirePOWER Services."

NGIPS Deployment Locations and Scenarios

The NGIPS can be deployed in various locations of an infrastructure. Figure 10-7 shows some typical NGIPS locations.

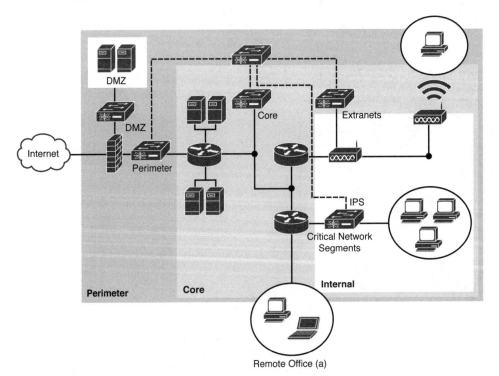

Figure 10-7 *NGIPS Deployment Locations*

In perimeter deployments, the device monitors attacks from the outside. It is usually deployed behind a perimeter access control device such as a firewall that is responsible for enforcing access policies so that the NGIPS does not spend resources inspecting traffic that should not be traversing the network.

A demilitarized zone (DMZ) is a partly trusted area where web and other servers reside. There is a certain risk for DMZ devices like servers, and thus an NGIPS is often deployed to protect them.

An NGIPS deployed at the core of a network detects insider threats and attacks. It also often identifies malware propagation, worms, and outbound malicious activity. Cisco NGIPS network discovery is more accurate when deployed closer to the core as internal network traffic is evaluated and provides more accurate discovery results.

Extranets provide connectivity from an enterprise to its partners', suppliers', and customers' networks. Such networks could carry concerns and threats that are not welcome to the enterprise. NGIPS can provide protection against those threats and secure sensitive information.

NGIPS can also be deployed in critical network segments—that is, parts of the network that contain highly valuable assets, also called "crown jewels." These assets could include valuable servers that contain sensitive data and private information and e-commerce systems that are highly regulated. NGIPS may also be used in the following locations:

- Branch office links

- Out-of-band management networks

- Cloud services (usually virtual NGIPS)

NGIPS Deployment Design Considerations

Security architects consider a number of different factors when designing and deploying NGIPS in an infrastructure. There are multiple questions to answer in the requirements definition phase to find the most efficient solution. This section discusses some basic considerations security engineers usually come across when designing the deployment of an NGIPS.

Threat Management and System Capabilities

The threat management and overall system capabilities provided by an NGIPS are important for security engineers. Multiple vendors offer systems with different features and protection capabilities. Even though each vendor can make claims about the system's efficacy, it is important to understand what the system can and cannot do in order to help customers maximize the protection of their investments.

It is vital to perform a *threat analysis* against the *security model* to determine how the NGIPS would perform against it. For the Cisco threat model, the NGIPS should provide protection before and during an attack, and it should offer the analysis functionality during and after. Retrospective historical analysis is also important for a protection system to offer a holistic approach to protection after an attack. A good understanding of the candidate system will help in evaluating the system against the security model and also against current and modern threats. You should perform threat analysis before evaluating the system against the security model as threats could significantly vary depending on the architecture.

The following are some of the features and capabilities security architects have to think about:

- **Mode:** You need to determine whether to use inline or passive mode and whether to use a physical or virtual sensor when designing an NGIPS solution.

- **Real-time contextual awareness:** The capability of looking through multiple contexts—such as applications, users, devices, operating systems, vulnerabilities, services, behaviors, and files—is important for modern systems.

- **Open standards:** It is important to be able to trust the rules and the efficacy of the system rules. Using open standards helps by allowing integration with third-party rules.

- **Manageability, visibility, and orchestration:** Ease of use reduces the cost of ownership and provides better efficacy in today's diverse environments. Capabilities such as automated impact assessment, IPS policy tuning, behavior analysis, anomaly detection and correlation, and user identification certainly increase the ability of operators to perform their jobs faster and more efficiently.

- **Advanced features:** Functions such as application control, URL filtering, and malware protection increase the security an NGIPS offers.

- **Security and regulatory compliance:** An NGIPS solution should be able to enable the enforcement of practices described in security standards (such as CISSP and the ISO 27000 series) in order to provide regulatory compliance (for example, with PCI, HIPAA, SOX, and FISMA).

- **Reporting:** The reporting requirements of an organization should be cross-referenced with the reporting capabilities of the system. Custom reporting is often required by modern NGIPS to allow quick analysis and response to security incidents.

Flow Handling

In order to be inspected, packet flows need to traverse the same device. Cisco ASA with FirePOWER Services, Firepower Threat Defense, and NGIPS appliances need to able to process and analyze protocols by performing analysis on traffic bidirectionally.

NGIPS devices traditionally are challenged when processing asymmetric flows because they cannot monitor the flow bidirectionally. In asymmetric flows, the forward and return paths are not the same. For example, packets flowing to a server do not follow the same hops as the returning packets. Asymmetric flows are often expected and designed in properly designed networks. They offer redundancy and take advantage of optimized switching fabrics and scalable uplinks. NGIPS devices cannot take action on packets they can't see, and they do not tolerate too many missed packets. The primary issue with asymmetric traffic and IPS is performance because unidirectional traffic needs to be buffered longer in order to wait for retransmissions and degraded detection because of missing packets in one direction. Figure 10-8 shows how the Link Aggregation Control Protocol (LACP) hashing algorithm of the port channel can end up creating asymmetric flows seen by two different NGIPS devices.

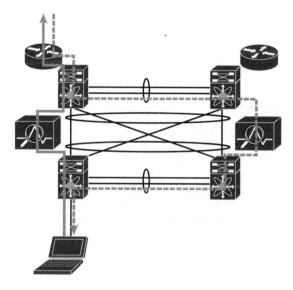

Figure 10-8   *Asymmetric Flows in a Redundant Data Center*

Network architects need to ensure that asymmetric packets flow in a deterministic manner and are properly handled. Specifically for Cisco ASA with FirePOWER Services, ASA Cluster Context Pairing allows for the packets of the same connection to be forwarded to the same firewall and thus be inspected by the same NGIPS device, ensuring better security.

Scale and Availability

A vary basic factor in network design is performance. With today's bandwidth-intensive, chatty applications and constantly increasing bandwidth requirements, an NGIPS scalable and extensible deployment is a requirement. In addition, in environments with high-traffic profiles and low-latency requirements (such as a data center), the integration with the fabric is important. For example, an NGIPS being able to integrate with virtual port channel (VPC) links in a data center allows for more integrated architecture.

For low latency, passive mode deployments would be more ideal, but they are not always possible due to security requirements. For example, what happens to a low-latency stock trading application in an overwhelmed NGIPS? The Cisco NGIPS offers a rule latency threshold option that can be configured to suspend the rules when processing time exceeds the configured limit. In addition, the Cisco NGIPS appliance has a feature called Automatic Application Bypass (AAB) that limits the time allowed to process packets through an interface.

Cisco offers high-performance NGIPS functionality that can serve today's applications. Performance and high-traffic processing are vital. For cases in which more processing power is required, Cisco ASA can allow multiple ASAs with FirePOWER Services to form a cluster (ASA Clustering Context Pairing) and serve much more aggregate bandwidth than a standalone device. Cisco Firepower NGIPS appliances themselves can be stacked together, and this more robust stack of systems then acts as one. In order to set up stacking, the primary device needs to be connected to all secondary devices using two stacking cables and a stacking module (see Figure 10-9).

Figure 10-9 *Cisco Firepower Appliance Stacking Module*

Downtime is important for networks. Some critical infrastructures have zero downtime requirements. The recovery time from a failure is important. In addition, the mean time between failure (MTBF) is often a good indicator of the average time a device stays up. Multiple high-availability features ensure that a whole network will not go down when a failure occurs.

Some features include hardware and link redundancy. For link redundancy, port channel support is widely used. For hardware redundancy, Cisco ASA Clustering combines multiple ASA devices (with FirePOWER Services) to provide high throughput and ensure that hardware failure can be properly handled by the other devices. Cisco ASA Clustering also ensures that the same flows are handled by the same device, thus eliminating asymmetric routing. Figure 10-10 shows how flows are transported over the cluster control link and processed by the same device. What's more, just for device pairs, the ASA offers the failover feature (active/standby or active/active failover pair) that automatically fails over to the healthy device in the event of a failure. The FirePOWER Services module state is not synced in this scenario.

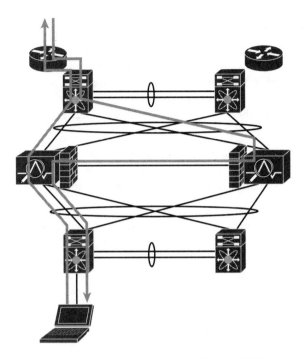

Figure 10-10 *ASA Cluster with FirePOWER Service Sending Packets to the Right ASA Through the Cluster Control Link*

Cisco Firepower NGIPS appliances also offer Firepower clustering (high availability), which differs from the ASA clustering mentioned previously. Firepower clustering establishes resiliency between two appliances or two stacks. Clustered devices synchronize state via a dedicated HA link. Both devices in a cluster must be the same model and have identical interfaces, software, and licenses. In the event of a failure, automatic failover takes place. Firepower clustering is a lot like having multiple standalone appliances, except duplicate events are suppressed.

If you have deployed a standalone device that has a zero downtime requirement, what happens if the device fails at some point? The fail-open feature offered in the Cisco NGIPS device allows you to bypass processing in the event of a failure and thus avoid downtime.

Thus, there are multiple options that can provide redundancy, performance, and extensibility. It is up to the security architect to consider the current and future network requirements and design for a highly scalable and failure-resilient NGIPS deployment.

Note   Firepower clustering and stacking are not supported on all models. We recommend using the Cisco configuration guides for platform-specific information.

Management Platform Integration

NGIPS management platforms aggregate and correlate information from the appliances and assess and control the overall activity that occurs on the network. Given the criticality of being able to manage and monitor the security of a network, you often want to plan for downtime in management platforms. Some management platforms offer high-availability capabilities to ensure that there is redundancy so that a failure does not render an NGIPS unusable.

Losing connectivity to a management platform should not render the NGIPS it manages unusable. Losing visibility of the events and configuration is acceptable, but the detection and blocking of malicious traffic should continue, and all collected events should be transmitted when the manager is recovered.

The Cisco FMC can operate in high-availability mode. Policies, user accounts, and more are shared between two Firepower devices. Events are automatically sent to both members of the redundant pair. If the FMC on one of them fails, the other one will take over. In redundant mode, two FMCs share the following information:

- User account attributes and user roles
- Authentication configuration
- Custom dashboards and workflows
- Intrusion detection, file control, access control, discovery, and correlation policies
- Device attributes

Scale is also important to the management platforms. Depending on the number of NGIPS devices, you can choose different management platforms. For the FMC, for example, a FS4000 can support up to 300 sensors with a maximum of 300 million events with 20,000 flows per second.

The ASDM is a standalone device management tool and thus does not include any redundancy scenario. Practically, ASDM is launched from the client application and connects to the ASA with FirePOWER Services or the NGIPS module for management.

Licensing and Cost

The overall cost of ownership is one of the most important factors in choosing the hardware that serves your security needs. For some vectors, licensing may be structured in ways that make the price of a product appealing, but the total end price after adding the necessary licenses ends up being much higher. Of course, you should purchase only licenses that enable the capabilities needed.

Although pricing is important, you should keep in mind that in today's complex infrastructures, standalone devices at high prices are not always the best way to go. Today's business is focused on generating results, and the infrastructure should align with that goal. Thus, implementing architectural approaches that deliver business outcomes is usually more important than purchasing purely cost-effective devices for the network without having a holistic architectural strategy.

Specifically for Cisco Firepower NGIPS, the following licenses are available:

- **Protection:** This type of license allows managed devices to perform intrusion detection and prevention and enables file control, as well as intelligence filtering, clustering, and stacking.

- **Control:** This type of license requires a Protection license and enables user and application control. It also allows devices to perform switching and routing.

- **URL Filtering:** This type of license enables cloud-based category and reputation URL filtering. It requires a Protection license and a Control license.

- **Malware:** This type of license enables network-based advanced malware protection.

- **FireSIGHT** is an additional license that comes with FMC. It allows host, application, and user discovery. If NGIPS management is performed with ASDM, a separate license is not required.

Note   Licenses are installed on the FMC and not on a managed device. FMCs in a high-availability pair do not share licenses. Therefore, each platform needs a separate FireSIGHT license. When using high availability, all FMC licenses must be replicated on both sides for high availability to work successfully.

NGIPS Deployment Lifecycle

IT and network deployment of NGIPS is an iterative process. It doesn't finish as soon as the equipment is installed on site. It continues after the implementation and constantly gets adjusted according to the organization's security needs and findings. The deployment lifecycle consists of four steps, as illustrated in Figure 10-11:

Step 1.   Policy definition

Step 2.   Product selection and planning

Step 3.   Implementation and operation

Step 4.   Evaluation and control

The policy definition phase dictates the product selection and deployment plan that are chosen to satisfy it. After the selection step, the system gets deployed in the network. The operation and continuous evaluation ensure that the system is performing its tasks efficiently and successfully. At times, adjustments need to be made either because of changes in the policy or based on findings. The following sections describe all the steps in the deployment lifecycle.

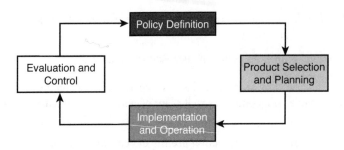

Figure 10-11   *The NGIPS Deployment Lifecycle*

Policy Definition

The security policy is the basis for security deployments. This policy defines what is considered important and how it will be protected in an infrastructure. Product and implementation are chosen in order to satisfy the security policy. Two organizations with exactly the same assets could have completely different security policies because of the way they assess risk. For example, a hospital with virtual servers in the DMZ needs to comply with HIPAA rules and thus could have a very different policy from a car repair shop that hosts its website in the DMZ. Thus, the deployment of an NGIPS or other security products starts with policy definition.

The policy definition phase includes *threat analysis,* as mentioned in Chapter 9, "AMP Threat Grid: Malware Analysis and Threat Intelligence." Before deciding on mitigations, the assets need to be identified, and the threats posed to them need to be defined. Then the threats are assigned risk (using risk analysis models). At this point, the *security model* is used to determine how the high-risk threats will be addressed (prevented or mitigated if they occur). After all potential mitigations are in place, there might still be risk (residual risk) that the security policy needs to address or accept. There will potentially be threats with mitigation costs higher than the cost of the risk occurring. In such a case, the risk may be accepted with no action taken. Of course, there are multiple tangible and intangible cost factors that can go into a security threat, and such risks should be evaluated carefully.

Compliance standards also influence the policy definition extensively. HIPAA, PCI, ISO, and other standards involve different rules that a security policy needs to satisfy in order for the organization to be compliant. Compliance audits focus on finding holes in the policy that could potentially render an organization not compliant.

After evaluating threats, risk, the security model, and compliance requirements, a security team finalizes the security policy that is used as the baseline for choosing the product and planning its deployment, as described next.

Product Selection and Planning

During the product selection and planning phase, a security team identifies the device that will fulfill the security policy requirements and puts in place a plan for implementation. This phase defines the details of how the security policy will be met. A write-up of all the requirements is created in order to help in the product decision and the implementation. After the product decision is made, having a detailed implementation plan in place helps ensure a successful installation with reduced complexity. The security team needs to account for predictability and risk awareness before proceeding with the installation.

Because the product selection dictates the success of the NGIPS installation, the requirements definition that serves as input to the decision process needs to be as detailed as possible. Some determining factors are device type, deployment size, cost, other security devices, scaling requirements, and responsibilities:

- Security architects start by identifying the use cases of the deployment. For example, an NGIPS deployed to prevent malware in a school is different than an NGIPS for preventing data exfiltration in a bank.

- The location of the NGIPS also plays a role in the requirements document as each location assumes different performance and security requirements. Potential locations could be Internet edge, data center, branch, and core. It is obvious that the performance and availability requirements in a data center are not the same as those in a branch office. For example, an NGIPS in a data center looking at only internal traffic will not identify as many threats as when sitting at the Internet edge, looking at the wild Internet traffic.

- The team needs to choose deployment options such as inline, passive, routed, switched, standalone appliance, or ASA with FirePOWER Services, Firepower Threat Defense, or virtual NGIPS, based on the use case and deployment locations.

- Connectivity is the next subject of interest. How many sensing interfaces are needed? Are they going to be passive taps or inline interface pairs? Copper or fiber? What are the speed, link aggregation, and wireless setup? The answers to all these questions need to be documented for comparison against the NGIPS vendor options available.

- Performance and scale are important considerations. How much traffic needs to be processed by the NGIPS? How much latency is acceptable? What is the peak number of connections, and what is the maximum connection rate? These questions need to be answered when scaling a deployment. Cisco ASA clustering and Firepower NGIPS stacking can be used to increase the aggregate NGIPS throughput.

  Vendor data sheets should cover device performance for engineers to use. Traditionally, the firewall industry has almost always published maximum throughput numbers in data sheets. Engineers should ensure that performance numbers are sufficient in the deployment environment. The IPS industry has generally been more conservative about throughput estimates on data sheets, partly because the performance range varies based on features used and traffic patterns. In general, using extra features increases processing load and decreases performance. For example, a Cisco Firepower NGIPS running malware inspection and application control could in some cases run below its nominal performance numbers. You should exercise caution when investigating published performance data sheets and ensure that they match the deployment use case in question.

■ Availability also needs to be in the requirements list. Is bypass (fail-open) or non-bypass going to be used? Is clustering going to be available for redundancy? Is the traffic profile many short-lived flows or long-lived ones? These availability questions to need be answered. For Cisco NGIPS specifically, clustering can provide high availability between two NGIPS devices.

■ The management platform is another consideration. Is the management platform going to manage multiple devices? How is it going to be accessible, and by whom? Is the management software going to be virtual or an actual appliance? These are some of the decisions you need to make. For Cisco, the FMC can be deployed in a virtual machine and as an appliance and supports redundancy, so there is no unmanageable NGIPS situation if one FMC fails.

■ The feature requirements needed to enforce the policy must also be identified. Is malware part of the problem to address? URL filtering, user discovery, vulnerabilities, application awareness, and control are some features that Cisco NGIPS supports and that contribute to enforcing the overall security policy.

A security team should revisit the design considerations when answering all of the preceding questions in order to cover all the potential holes and ensure a smooth implementation phase.

After you answer all these questions, you need to check the long list of information against vendor products, product support, and licensing costs in order to make a decision. In making a vendor decision, you should also consider the future. Focusing purely on current requirements might lead to poor choices for years to come. What is more, integrating NGIPS into the whole network architecture in order to bring the business outcomes desired is how product selection should be viewed. Just focusing on a cost-effective piece of equipment with features that will solve security problems today is not the way to go.

After the vendor selection, a planning document is produced from the requirements document that will dictate how the deployment will take place, what features will be used, and in what timeframes. The plan needs to be as detailed as possible in order for the deployment to go smoothly and for the NGIPS operation to be efficient and successful.

Implementation and Operation

During the implementation and operation phase, the NGIPS is put in place in the network and starts inspecting traffic. The operation steps follow the initial installation and can take quite a bit of time as the process involves configuration and fine-tuning.

The implementation phase involves the following hardware and software installations:

- **Installation of the management platform:** This installation happens first because the management platform needs to be ready to discover the device to manage and start configuring it. This step involves going through the initial configuration, giving the device an IP address and a gateway in order to be reachable.

  Specifically for Cisco Firepower NGIPS, the FMC needs to be installed in the network and configured. Either in hardware (appliance) or software (virtual machine), the FMC needs to be accessible from the network. If ASDM is the management software of choice, it can be launched and installed only after the following installation is done.

- **Installation of the Firepower appliance, the Firepower Threat Defense, the virtual appliance, or the Cisco ASA with FirePOWER Services:** This installation involves going through the initial configuration, giving the device an IP address and a gateway in order to be reachable. If the device is Cisco ASA with FirePOWER Services, then ASDM can be launched and installed by establishing an HTTPS session into the firewall's management IP address.

The initial device configuration and operation includes the following steps:

Step 1.   **Addition of the NGIPS appliance/module to the management platform:** This step includes establishing connectivity between the management platform and the device in order to begin managing it.

Step 2.   **Application of licenses and basic configuration:** After establishing connectivity, the management platform connects to the device to provision licenses that allow it to operate. Then a basic configuration is placed on the device, making sure that the policy is not very aggressive if the NGIPS is installed inline. At this stage, the NGIPS device might also be used in passive mode to prevent inadvertent packet loss.

Step 3.   **Tuning:** Initially, many of the policies need to be tuned to the needs of the network. Sometimes, especially in inline deployment, a minimal set of features is deployed to avoid inadvertent outages due to misconfigurations. Later, the configuration can be adjusted to gradually take advantage of the whole set of NGIPS features. After the initial learning phase (specifically for Cisco), Firepower NGIPS devices offer a number of recommendations to make sure the policies align with the network condition.

Step 4.   **Operation:** The final step is device operation. After finishing the tuning of the device and after ensuring a smooth transition, the NGIPS that was proactively put in passive mode can be converted to inline mode. Operation is a continuous process that requires proper planning and organization. Operating the NGIPS and using it to act appropriately or generate useful reports requires a certain amount of planning and organization. Operations teams need to be assigned and take their place in the day-to-day NGIPS operation and support.

Evaluation and Control

The final phase in the deployment lifecycle process is evaluation and control. That is the phase that verifies all previous steps and serves as feedback to the policy definition step. Findings and lessons learned from the evaluation are fed into the policy, which can be adjusted to accommodate make the environment more secure.

Specifically for Cisco Firepower NGIPS, all features that apply to the after phase in the security model fall under evaluation and control. Some of these features include:

■ **Snort rule tuning:** Snort signature tuning happens initially after NGIPS implementation.

■ **Signature updates:** SourceFire Rule Updates (SRU) take place continuously in the NGIPS. The updates ensure that there is coverage for the most recent threats and exploits.

■ **Firepower recommendations:** The FMC uses host profile information to make recommendations about the rules that should apply to your environment. It can associate the host, OS, and applications with the rules that apply to them. It also revisits the rules that are already applied in the system. The Firepower recommendations should be used continuously to improve the security of the system.

■ **Vulnerability scans:** These scans should be leveraged in Cisco NGIPS occasionally in order to identify vulnerable devices and patch them. Periodically finding vulnerable hosts helps prioritize and keep the system up-to-date.

When the system identifies an incident, investigation needs to take place to mitigate it and find the root cause. Analytics and NGIPS reports can be used to investigate the incident. After the root cause is identified and addressed, lessons learned should be collected in order to update the security policy. If misconfiguration or issues were responsible, then the NGIPS policy also needs to be updated.

Obviously, NGIPS deployment is not finished as soon as the equipment is installed. It is an iterative process that involves ensuring that the security policy and the NGIPS are up-to-date and proved the best protections possible.

Summary

As you have seen in this chapter, if IPS was important for the security of legacy networks, NGIPS is essential in today's security landscape. Features such as application and contextual awareness, file control, and intelligence correlation can reduce complexity and increase the security of a modern infrastructure.

Specifically for Cisco, NGIPS is available in the ASA with FirePOWER Services, with Firepower Threat Defense, and also as a standalone virtual or physical appliance. There are multiple deployment options to fit different customer needs, depending on the deployment use case and location. When designing the deployment of NGIPS, network architects need to consider various factors, including system capabilities, traffic flow, and scale and availability. The deployment process is not a one-and-done step. It is an iterative process of defining the security policy, choosing products, and planning, operating, and evaluating the efficacy of the system.

Chapter 11

Configuring Cisco
Next-Generation IPS

This chapter covers the following topics:

■ Policy

■ Snort rules

■ Performance settings

■ Stack/cluster

You learned in Chapter 10, "Introduction to and Deployment of Cisco Next-Generation IPS," how security architects can use next-generation intrusion prevention systems (NGIPS) in modern networks. A simple and efficient configuration interface allows administrators to use a wealth of NGIPS functions easily. The Cisco NGIPS product is not only properly architected to offer the best functionality in the industry but also comes with an intuitive management platform, the Firepower Management Center (FMC).

This chapter introduces the configuration options available in the FMC. It describes policy configuration options, IPS rules, Snort, and NGIPS preprocessors. Finally, it goes over performance settings as well as stack and cluster configuration.

Note You can also use Adaptive Security Device Manager (ASDM) with FirePOWER services and Firepower Threat Defense (FTD) to configure NGIPS features in Cisco ASA with FirePOWER Services. ASDM is presented in Chapter 4, "Troubleshooting Cisco ASA with FirePOWER Services and Firepower Threat Defense (FTD)."

Policy

In Cisco Firepower NGIPS, an IPS policy consists of a set of settings that control the features available in Cisco NGIPS products. The FMC is built to efficiently manage all the features and allow security engineers to leverage the tools at their disposal in a simple and consistent manner. As NGIPS features keep growing, the management interface adds extra functionality but keeps complexity for administrators to a minimum.

Note   Cisco ASA with FirePOWER Services, Firepower Threat Defense and Cisco NGIPS appliances (after version 5.4) have the capability to locally manage SSL/TLS communications and decrypt the traffic before applying attack, application, and malware detection policies. SSL decryption can be used in passive and active mode and supports HTTPS- and StartTLS-based protocols like SMTPS and FTPS. Thus, the NGIPS policy configuration options presented in the following sections can also be applied to encrypted traffic that is first processed by the SSL decryption engine.

Policy Layers

An intrusion policy in Cisco NGIPS consists of the base policy and a set of other policies that customize the base policy. These policies are applied to the system in a layered order as the overall intrusion policy (see Figure 11-1).

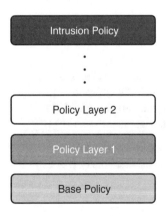

Figure 11-1   *NGIPS Layered Approach*

In FMC, you can see the policy layers by going into a policy and editing the Policy Layers settings (see Figure 11-2). The base policy is the bottom policy and contains a summary of the rules in it. The Policy Layer page has multiple options to edit or reorder the policy layers in the IPS.

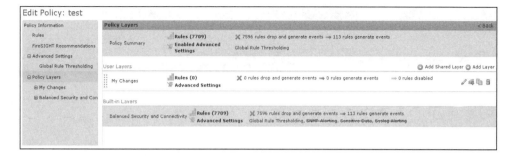

Figure 11-2 *A Layered NGIPS Policy Configuration*

Variables

Variables are used in multiple locations in Cisco Firepower NGIPS. IPS rules use precon-figured variables representing networks and ports. For example, the inside (protected) network is represented by the variable $HOME_NET, and the outside (unprotected) network is represented by the variable $EXTERNAL_NET. Other variables are used in more specialized rules. For example, $HTTP_SERVERS represents the web servers and $HTTP_PORTS the ports used by these servers.

There are two types of variables:

■ **System default variables that are the preconfigured variables in the system:** These include $AIM_SERVERS, $DNS_SERVERS, $EXTERNAL_NET, $FILE_DATA_PORTS, $GTP_PORTS, $HOME_NET, $HTTP_PORTS, $HTTP_SERVERS, $ORACLE_PORTS, $SHELLCODE_PORTS, and more.

■ **Policy variables that override default variable:** They are used in specific policies.

You can manage variables can in the FMC's Variable Set section of the Objects tab. Here you can edit or create the default and other variable sets to be used in an IPS policy.

If you click the Add Variable Set button shown in Figure 11-2, you get the screen shown in Figure 11-3, where you can create new network or port variables and assign them to the default or policy-specific (customized) variable sets used in an IPS policy, as shown in Figure 11-4.

When creating a network variable, you can use more than one address; just separate addresses with commas—for example, [192.168.1.2, 10.10.10.2, 172.18.1.2]. You can also use CIDR representation—for example, [192.168.1.2, 10.10.10.2, 172.18.1.0/24]. In addition, you can exclude addresses from a list by using an exclamation point—for example, [192.168.1.2, !10.10.10.2, 172.18.1.0/24].

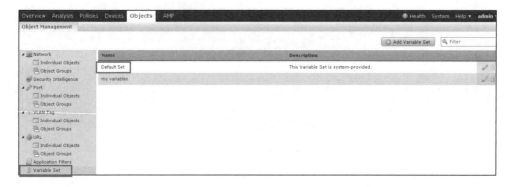

Figure 11-3   *Variable Sets in FMC's Objects Screen*

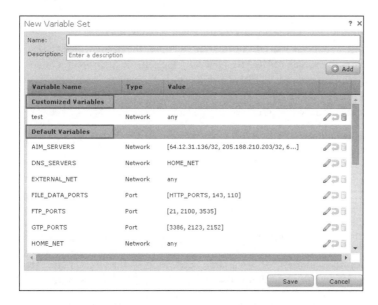

Figure 11-4   *Creating New Variable Sets in FMC*

When creating port variables, you can use ranges, such as [25-121]. The following are some other possibilities:

■ **For p**orts less than a number, you can use this format: [-1024].

■ **For p**orts more than a number, you can use this format: [1024-].

■ To exclude ports, you can use this format: [!25].

■ To list ports, you can use this format: [25, !21, 80-].

When you accurately define variables, the processing of the rules using them is optimized and the right systems are monitored for illegitimate traffic. By leveraging variables, you can more efficiently change the variable value without changing all the rules

for which that variable is used. For example, if multiple rules are defined to protect the web servers, you would need only to define or update variable $HTTP_SERVERS instead of updating all the rules.

Configuring a Cisco Firepower Intrusion Policy

A Cisco Firepower intrusion policy is configured in the IPS Policy tab in the FMC (see Figure 11-5). A policy is applied in an access control policy, which in turn is enforced in the Cisco Firepower system. This section assumes that the NGIPS system interfaces are already configured and the access policy that will use an IPS policy for inspection is set with an Allow action, as shown in Figure 11-6. (Other actions cannot be used with IPS policies.) Depending on the software version of the system, the policies in the intrusion policy could be in the Access Control dropdown instead of in a separate Intrusion dropdown.

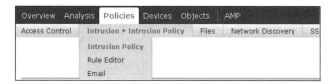

Figure 11-5 *IPS Policy Configuration*

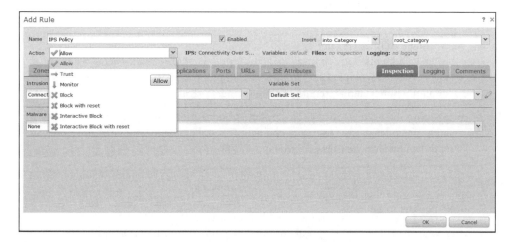

Figure 11-6 *Allow Action Used in an Access Policy That Will Leverage an IPS Policy*

You can click the Create Policy button to create a new policy. The next prompt, shown in Figure 11-7, allows you to set a name, a description, whether to drop and trigger an event when deployed inline and a rule with an action of Drop and Generate Event is matched, and the default policy used as a base policy.

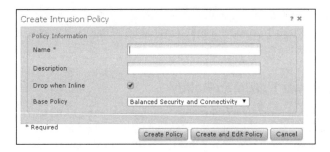

Figure 11-7 *New Policy*

The default intrusion policies are policies that exist in the system by default and can be used as starting points for new configurations. These are the available default intrusion policies:

- **Balanced Security and Connectivity:** This policy is built for both speed and detection. It serves as a good starting point for most organizations and deployments.

- **Connectivity over Security:** This policy is for organizations where connectivity takes precedence over network infrastructure security. It enables far fewer rules than does the Security over Connectivity policy.

- **Maximum Detection:** This policy is built to encompass a selection of critical recent vulnerabilities with CVSS scores of at least 7.5. This policy favors detection over throughput.

- **No Rules Active:** This policy has all rules and preprocessors disabled. It is used when an administrator chooses to create a policy from scratch. This is not true for FirePOWER version 5.4 and later, where all preprocessors have been abstracted out of an IPS policy and are configured in the network analysis policy.

- **Security over Connectivity:** This policy is built for organizations where security takes precedence over user convenience. This policy could generate false positives and disruptions when first deployed.

A newly deployed Firepower system comes with two custom default policies provided by Cisco: Initial Inline (see Figure 11-8) and Initial Passive. They are not default policies applied by default.

After you create a policy, it appears in the Policy Information section in the IPS Policy tab, as shown in Figure 11-9.

When using a default policy as the base policy, an administrator can edit the base policy (using the Manage Base Policy option) and choose whether to allow rule updates to modify the base policy. Note that rule updates change rules, preprocessor rules, and default policy settings for rules that have not been customized by the administrator.

Policy Information   < Bac

Name   Initial Inline Policy

Description   Default policy

Drop when Inline   ☑

🗔 **Base Policy**   Balanced Security and Connectivity ▼   ✎ Manage Base Polic
   ⊙ The base po   --System-Provided Policies--   3-001-vrt)
                    Balanced Security and Connectivity
   📊 **This policy h** Connectivity Over Security   ✎ Manage Rule
      ➡ 355 rules ge Maximum Detection   🔍 Vie
      ✕ 7756 rules d No Rules Active   🔍 Vie
                      Security Over Connectivity
   No recommendatic   --User Created Policies--   et up FireSIGHT recommendations.
                      Initial Inline Policy
                      Initial Inline Policy - Non Default
                      test   Commit Changes   Discard Changes
                      test2

Figure 11-8   *Default Inline Policy*

Figure 11-9   *Policy Information*

The rules deployed by the default policy in use can be edited by using the Rules option in the Policy Information section. When you're editing a rule, it appears in the My Changes section of the Policy Information. You'll learn more about editing and creating IPS rules later in this chapter.

Committing a Policy

The preceding sections explain how to configure various aspects of an IPS policy. After all the changes have been made, the policy doesn't take effect unless it is committed. When you click the Commit Changes button (refer to Figure 11-8), you might be prompted to insert a comment that describes the change. The comment is a configurable option under the intrusion policy preferences. Comments are stored in the audit logs and thus are searchable. Alternatively, you can choose to discard the changes, in which case you remove the changes since the last commit. Finally, if you choose to leave the Intrusion Policy screen with uncommitted changes, the changes are not lost. They remain uncommitted and can be revisited later to be committed or discarded.

After a policy is committed, Firepower performs a validation check to make sure there are no incorrect or invalid settings. For example, enabling a rule that uses a disabled pre-processor would be flagged after the commit. For version 5.4 and later, the preprocessor check does not happen.

The committed policy configuration or changes further need to be applied to an access control policy (see Figure 11-10).

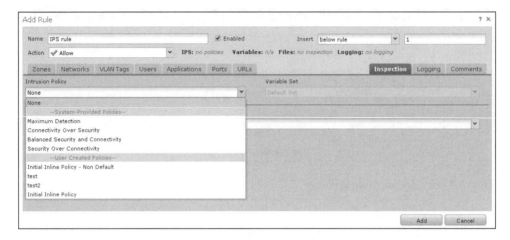

Figure 11-10 *IPS Policy Applied in the Inspection Tab of a Rule in the Access Control Policy*

The access control policy that contains the IPS policy is then applied to a device in the Targets tab of the policy, as shown in Figure 11-11.

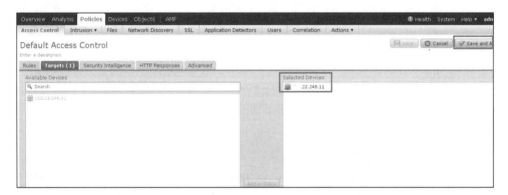

Figure 11-11 *Applying an Access Control Policy to a Device*

Snort Rules

The core of Cisco Firepower system's IPS capability is the IPS rule base and the detection engine, which includes preprocessors. When a Cisco NGIPS is booted, the engine is initialized, the rule structures are initialized, and then traffic is matched against the rules.

The Cisco Firepower NGIPS engine is based on Snort. Snort is an open source IPS tool, originally created by SourceFire, that is widely used in the industry. Snort identifies malicious traffic that is subjected to deep inspection according to the enabled rules in the IPS policy.

A rule defines a set of keywords and options to match against in order to identify security policy violations, known network attack patterns, and other malicious activity. The IPS engine matches packets against the criteria specified in each rule, and if a rule is matched, the rule action field is triggered. For example, if a rule matches on an exploit with the action Drop, the offending packet is dropped. After the offending packet is dropped, the flow is blacklisted, and no new packets from the flow are passed.

During initialization, the Firepower NGIPS engine groups rules into sets on Snort rule headers and options properties. These sets are organized so that the rule options for all the rules with common unique characteristics are listed together.

A malicious packet could possibly match more than one rule and trigger event. As rule options are matched, events are queued until all options are processed. The final selection of the event triggered is chosen based on the following criteria:

- Event processing order is considered.

- Rules generating events supersede those set to Drop and Generate.

- Content-matching events supersede anomaly detection events.

- Protocol content events supersede generic content events.

- Longer content length matches supersede shorter content matches.

The events are sent from the NGIPS device to FMC, and they are stored in the database of all intrusion events and can be queried later.

Rule Anatomy

Snort uses a simple and flexible description language that is powerful for defining the indicators that the IPS policy should be matching against. Although most Snort rules are written in a single line, you can have rules span multiple lines by adding a backslash (\) to the end of each line, as in this example:

```
alert top $EXTERNAL_NET any -> HTTPS_SERVERS $HTTPS_PORTS \
   (msg: "Example rule"; flow: to_server, established; \
   uricontent: "cgi/test/mal.exe"; reference: cve-1991-1345; \
   classtype: web-application-activity; sid: 9991; rev:1;)
```

A Snort rule has two sections: a header and a body. The header contains the action, protocol, source, and destination IP addresses and netmasks, as well as the source and destination port. The body contains keywords that define the criteria to trigger an alert. The body keywords contain event messages, patterns in the payload to match, and specifications of which parts of the packet to match on. In the preceding rule, this is the header:

```
alert top $EXTERNAL_NET any -> HTTPS_SERVERS $HTTPS_PORTS
```

And this is the body:

```
(msg: "Example rule"; flow: to_server, established; \
uricontent: "cgi/test/mal.exe"; reference: cve-1991-1345; \
classtype: web-application-activity; sid: 9991; rev:1;)
```

As you can see, the rule content is included in parentheses. The keywords are separated by semicolons.

In the FMC, all IPS policy rules are available in a policy under Policy Information (see Figure 11-12). Rules are grouped based on categories. Multiple other rule classification options can be used to look through the rules. For example, you can view the rules according to the rule configuration in order to match on the rule state. Using the Rule Content option allows you to view the rules based on the matched content. The Platform Specific option allows you to look for rules based on the platform of interest. Many more options are available.

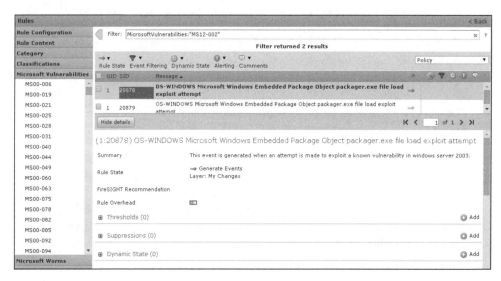

Figure 11-12 *IPS Policy Rules*

The following sections provide more information of the anatomy and the details of rules.

Rule Headers

In the previous rule example, this is the header:

```
alert tcp $EXTERNAL_NET any -> HTTPS_SERVERS $HTTPS_PORTS
```

As you can see, these are the header options:

- **alert:** Generates an event when triggered. Other options are **pass, generate events, drop and generate event,** and **disabled.**

- **tcp:** Matches TCP traffic only. Other protocols are **udp, icmp,** and **ip.**

- **$EXTERNAL_NET:** Matches traffic from any host that is not on the internal network.

- **any:** Matches traffic sent to any destination.

- **-> :** Matches external traffic destined for the TLS servers on the network. A bidirectional operator <> is also available.

- **$HTTPS_SERVERS:** Matches traffic to be delivered to TLS servers.

- **$HTTPS_PORTS:** Matches TLS port traffic.

You can access Snort rules in the FMC by selecting **Policies > Intrusion > Intrusion Policy > Rule Editor** (shown later, in Figure 11-16). Figure 11-13 shows how an IPS rule header is accessible and editable in the rule editor. You can see all the header options and how they can be configured according to the rule author's needs.

Note The Classification field is from the rule body and belongs in the **classtype** Snort option.

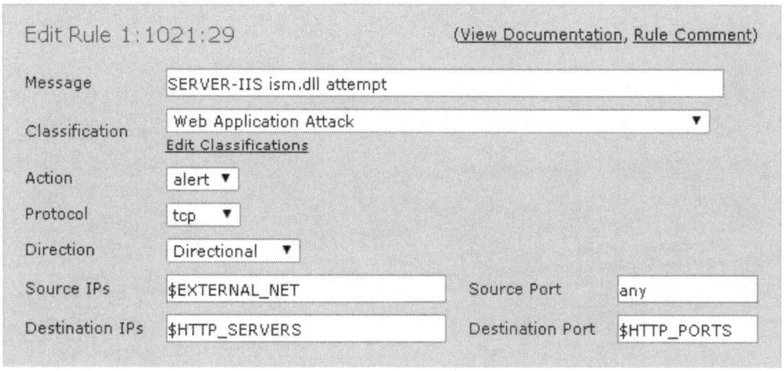

Figure 11-13 *Editing a Snort Rule's Header Fields*

Rule Body

The body of a rule looks like this:

```
(msg: "Example rule"; flow: to_server, established; \
uricontent: "cgi/test/mal.exe"; reference: cve-1991-1345; \
classtype: web-application-activity; sid: 9991; rev:1;)
```

The **flow** value can be set to **to_client**, **to_server**, **from_client**, or **from_server**, based on who initiates the connection. **flow** can also be set to **established**, **stateless**, **no_stream**, or **only stream** based on the type of connection.

Content rules contain the **content** keyword. More than one **content** condition can exist in a rule. **content** can use an **offset** and a **depth** for where and how long to match in the packet.

sid is a unique Snort identifier. **rev** is the revision of the rule.

A **flags** keyword can be used to match on the TCP flags of the packet.

Another option that can be added to the rule is **metadata** that signifies the service the rule is matching on. It can also affect **impact_flag**. **metadata** is not necessarily a required match. Until the service is identified for a flow or until there is not a service identified, the IPS falls back to ports to identify a service. If the service is identified, the ports the traffic traverses from are ignored.

Other options are **file_data** to match on HTTP or email response data, **detection_filter** to define the rate that must be exceeded by a source or destination host before a rule can generate, **fast_pattern** to define patterns that qualify for further inspection, **flowbits** for tags to be used in subsequent rules, and **byte_jump**, **byte_test**, and **byte_extract** to extract and test through certain bytes in the packet payload.

Figure 11-14 shows the rule's body options as they appear when editing a rule in rule editor. You can change the option order in the rule. Also, you can add more options to match different packet fields.

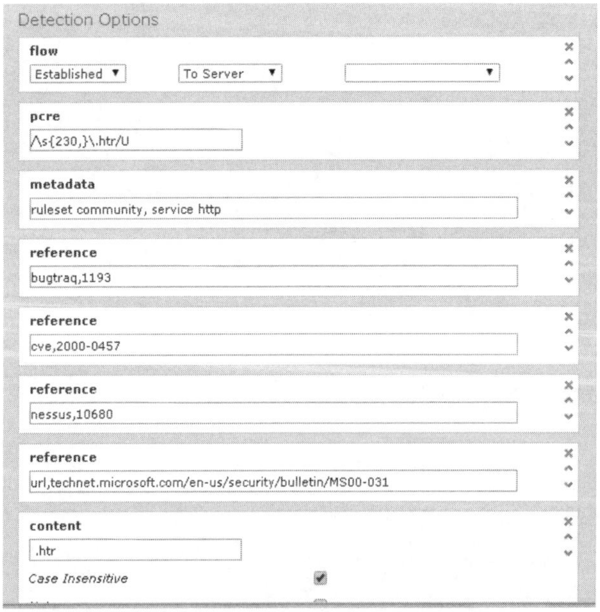

Figure 11-14 *Editing a Snort Rule's Body*

Writing a Rule

The process of authoring a rule is not complicated:

Step 1.   Clearly identify the problem that requires a rule. If the issue is a security vulnerability, for example, then that malicious indicator of compromise needs to be written to alert on exploit attempts.

Step 2.   Capture the offending traffic in question by using packet captures.

Step 3.   Look into the captured traffic to identify common characteristics, such as ports, protocols, and source or destinations.

Step 4.   Identify unique characteristics in the traffic. For example, are you looking for a specific pattern in the packet payload?

Step 5.   After completing the analysis, write a rule in the FMC that satisfy all the criteria defined in the previous steps.

Step 6.   Push the rule to the IPS and, after generating the offending traffic, make sure the rule operates as expected.

Because Snort is an open source language, custom rules can be written by anyone and reused in the Firepower NGIPS configuration. Cisco Firepower can use third-party rules. You can import them by clicking the Import button in the Rule Updates tab in the FMC (see Figure 11-15).

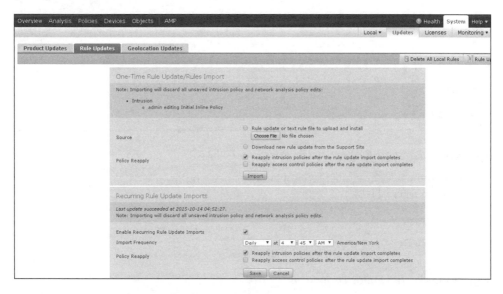

Figure 11-15   *Importing Snort Rules in the FMC*

You can further use and edit the imported rules in the layered IPS policy. You can configure the Rule Update function to perform periodic updates of Cisco-authored SourceFire Rule Updates (SRU) from an external location (feed).

Managing Snort Rules in FMC

You can access and manage Snort rules in an IPS policy in the FMC by using **Policies >
Intrusion > Intrusion Policy > Rule Editor**, as shown in Figure 11-16, or in an intrusion
policy found under **Policy > Access Control > Intrusion** in versions 5.4 and later.

Figure 11-16   *Policies > Intrusion > Intrusion Policy > Rule Editor*

Figure 11-17 shows the rules as they appear in the IPS policy editor.

Rules									< Back
Rule Configuration		Filter:							?
Rule Content									
Category								Policy ▼	
app-detect		Rule State	Event Filtering	Dynamic State	Alerting	Comments		Policy	
blacklist		GID	SID	Message ▲				Layer: My Changes	
browser-chrome		1	32845	APP-DETECT Absolute Software Compudrace outbound connection - 209.55.113.223				Base Policy	
browser-firefox		1	32846	APP-DETECT Absolute Software Computrace outbound connection - absolute.com	⇒				
browser-ie		1	32847	APP-DETECT Absolute Software Computrace outbound connection - bh.namequery.com	⇒				
browser-other		1	32848	APP-DETECT Absolute Software Computrace outbound connection - namequery.nettrace.co.za	⇒				
browser-plugins		1	26286	APP-DETECT Absolute Software Computrace outbound connection - search.dnssearch.org	⇒				
browser-webkit		1	26287	APP-DETECT Absolute Software Computrace outbound connection - search.namequery.com	⇒				
content-replace		1	32849	APP-DETECT Absolute Software Computrace outbound connection - search.us.namequery.com	⇒				
decoder		1	32850	APP-DETECT Absolute Software Computrace outbound connection - search2.namequery.com	⇒				
exploit-kit		1	32851	APP-DETECT Absolute Software Computrace outbound connection - search64.namequery.com	⇒				
file-executable		1	25358	APP-DETECT Acunetix web vulnerability scan attempt	⇒				
file-flash		1	25360	APP-DETECT Acunetix web vulnerability scanner authentication attempt	⇒				
file-identify		1	25362	APP-DETECT Acunetix web vulnerability scanner base64 XSS attempt	⇒				
file-image		1	25359	APP-DETECT Acunetix web vulnerability scanner probe attempt	⇒				
file-java		1	25364	APP-DETECT Acunetix web vulnerability scanner prompt XSS attempt	⇒				
file-multimedia		1	25361	APP-DETECT Acunetix web vulnerability scanner RFI attempt	⇒				
Classifications		1	25363	APP-DETECT Acunetix web vulnerability scanner URI injection attempt	⇒				
Microsoft Vulnerabilities		1	25365	APP-DETECT Acunetix web vulnerability scanner XSS attempt	⇒				
Microsoft Worms		1	23616	APP-DETECT Amazon Kindle 3.0 User-Agent string requested	⇒				
Platform Specific		1	23617	APP-DETECT Amazon Kindle chrome scriptable plugin attempt					

Figure 11-17   *Snort Rules in an IPS Policy in the FMC*

To view the rules in another layer of an IPS policy, you can use the Policy dropdown, as
shown in Figure 11-18.

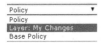

Figure 11-18   *IPS Policy Dropdown*

The rule options bar, shown in Figure 11-19, allows you to set various options to multiple rules at the same time. For example, you can set comments or alerts, change the
temporary state, or filter rules.

Figure 11-19 *Rule Options Bar*

Other rule management capabilities the FMC offers are rule filtering with the filter bar, rule grouping with the rule grouping accordion, rule querying, setting of rule state, event filtering to limit the events triggered based on certain criteria, setting of dynamic state to rate limit the events triggered, alerting (SNMP), and comments.

You can see that the FMC allows for fine-grained and efficient management of all IPS rules used in Cisco NGIPS devices.

Cisco NGIPS Preprocessors

IPS pattern matching is almost impossible because of the different protocols and their intricacies. For example, matching a file pattern in SMTP email traffic is not performed the same way as matching it when flowing through HTTP with compression enabled. For that reason, the Cisco NGIPS offers a variety of preprocessors that normalize traffic so that it can be matched against the defined Snort rules.

The preprocessors attempt to make the streams of packets as much as possible like the reassembled packets that will be seen by the endpoints receiving them. For example, the preprocessors perform checksum calculation, stream and fragment reassembly, stateful inspection, and more. Each preprocessor has a variety of settings to be configured in order to minimize false positives and false negatives. In addition, customized ones perform dedicated resources to detect specific suspicious attack activity to avoid burdening the system with these tasks.

The following preprocessors are available in the Cisco Firepower NGIPS:

- **DCE/RPC:** The DCE/RPC preprocessor monitors DCE/RPC and SMB protocol streams and messages for anomalous behavior or evasions.

- **DNS:** The DNS preprocessor inspects DNS responses for overflow attempts and for obsolete and experimental DNS record types.

- **FTP and Telnet:** The FTP and Telnet preprocessor normalizes FTP and Telnet streams before they are passed to the IPS engine. It requires TCP stream preprocessing.

- **HTTP:** The HTTP preprocessor normalizes HTTP requests and responses for IPS processing, separates HTTP messages to improve IPS rule performance, and detects URI-encoding attacks.

- **Sun RPC:** The Sun RPC preprocessor normalizes and reassembles fragmented SunRPC records so the rules engine can process the complete record.

- **SIP:** The SIP preprocessor normalizes and inspects SIP messages to extract the SIP header and body for further rule processing and generates events when identifying out-of-order calls and SIP message anomalies.

- **GTP:** The GTP preprocessor normalizes General Service Packet Radio (GPRS) Tunneling Protocol (GTP) command channel signaling messages and sends them to the rules engine for inspection.

- **IMAP and POP:** The IMAP and POP preprocessors monitor server-to-client email traffic and alert on anomalies. They also extract and decode email attachments and allow further processing by the NGIPS rules engine and other Cisco Firepower features.

- **SMTP:** The SMTP preprocessor inspects SMTP traffic for anomalous behavior and extracts and decodes email attachment for further processing.

- **SSH:** The SSH preprocessor detects SSH buffer overflow attempts and monitors for illegal SSH versions.

- **SSL:** The SSL preprocessor monitors the SSL handshake transactions. After the SSL session is encrypted, the SSL preprocessor stops inspecting. It requires TCP stream preprocessing. The SSL preprocessor can reduce the amount of false positives and save detection resources from the IPS system.

- **SCADA:** There are two supervisory control and data acquisition (SCADA) protocols for which the Cisco Firepower NGIPS offers preprocessors: DNP3 and Modbus. These protocols monitor and control industrial facilities. The SCADA preprocessors monitor the DNP and Modbus protocols for anomalies and decode their messages for further rule inspection.

- **Network:** Multiple network and transport layer preprocessors detect attacks exploiting the following:

  - Checksum verification

  - Ignoring VLAN headers

  - Inline normalization

  - IP defragmentation

  - Packet decoding

  - TCP stream

  - UDP stream

The packet decoder normalizes packet headers and payloads for further processing. The inline normalization preprocessor normalizes traffic to prevent evasion techniques in inline deployments. The rest of the network preprocessors detect anomalous network or transport layer behavior.

■ **Threat detection:** The threat detection preprocessors detect specific threats and include the following:

- Back Orifice Detection

- Portscan Detection

- Rate-Based Attack Prevention

- Sensitive Data Detection

The FMC offers a wealth of settings for each preprocessor that are available in the IPS policy Advanced Settings view. Rules can also be viewed based on the preprocessor they are using (see Figure 11-20). For version 5.4 and later, the rules can be edited under **Policy > Access Control > Intrusion.**

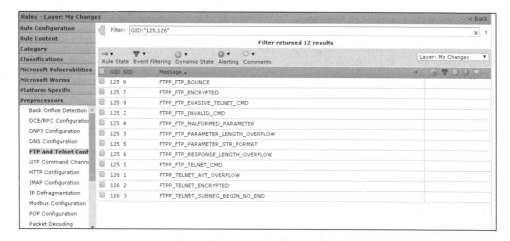

Figure 11-20   *Rules View Categorized by Preprocessor*

Firepower Recommendations

Firepower can offer recommendations about rules that apply to the operating systems and the server and client applications detected by the system. When you configure the Recommendations feature, Firepower searches through the base policy to find the rules that protect against vulnerabilities that have been identified for the discovered assets.

Based on the base policy rules, the system identifies the states in the policy and proposes new states. It optionally can automatically set the rules to the recommended settings. The rules that are disabled or that generate events and apply to the vulnerabilities discovered are set to generate events; the rules that drop and generate events and protect the assets are set to drop and generate events. Finally, the rules that do not protect identified assets are disabled. The proposed changes can be for rules and preprocessor settings as well. You can also automate generation of recommendations by using task schedules.

You can enable the Recommendations feature under IPS Policy Information as shown in Figure 11-21. In versions 5.4 and later, the Recommendations feature is set via **Policy > Access Control > Intrusion Policy**. There are two options: one to generate and preview the recommendations and the other to generate and use the recommendations. When generating recommendations, the system displays filtered views of the rules recommended to be set to Generate Events, Drop and Generate Events, or Disable. After previewing the recommendations, you can manually set the recommended options. Rules that have been set manually are not updated by the Recommendations feature. After using the proposed changes, Firepower adds a read-only Recommendations layer to the intrusion policy. Choosing not to use recommended rule states removes the layer.

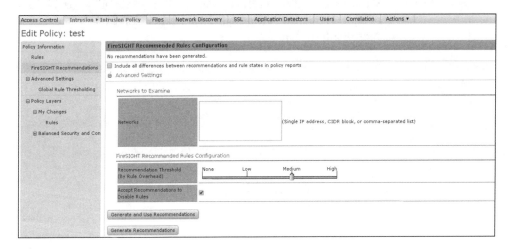

Figure 11-21   *Firepower Rule Recommendations*

The FMC also provides advanced settings in the Recommendations configuration. If the advanced settings are not used, the system applies all the recommendations to all the hosts in the system. When using the advanced settings, you can define which hosts (networks) on the network are monitored for vulnerabilities in order to provide recommendations. That influences which rules are recommended based on rule overhead and which are disabled.

In Firepower, each rule is categorized based on the rule's potential overhead introduced to the system: none, low, medium, high, or very high. In the advanced settings, you can choose the overhead level that is taken into consideration when making rule recommendations. For example, when you set medium overhead in the advanced settings, the system makes recommendations based on all rules with an overhead rating of none, low, or medium and does not make any recommendations for rules with high or very high overhead.

Performance Settings

You can improve performance of a Cisco NGIPS sensor by leveraging some performance settings in the advanced policy configuration. In version 5.4 and later, the performance settings are in the advanced settings, under **Policy > Access Control > Intrusion:**

- **Event Queue Configuration:** You can set the Event Policy configuration in the Advanced tab when editing an access control policy. You can set the maximum packet states per packet and disable content checks that will be inserted through the stream reassembly process (see Figure 11-22).

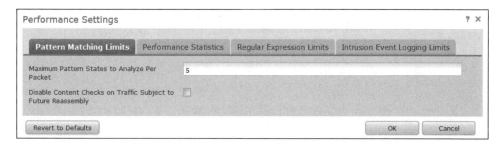

Figure 11-22   *Event Queue Configuration*

- **Latency-Based Packet Thresholding:** Many applications are not tolerant of latency. For example, high-frequency-trading traffic has a very low latency requirement. The IPS operations, especially when processing through rules and preprocessors, can introduce latency to the streams. In cases where latency is an issue, latency-based packet thresholding can be used (see Figure 11-23). Packet latency thresholding measures the total time taken to process a packet by IPS decoders, preprocessors, and rules, and it stops inspection if the processing time exceeds the configured threshold. For more accuracy, packet latency thresholding measures elapsed time from the time the packets enters the decoder; it does not measure processing time. It is obvious that when used, latency packet thresholding can let attacks pass when the threshold is met and traffic is allowed through uninspected. The options are set in the Advanced tab when editing an access control policy in the FMC.

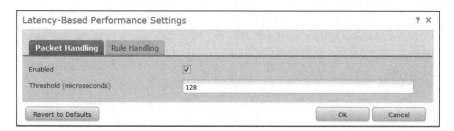

Figure 11-23   *Latency-Based Packet Thresholding*

■ **Latency-Based Rule Thresholding:** Latency-based rule thresholding is also set in the advanced settings of the IPS policy or under **Policy > Access Control > Intrusion** in version 5.4 and later. It measures and enforces a maximum processing time of packets through a rule. If a rule takes more time than the threshold specifies, a counter gets incremented, and when the counter reaches a limit, the rule is suspended for a specified period and an alert is triggered (see Figure 11-24). Latency rule thresholding is a software-based latency implementation that does not enforce strict timing. Latency rule thresholding could, of course, let attacks pass while the rule is disabled.

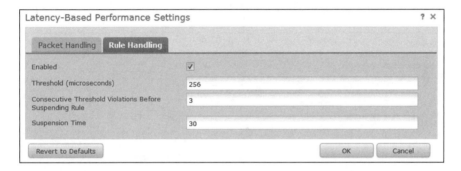

Figure 11-24   *Latency-Based Rule Handling*

■ **Performance Statistics Configuration:** The Cisco Firepower IPS maintains statistics In the IPS policy advanced settings, to alleviate processing load, you can set the intervals at which the performance statistics of the device are updated. These intervals are in seconds and number of packets analyzed.

■ **Regular Expression Limits:** Perl Compatible Regular Expressions (PCRE) are often used in Snort rules to match on packet payloads. Regular expression processing can add processing load to a device. The default regular expression match and recursion limits can be overridden in the Regular Expression Limits setting in the advanced settings of an IPS policy. Increasing the default limits could improve security but could also degrade the performance of the device.

■ **Event Logging Limits:** A packet could be matched against more than one IPS rules that generate events. When more than one events are generated by a packet, they are placed in the event queue, and the top events are logged by the device. The rule processing configuration can be set in the Advanced tab when editing a policy access control and allows you to set the queue size, the number of top events to be logged, and how the events are prioritized in the queue, as illustrated in Figure 11-25.

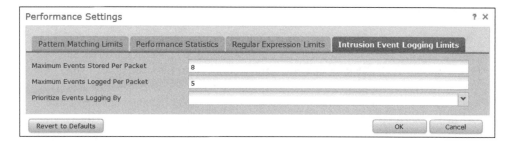

Figure 11-25 *Event Logging Limits*

The advanced settings also allow you to set a global threshold (see Figure 11-26) to manage the number of events generated by each rule over a period of time. When you're using the global threshold, that threshold applies to all rules that do not have an overriding specific threshold set.

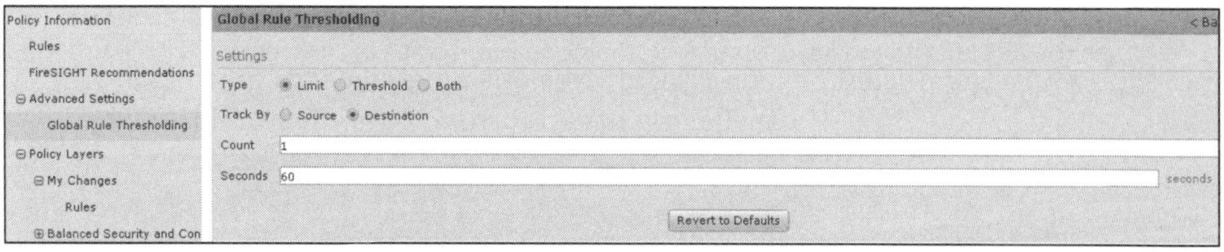

Figure 11-26 *Global Rule Threshold*

Stack/Cluster

As described in Chapter 10, Firepower NGIPS offers stacking of multiple devices that can offer much higher IPS throughput and clustering that allows for redundancy. Both options can be configured in the FMC's Devices tab.

Clicking Add brings up cluster and stack options, as shown in Figure 11-27. For either feature, more devices must be managed in the FMC in order to be configured.

Refer to Chapter 10 for more information on clustering and stacking.

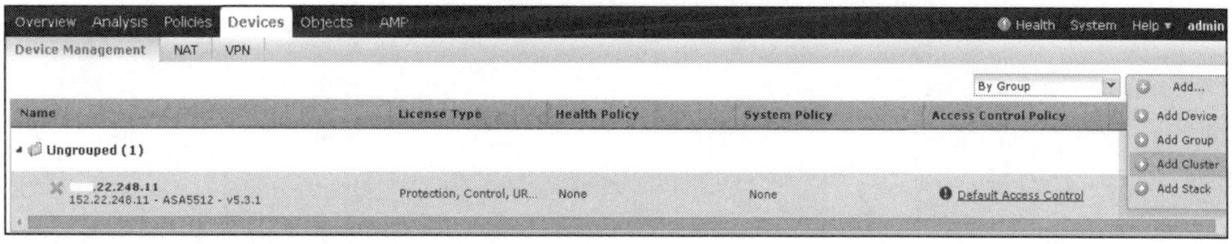

Figure 11-27 *Stack and Cluster Dropdown in the FMC's Devices Tab*

Summary

As you have seen in this chapter, Cisco NGIPS products can be fully managed using the FMC. You have seen how IPS policies can be configured and customized for each network's needs. In this chapter you also learned about Snort rules and how to write new ones. You have also learned how preprocessors are used for more efficient protocol processing in the system. You have also seen the intelligent recommendations Cisco NGIPS can offer for more efficient configuration and how to configure redundancy and stacking.

ASDM is another management platform specifically for Cisco ASA with SourceFire Services. It is covered in Chapter 12, "Reporting and Troubleshooting with Cisco Next-Generation IPS."

Reporting and Troubleshooting with Cisco Next-Generation IPS

This chapter covers the following topics:

- Analysis of IPS-related events that can help an administrator analyze malicious or suspicious activity identified by next-generation intrusion prevention systems (NGIPS)

- Troubleshooting and monitoring of an NGIPS to ensure that it is functioning properly

This chapter discusses the reporting and troubleshooting capabilities of Cisco NGIPS. As discussed in previous chapters, a Cisco NGIPS offers a wealth of intrusion prevention techniques that can be configured using the Firepower Management Center (FMC). The events and IPS activities taking place in an NGIPS are collected in the FMC logs that are available for analysis. This chapter describes basic NGIPS analysis you can perform to assess the security of an environment. In addition, when a system is facing issues, an administrator can use troubleshooting tools in the FMC to investigate the health and problems of the system.

Analysis

The FMC provides robust reporting capabilities that can help administrators investigate intrusions, indicators, or compromise and suspicious activity identified by NGIPS. An intrusion policy that is tied to an access control policy by default generates a log in the FMC at the end of every connection that triggers an IPS event. That log is unrelated to any IPS logging actions generated in the rule. When a possible intrusion or malicious activity is identified, an intrusion event is triggered that records the date, the time, the type of exploit, as well as contextual information about the source of the attack and its target. IPS rules generate connection events according to their configured default action. When a rule generates an event, the system does not automatically generate a connection event at the end of the connection that triggered the rule unless it is configured in the default action. These logs can further be used in the analysis. Any sort of connection analysis requires connection log collection on the FMC.

The FMC can help an investigator look into the NGIPS-collected data with a variety of tools:

- Event information and statistics

- Time-based reports

- Alerting

- Incident handling

- Workflows

- Correlation policies

Intrusion Events

You can use the FMC to view, review, search, and analyze intrusion events in the FMC. **Overview > Summary** offers an Intrusion menu that provides a summary of the intrusion events identified by the NGIPS (see Figure 12-1). You can adjust the time interval the events refer to by using the time range link at the top right of the page.

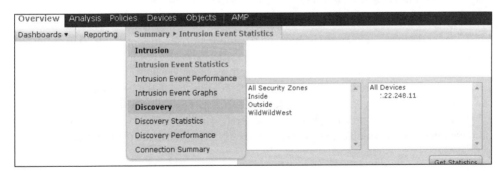

Figure 12-1 *Intrusion Event Summary Dropdown*

There are three options to review in the Intrusion menu:

- Intrusion Event Statistics

- Intrusion Event Performance

- Intrusion Event Graphs

By selecting Intrusion Event Statistics, you can see a summary of the intrusion events triggered, as shown in Figure 12-2.

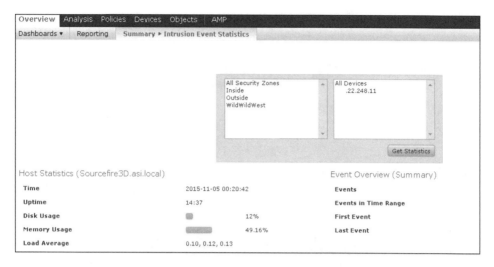

Figure 12-2 *Intrusion Event Statistics*

As shown in Figure 12-2, the Intrusion Event Statistics page includes the following:

- Host statistics, with information about the NGIPS and FMC

- An event overview, with information about the total events in the event database that stores the events triggered within the time interval

- Event statistics, with details about the event database, such as the most heavily triggered events, the zones that trigger most events, and the NGIPS that generate them

Selecting Intrusion Event Performance brings up the Intrusion Event Performance page, shown in Figure 12-3. This page allows you to generate graphs with performance statistics over time, intrusion events per second, blocked packets, bytes per packet, and more.

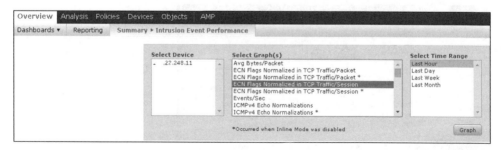

Figure 12-3 *Intrusion Event Performance*

Selecting Intrusion Event Graphs brings up the Intrusion Event Graphs page, shown on Figure 12-4. This page allows you to plot the intrusion events generated over time. You can filter the events based on NGIPS, destination ports, addresses, messages, and time. The end result is a graph that shows how the events trend over time and which intrusion events were most prevalent.

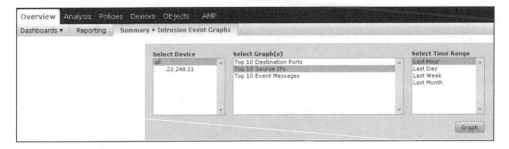

Figure 12-4   *Intrusion Event Graph*

For more detailed analysis of the event information, FMC offers the Analysis tab, which provides an Intrusions dropdown, as shown in Figure 12-5.

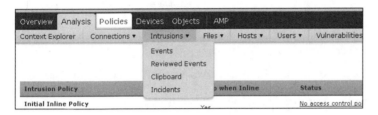

Figure 12-5   *Analysis > Intrusions in the FMC*

The Events default workflow, shown in Figure 12-6, shows the events triggered by the system in a specific time frame. The time can be adjusted using the time range link at the top right of the page. The Jump To dropdown allows you to go to various event types. Specific buttons also allow you to view, copy, delete, or download the packets that triggered the events. If you are certain that an event was not malicious, you can mark it as Reviewed to move it to the reviewed events.

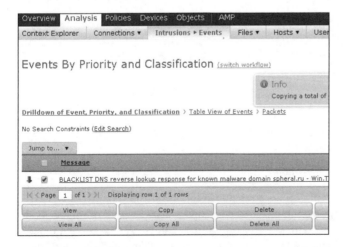

Figure 12-6   *Events Workflow*

You can see the reviewed events can by selecting **Intrusions > Reviewed Events** (refer to Figure 12-5). From the Reviewed Events page you can view, unreview, copy, delete, or download the packets that triggered the event.

You can further investigate the events shown in the Events page by associating them with logged connections, if any. To do this, you click the link of the event message name, as shown in Figure 12-7. This way, you can view the actual flows that generated the events.

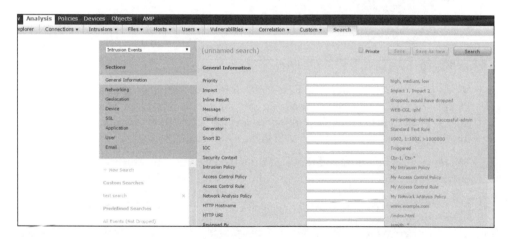

Figure 12-7 *Events in Relation to Connections*

You can search events by selecting **Analysis > Search**. You can save the search options in the Events or Reviewed Events workflows and then revisit them later by clicking the **Search** button in the workflow. The custom search page, shown in Figure 12-8, allows you to save various search criteria so that you can rerun a particular search.

Figure 12-8 *Custom Intrusion Event Search*

You can load a saved search from the save search panel on the left of the **Analysis > Search** page, which shows all the saved searches. After you load a particular search, you can run it and find the results at **Analysis > Events**.

You can use the search results on the Events page to generate new reports. Suppose you have one or more events in the Events page. You can copy them by using the Copy button (refer to Figure 12-6). Those events are then stored in the Clipboard, and you can view them by selecting **Intrusions > Events > Clipboard**, as shown in Figure 12-9.

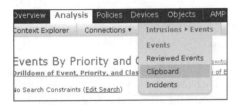

Figure 12-9   *Intrusions > Events > Clipboard*

You can use the events in the Clipboard to generate reports, as shown in Figure 12-10. You have two available options: generate a report for only the checked events or generate a report for all the events.

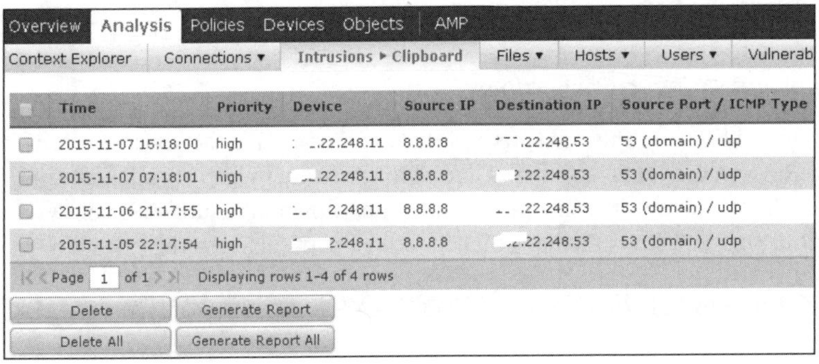

Figure 12-10   *Generating Event Reports*

When you generate a report, the next screen is Report Templates, shown in Figure 12-11. Here you can choose from the available report options and generate the report. You can then run the report immediately or save it to be run later. There are three report formats available in FMC: PDF, HTML, and CSV.

The reports can be stored and reviewed from the Overview tab. The following section provides more information on reports.

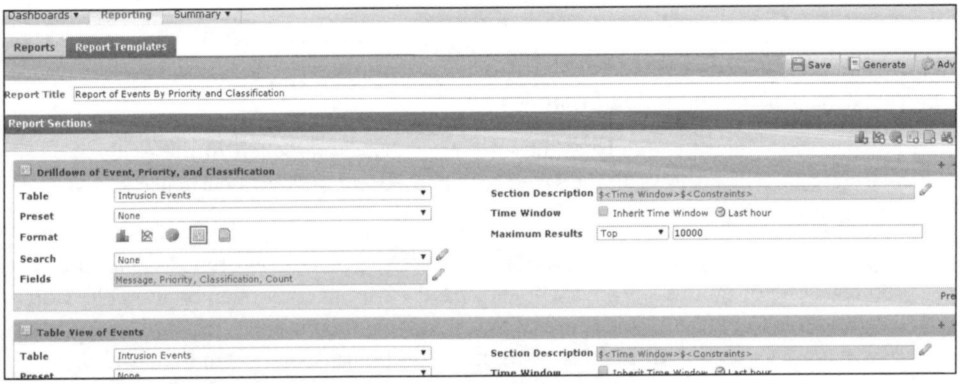

Figure 12-11   *Report Template*

Intrusion Event Workflows

A workflow, like the event workflow shown earlier, is a series of data pages in the FMC that you can use to evaluate events generated by the managed NGIPS devices. As shown previously, the FMC provides predefined event workflows that can be used for analysis of the events in the event database. You can edit the default event workflow shown in the Events page along with other workflows by selecting **Admin > User Preferences > Event View Settings, as** shown in Figure 12-12.

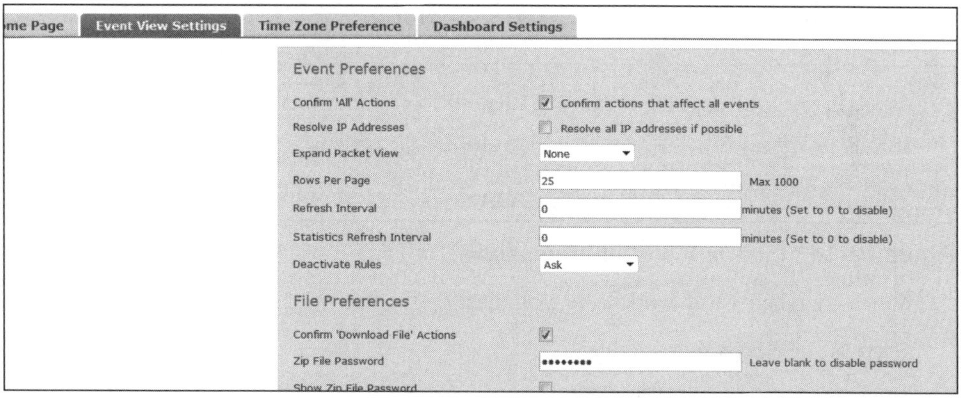

Figure 12-12 *Event View Settings*

A workflow consists of table views, detail pages, graphs, and final pages. You can change the intrusion event workflow used in the Event View Settings page with the Switch Workflow link, as shown in Figure 12-13. You can then view events based on the pages and tables in the predefined workflow chosen.

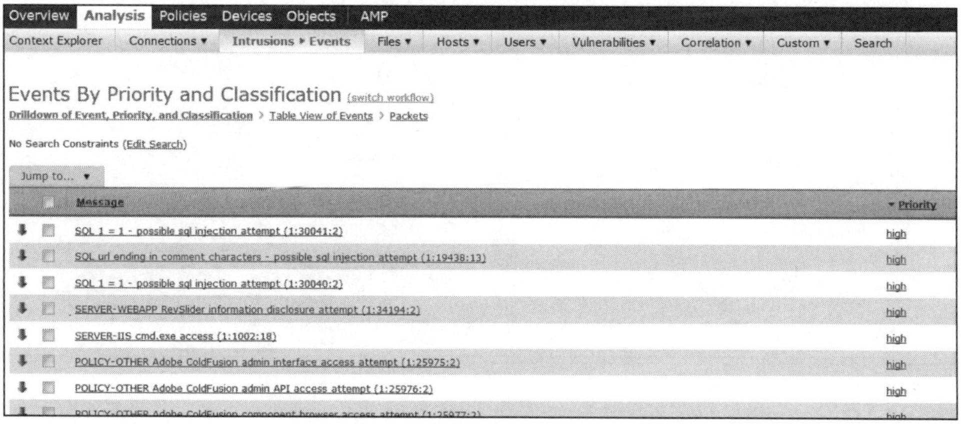

Figure 12-13 *Predefined Workflows Dropdown*

Some of these predefined workflows group events based on destination ports, destinations, impact, and priority and source or destination addresses, based on event-specific criteria or IP criteria.

If the predefined workflows are not satisfactory, you can create custom workflows by selecting **Analysis > Custom > Custom Workflows** (see Figure 12-14).

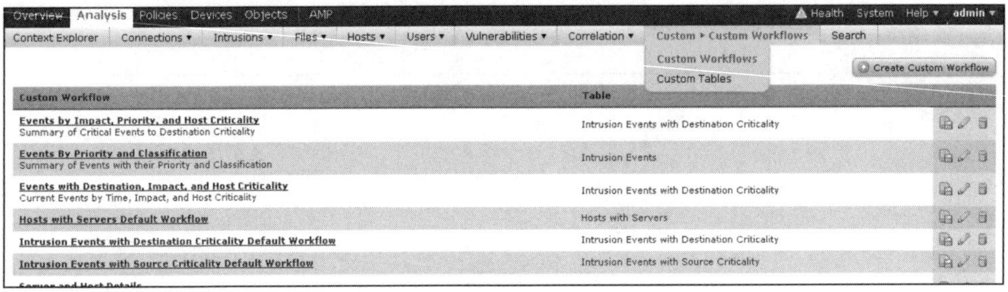

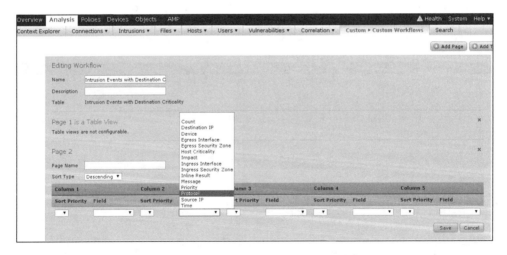

Figure 12-14   *Custom Workflows Dropdown*

When creating custom workflows, you must do the following:

Step 1.   Select a source table.

Step 2.   Define a workflow name.

Step 3.   Add pages to the workflow. You can customize pages based on the columns that should be present in the page (see Figure 12-15).

Figure 12-15   *Editing a Custom Workflow*

You can export a custom workflow from an NGIPS device and reuse it in another one by clicking the Export icon in the Custom Workflows page or by selecting **System > Tools > Import/Export**.

Reports

Cisco FMC can provide multilevel reports with event views and dashboards that can help you identify potential security threats and monitor security. It also supports custom reports. An FMC report is in PDF, HTML, or CSV format. A default report template defines the data searches and formats for the report sections. It also defines the sections, the source database with the content, and the presentation format. You can build custom report templates by using a powerful template designer. Reports can be exported and imported so they can be reused within the FMC. Input parameters can be imported in a report to expand its usefulness.

You can adjust the default template available in the FMC to include new or remove existing sections. In order to create a template, you first need to go to the Events page (see Figure 12-16) and navigate in the events so that only interesting events are included in the viewer. Then you click Report Designer, highlighted in Figure 12-16. You can also create event reports by selecting **Overview > Reporting > Report Templates** and using saved searches.

Figure 12-16 *Report Designer Option in the Events Page*

Figure 12-17 shows the first sections of the report template built from the intrusion event workflow. You can set a report title, delete any unwanted sections, adjust titles and formats of sections, change settings of section fields, add page breaks and text, and add tables of contents and cover pages through the advanced settings. Then you can save the template.

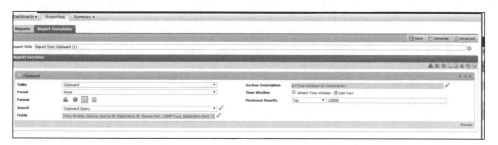

Figure 12-17 *Report Template*

You can also export a report template, by clicking the Import button to import a previously exported template.

When you complete the report design, you can generate it by using the Generate button. The Generation popup page allows you to set the report name, the global timeframe that will be applied to all sections in the report, and the format (PDF, CMV, or HTML).

If input parameters are used in the report, then the generation process prompts for these parameters. For example, Figure 12-18 demonstrates setting the report template in a report.

You can also schedule reports to run at later time from the task scheduler available at **System > Tools > Scheduling > Add Task.** You can schedule the tasks to run once or to recur at certain times. A status email can be sent to the administrator to confirm report completion.

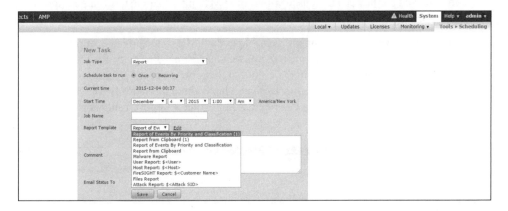

Figure 12-18   *Report Scheduling*

Finally, the Reports tab, available at **Overview > Reports**, includes all the previously run reports. You can download or delete any of the stored report files.

Incidents

An incident is a violation of a security policy. Certain events could be considered incidents for one environment and normal behavior for others. For example, port scanning activity could be part of a monitoring system and would therefore not need to be flagged as malicious. Other events, like a compromised host exfiltrating Social Security numbers, should definitely be flagged as an incident to be investigated. It is up to the system administrator to define what suspicious behavior constitutes an incident and what security options are available.

In order for an organization to respond to incidents appropriately, it needs to be properly prepared and organized for incident response. After a defined incident is observed, a system should notify the administrator, who then starts the investigation process. A communication plan needs to be in place in order to inform the parties involved. The next step is containment and remediation of the threat. Finally, a debriefing process identifies the lessons learned from the incident.

The Cisco FMC by default supports and can alert based on the following type of incidents:

- Compromise of system integrity

- Damage

- Denial of service

- Hoax

- Intrusion

- Theft

- Unauthorized administrative access

- Unknown

- Website defacement

In order to create an incident in the FMC, you go to **Analysis > Intrusions > Incidents** (see Figure 12-19). If there are stored events in the Clipboard, when creating a new Incident, the clipboard events show in clipboard table in order to be added to the incident if necessary. As with any other report, incident reports can be run and generated on the fly in HTML, PDF, or CSV.

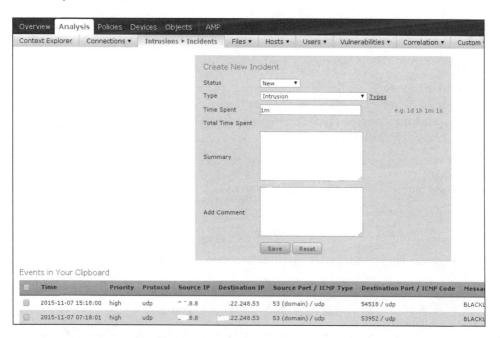

Figure 12-19 *Incident Creation*

While you are at **Analysis > Intrusions > Incidents**, you can create new incident types other than the predefined ones while creating a new incident and by editing the incident type field.

You can run a report on a defined incident by using the Generate Report button shown in Figure 12-20. You can also schedule incident reports.

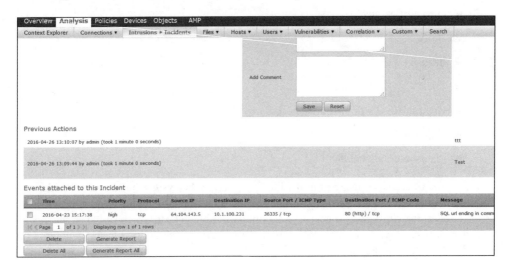

Figure 12-20   *Incident Report Generation Button*

Alerts

Although the FMC can provide various types of analytics to enable you to monitor the health of the network, you might prefer to receive alerts about certain events so you can act quickly to remediate them. The FMC allows you to configure email alerts, logging to a server, and SNMP traps.

The system can generate alerts when one of the following happens:

- An intrusion event with a specific impact flag

- A discovery event

- A malware event or retrospective malware event

- A correlation event from a specific correlation policy violation

- A connection event from an access control rule

- A specific status change for a module in a health policy

You set intrusion alerts in the advanced settings in an intrusion policy configuration. You can do this at either **Policies > Intrusion > Intrusion Policy** (see Figure 12-21) or **Policies > Intrusion > Email** (shown later, in Figure 12-24).

Figure 12-21 *Alert Settings in Intrusion Policy Configuration*

The email, SNMP, and syslog alert settings used in various alert configurations in the system are configured at **Policies > Actions > Alert**, as shown in Figure 12-22.

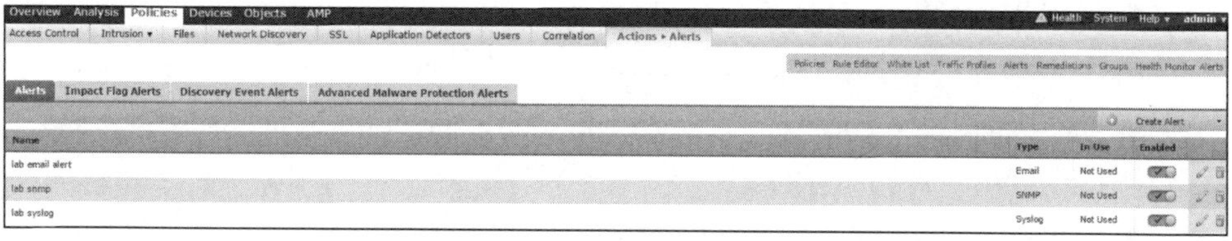

Figure 12-22 *Alert Server Profile Configuration*

SNMP Alerts

Each SNMP alert generated by the NGIPS contains the following information:

- Name of the server generating the trap
- IP address of the device that detected it
- Name of the device that detected it
- Event data

By clicking the Edit button in the policy's advanced settings, you can set the SNMP trap settings as shown in Figure 12-23. These include binary or string rendering of the IP addresses, SNMP version, server address, authentication password, encryption password, and username. The configuration fields change depending on the SNMP version.

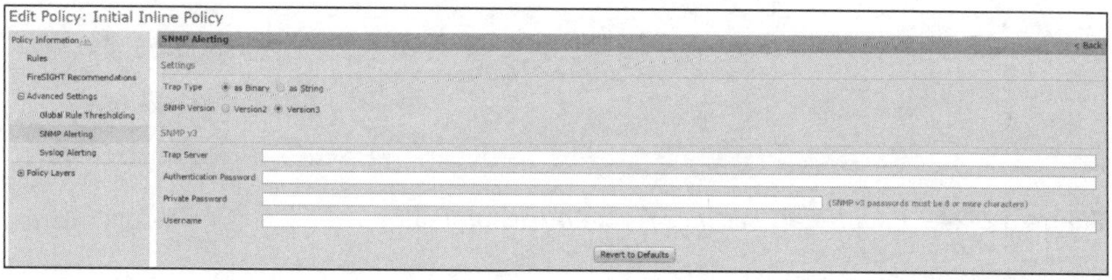

Figure 12-23 *SNMP Trap Configuration in IPS Policy*

For SNMP traps and syslogs, the actual events are generated by the sensor itself. The alerts configured at **Policies > Actions > Alerts** are generated by the FMC and leverage the correlation engine.

Email Alerts

Email alerts generated by the NGIPS contain the following information:

- Total alerts in the database
- Last email time
- Current time
- Total new alerts
- Number of events that matched specified email filters
- Timestamp, protocol, event message, and source and destination IP addresses and ports, with traffic direction information for each event
- Number of events per destination port
- Number of events per source IP address

By configuring the email fields at **Policies > Intrusion > Email**, you can set the sender and receiver, the maximum events, and frequency per email; enable summarization and coalescing of the alerts; set the time zone; and enable alerting for specific IPS rules (see Figure 12-24).

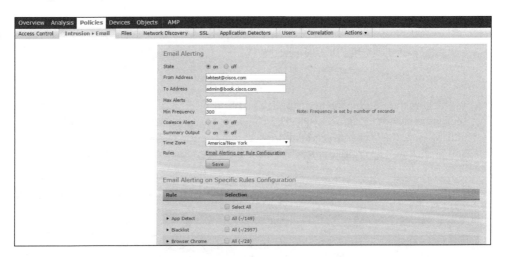

Figure 12-24   *Email Alert Settings for an Intrusion Policy*

Syslog Alerts

Syslog alerts generated by the NGIPS contain the following information and more:

- Date and time of alert generation

- Event message

- Event data

- Generator ID of the triggering event

- Snort ID of the triggering event

- Revision

As shown in Figure 12-25, editing the syslog settings in the policy's advanced settings brings up the host IP address, the syslog facility (as a categorization at the syslog server), and the syslog level (priority). You can use these settings at the syslog level to look for events of certain categories and priority levels.

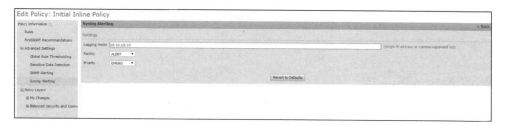

Figure 12-25 *Syslog Alert Settings for an Intrusion Policy*

The FMC platform can also alert based on event impact. You set the impact in the FMC based on the correlation between the IPS policy rules and the network discovery. The FMC shows the relevance of the attack to the host that is actually targeted. Higher-impact events are of more importance for the host in question than are lower-impact events. As shown in Figure 12-26, under **Policies > Actions > Alerts,** you can configure syslog, email, and SNMP alerts based on triggered event impact.

You configure the syslog, email, and SNMP profiles on the Alerts tab (refer to Figure 12-22). In addition, you can configure discovery event and malware alerts on other tabs, as discussed in Chapter 6, "Cisco AMP for Networks."

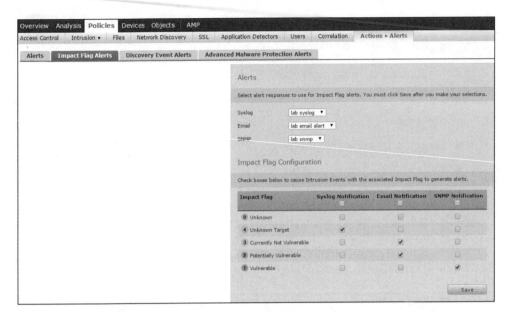

Figure 12-26   *Impact Alert Settings*

Correlation Policies

Correlation policies are policies that can perform actions based on correlation criteria met. They consist of correlation rules, compliance whitelists, and responses that are triggered when a certain event takes place or other criteria are met.

You create correlation policies at **Policies > Correlation** in the FMC. Figure 12-27 shows a correlation policy rule added in the Rule Management tab; it signifies the event that needs to happen for the correlation policy to be triggered. Correlation policy rules can include IPS events and many other options, such as a discovery event, a user activity, a host event, a malware event, a connection event, or a traffic profile change. If a correlation rule or a compliance whitelist is violated, a remediation or an alert can be generated. Note that correlation rules that are not added to a correlation policy do not actually take effect. They must be added to a correlation policy and assigned an action before they become active.

You can also define a whitelist and a profile by using the corresponding tabs. A compliance whitelist is a list between a destination and the host profiles discovered in the network. If traffic that violates the whitelist is identified, a whitelist alert is generated, and the appropriate remediation action takes place (see Figure 12-28).

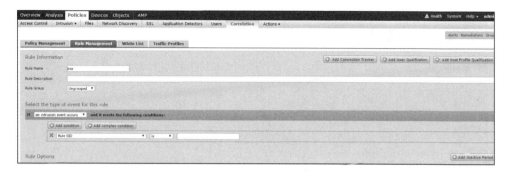

Figure 12-27   *Correlation Policy Rule Management*

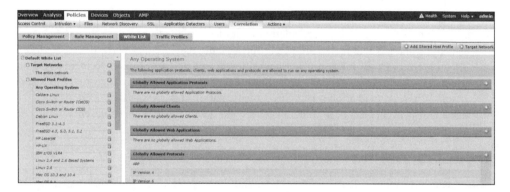

Figure 12-28   *Correlation White List*

A traffic profile is a profile of the traffic on a network, based on connection data logged over a time span that the administrator specifies.

The FMC can also send an alert based on the correlation policy. The Policy Management tab has a response icon (see Figure 12-29) for each correlation rule that brings up the available responses, as shown in Figure 12-30. As you saw previously in Figure 12-22, the responses are set at **Policies > Actions > Alert**.

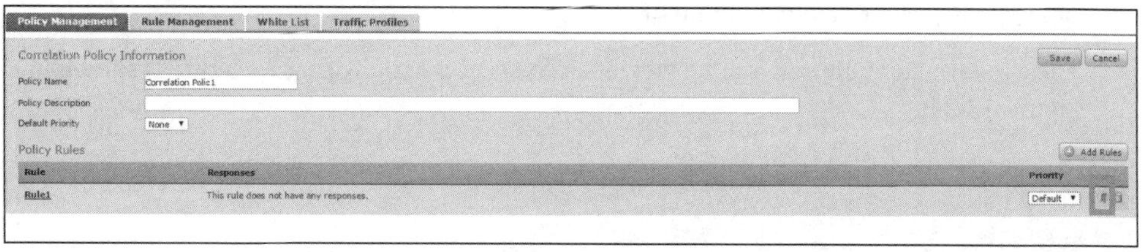

Figure 12-29   *Correlation Response Button in Correlation Policy*

Responses for Rule1

Assigned Responses

⌄ ⌃

Unassigned Responses

lab email alert
lab snmp
lab syslog

Update   Cancel

Figure 12-30   *Correlation Policy Response*

Moreover, other than responses, a correlation policy remediation can be applied when a violation occurs. There are preloaded modules for remediation in the FMC: IOS null route, PIX shun, Nmap remediation, and set attribute date. You can create remediation instances for the available remediation modules at **Policies > Actions > Remediations > Instances.** You can then use a remediation instance in a correlation rule as the response action. When a remediation is launched, a remediation status event is generated. Remediation events can be searched, viewed, and deleted just like other events.

Troubleshooting

At times you might experience issues or failures in a system. To troubleshoot such issues, the FMC provides troubleshooting tools and features. The following sections summarize some of the troubleshooting tools available for trying to find the root cause of an issue in the FMC.

Audit

Audits are used to examine user interaction with the FMC web interface and system logs. Audits are presented like an event view that allows for the analysis of audit log messages. Only 100,000 logs are stored at a time in the audit log. Beyond that limit, the older messages are removed in favor of the new ones.

The predefined audit logs can be viewed at **System > Monitoring > Audit,** as shown in Figure 12-31.

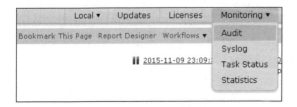

	Local ▼	Updates	Licenses	Monitoring ▼
Bookmark This Page	Report Designer	Workflows ▼		Audit
				Syslog
		‖ 2015-11-09 23:09:‖		Task Status
				Statistics

Figure 12-31   *Audit Log Dropdown*

The predefined audit log view shown in Figure 12-32 displays all interactions of the administrator using the GUI interface. It also includes the time, the action, the address of the administrator, and the event description.

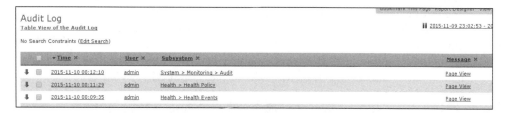

Figure 12-32 *Audit Logs*

The Edit Search button in a log view allows you to do custom searches based on different criteria, such as user, message, time, source IP address, or change.

Health Monitoring

The health of a device is important to ensure that there are no issues with its operation. FMC's health monitor provides numerous ways of keeping track of the health of an NGIPS. A series of tests define a health policy that can be applied to multiple devices to monitor their health. Tests can be scheduled and run periodically or at will. You can check the health status of a device from FMC health charts and status tables. Figure 12-33 shows the Health tab options:

- Monitor

- Policy

- Events

- Blacklist

- Monitor Alerts

Figure 12-33 *FMC's Health Tab*

A health policy consists of health modules, which are test scripts you run to test the health of the device. The FMC offers a variety of health modules, such as AMP, appliance heartbeat, disk usage, disk status, CPU, and more. As shown in Figure 12-34, the Health Policy tab has all the modules available on the left side. You can choose a module to enable it and set preferred values. For example, for the CPU, Memory, and Disk usage module, there is a warning and critical CPU threshold that triggers warning or critical syslog messages, respectively. Specifically for IPS, the IPS event rate option configures the event thresholds that trigger warnings and critical messages. There are many more modules that can be configured under the health policy.

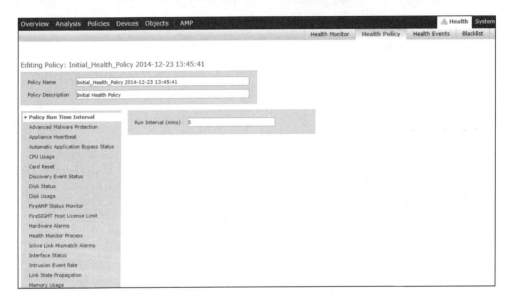

Figure 12-34 *Health Policy Configuration*

The FMC also allows you to compare a health policy against older health policies.

On the Health tab, the Blacklist option allows you to disable health monitoring for specific devices or health modules (see Figure 12-35). For example, if there is a network update that will bring the network down or an interface status is expectedly flapping, a blacklist could disable the alerts on the segment or the interface status. You can apply blacklists to a device or a module.

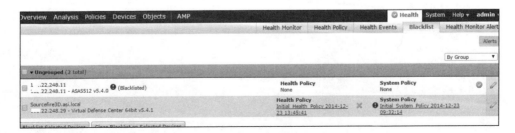

Figure 12-35 *Health Blacklist*

The Health Events tab, shown in Figure 12-36, displays all the health-related events from the system. To view only the events specific to one device, you can go to the Health Monitor and click the device name link. When you choose the alert level, the table shows only the health alerts related to that alert level.

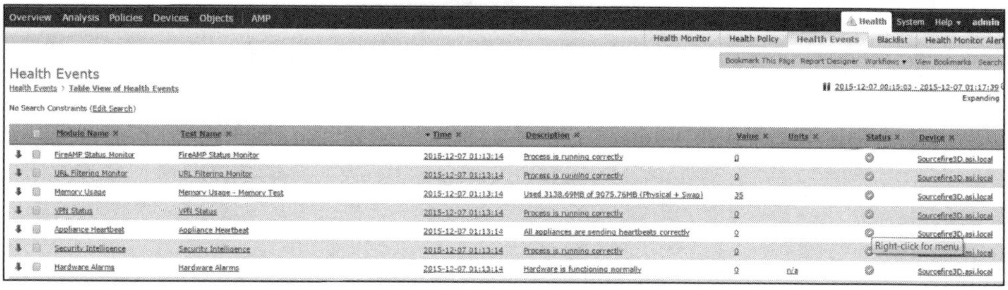

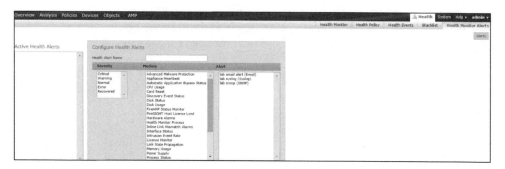

Figure 12-36   *Health Events*

By using the Health Monitor Alerts tab, you can configure notifications through email, SNMP, or remote syslogs about changes in a health module status. For example, an email can be sent when a CPU meets a warning level. A second email can be sent for a CPU of critical level. Figure 12-37 shows how you can set up a module to alert using one of the three options (right column) and severity (left column).

Figure 12-37   *Health Alerts*

Syslogs

For troubleshooting purposes, you can view the syslogs from the FMC at **System > Monitoring > Syslog**. The syslog displays each message generated by the system. Each syslog contains the date that the message was generated, the time it was generated, the host that generated the message, and the message itself. System logs are not generated by the devices themselves; they refer to the FMC appliance or VM.

There is also a search field you can use to search through the logs by using grep-like regular expressions, as illustrated in Figure 12-38. You can set the syslog filter to be case sensitive and to exclude the syslog that matches the filter.

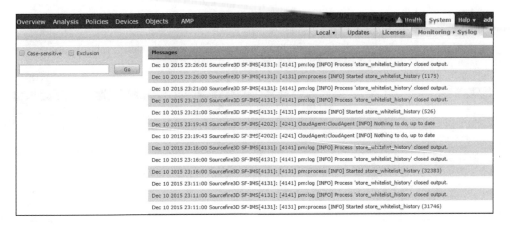

Figure 12-38   *Syslogs*

Summary

This chapter demonstrates how an analyst can use the FMC to analyze and investigate
information generated by an NGIPS. You have seen how to review and look into intrusion events, create reports, analyze incidents, and generate alerts. You have learned
how to create custom workflows and correlation policies. You have also learned about
the troubleshooting capabilities of an NGIPS. You have learned how to monitor the
health of a system, use health alerts, and audit the status of a device to ensure its
smooth operation.

Index

D

E

east-to-west communication, 58

email alerts, 320

email authentication, 14

email encryption, 14

email security, 13–16

   Cloud Email Security, 15

   Email Security Appliance, 13–15

   Hybrid Email Security, 16

Email Security Appliance. *See* ESA

enable password command, 83

encryption

   email, 14

   password, 83

endpoint IOC downloads, 198

endpoint protection. *See* AMP for
   Endpoints

engines

   AMP for Mac, 232

   AMP for Windows, 223–224

Enhanced Interior Gateway Routing
   Protocol (EIGRP), 5

error reporting connectivity, 198

ESA (Email Security Appliance), 13–15

   AMP report from, 192

   configuring for AMP, 189–191

   ESA models list, 13–14

   features supported by, 14–15

Ethos engine, 145, 224

evaluation of NGIPS, 282

events

   impact alerts, 321, 322

   logging limits, 304–305

   queue configuration, 303

   server connectivity, 198

   statistics, 309

   See also intrusion events

exclusion sets, 209 211

expert command, 133

exploits, 10

extension exclusions, 209

$EXTERNAL_NET header, 295

extranets, 271

F

fail-open capability, 49, 269, 275

failover in Cisco ASA, 45–49

   active/active failover, 47–49

   active/standby failover, 45–46

   fail open vs. fail close, 49

   stateful failover, 47

failover replication http command, 47

fast_pattern keyword, 296

file analysis

   ESA for AMP configuration, 189–191

   WSA for AMP configuration, 188

File Analysis report, 192

file control, 28

file dispositions, 150, 177

file policies, 108–110

   advanced, 178–180

   AMP configuration of, 174–180

   creating new, 108–109, 174

   file dispositions/types and, 177–178

   setting rules for, 110, 174, 176–177

   zip/archive files and, 178

file reputation, 19, 142, 196

   ESA for AMP configuration, 189–191

   WSA for AMP configuration, 185–188

file retrospection, 20, 142, 196

file sandboxing, 20, 142, 196, 256

file trajectory, 196

file_data keyword, 296

FireAMP. *See* AMP for Endpoints

K

L

M

S